General prisons Board

General Prisons Board (Ireland) : fourth report, 1881-82, with appendices

General prisons Board

General Prisons Board (Ireland) : fourth report, 1881-82, with appendices

ISBN/EAN: 9783741104497

Manufactured in Europe, USA, Canada, Australia, Japa

Cover: Foto ©ninafisch / pixelio.de

Manufactured and distributed by brebook publishing software (www.brebook.com)

General prisons Board

General Prisons Board (Ireland) : fourth report, 1881-82, with appendices

FOURTH REPORT

OF THE

GENERAL PRISONS BOARD, IRELAND,

1881–82;

WITH APPENDICES.

Presented to both Houses of Parliament by Command of Her Majesty.

DUBLIN:
PRINTED BY ALEX. THOM & CO., 87, 88, & 89, ABBEY-STREET,
THE QUEEN'S PRINTING OFFICE.
FOR HER MAJESTY'S STATIONERY OFFICE.

1882.

[C.—3360.] *Price 9½d.*

CONTENTS.

A 2

FOURTH REPORT

OF THE

GENERAL PRISONS BOARD, IRELAND.

TO HIS EXCELLENCY JOHN POYNTZ, EARL SPENCER, K.P., K.G.

LORD LIEUTENANT GENERAL AND GENERAL GOVERNOR OF IRELAND.

Dublin Castle, July, 1882.

MAY IT PLEASE YOUR EXCELLENCY,

1. We, the General Prisons Board, submit to your Excellency this our Fourth Annual Report on the condition of the prisons and prisoners within our jurisdiction, and with respect to the registration of criminals during the year ending March 31, 1882.

I.—LOCAL PRISONS.

2. In our last Report we had occasion to refer to the great increase of labour and responsibility thrown on this Department by the operations under the Act, 44 Vic., cap. 4, for "The Better Protection of Person and Property in Ireland," and we at the same time explained the nature of the arrangements adopted up to that date, for the special custody and treatment of the prisoners arrested under its provisions.

Extended arrangements under the Act.

3. A very considerable extension of those arrangements was however, subsequently necessitated by the course of events, the Local Prisons either wholly, or chiefly appropriated to this particular purpose having been gradually increased as occasion required from five—the number so made use of at the date of our Report—to twelve, viz.:—

I. IN ULSTER.—Armagh, Enniskillen, Monaghan and Omagh.
II. IN LEINSTER.—Dundalk, Grangegorman, Kilkenny, Kilmainham, and Naas.
III. IN MUNSTER.—Clonmel, and Limerick.
IV. IN CONNAUGHT.—Galway.

Special Regulations issued under the Act 44 Vic. cap. 4.

4. In our last Report, we gave in full the special regulations framed by the Lord Lieutenant—pursuant to the provision contained in Sec. 1, sub-sec. 3, of the Act—and which it has been seen differ materially from the rules applicable to the ordinary classes of unconvicted prisoners.

Extra expenditure.

5. A considerable outlay was incurred in boarding and otherwise preparing for occupation the cells and rooms appropriated to the use of this class—and in providing suitable yards and sheds for their out-door exercise and association, as well as in supplying them with furniture, bedding, utensils, &c., of a description superior to that which it has been hitherto the practice to allow to ordinary prisoners either in this country, or in England.

Increased duties of officers.

6. The large increase in the time allowed to the "Suspect" prisoners for daily exercise and association, as well as the great extent of their correspondence, and the number of visits paid to them, involved, it is almost unnecessary to point out, a very great strain upon the officers charged with the supervision of the arrangements, and responsible for the strict observance of the prescribed Rules.

Governors, &c. &c.

Other officers.

7. This great and sudden addition to the usual duties of our staff was met, in the case of the superior officers, by redoubled energy, labour, and application on their parts, while in regard to the officers of the several other grades, upon whom, we may observe, the strain was likewise most serious, as well as almost incessant, it was sought, as far as practicable, to mitigate it by temporarily increasing the number of those employed.

Extra staff.

8. The Board with this view sought for and obtained the necessary Treasury authority for the temporary employment, in particular prisons, of extra officers, in addition to those already sanctioned, for the ordinary exigencies of the service, viz., 16 temporary chief warders, 81 temporary ordinary warders, and 57 temporary pensioner warders.

Temporary officers.

9. Officers called thus suddenly into requisition could not, of course, be expected to prove equal in efficiency or usefulness to the ordinary prison staff, but it was, as far as possible, arranged that the charge of the "Suspect" prisoners, as the most important class, should be confined to our most experienced and reliable officers, and we have every reason to feel satisfied that, as a rule, the confidence reposed in the intelligence and discretion of those selected for this difficult and delicate duty was not misplaced.

Reduction of Local Prisons.

10. In our first and second Annual Reports we have fully explained the measures proposed and subsequently carried out by us for the reduction of the number of Local Prisons transferred to our control in 1878, and in the latter—paragraph 6—we have detailed the particular prisons, eleven in number, selected for this purpose.

Temporary re-opening of certain Local Prisons.

11. During the recent emergency, however, it was found necessary to temporarily re-open three of these, viz., Ennis, Enniskillen, and Monaghan, as the readiest and most satisfactory mode of meeting the exceptional pressure with which we were called upon to cope.

Of these we have already felt ourselves in a position to discontinue the use of Ennis and Monaghan Prisons, and to dispense with the temporary staff attached to each; and the same course will be shortly followed in regard to the third—Enniskillen.

12. The operations under this Act are now drawing rapidly to a close, and as it will cease to be in force at all after the 30th September next, it may be of interest that we should here explain that between the passing of the Act, 2nd March, 1881, and the present time the total number of persons arrested under its provisions was 987, and that the largest number in custody at any one time was 624—during the week ended 6th March, 1882. **Close of operations under the P. P. P. Act.**

13. Since that date there has been a steady and almost continuous diminution in the number remaining in custody, and which at the present time is only 159.

We may observe that the expenditure incurred in every way by the General Prisons Board during the year ended 31st March, 1882, by the detention of prisoners under this Act is estimated at about £12,733. **Total expenditure under Act.**

14. In our Second Report, par. 8, and our Third Report, par. 20, we have described the successive steps by which the number of "Bridewells" had been since they came under our control gradually reduced from the original total of 93, to 35. **Bridewells.**

We had contemplated making some further reductions during the past year, but in deference to the adverse opinions of the local authorities, and having regard to the existing condition of things generally in the country, we have deemed it best, except in the case of Skibbereen, to defer any further action in this direction for the present, without, however, at all abandoning the fulfilment of our purpose, whenever circumstances admit of this, without risk of causing any serious local inconvenience. **Skibbereen.**

15. The revised Dietary for Local and Convict Prisons referred to in paragraphs 6 and 7 of our last Report is now in general use throughout the various prisons, and appears to have given very general satisfaction, without, upon the whole, occasioning any serious addition to the expenditure. **New Dietary.**

16. We beg to refer your Excellency to Table XIX. in the Appendix for the usual detail of the various works of reconstruction and repair, &c., undertaken by us during the past year. **Execution of works of reconstruction and repair, &c.**

As far as possible it has been our practice to provide through the agency of our prison labour for the execution of all works of this description, but in the present instance it will be seen that what has been done had reference in a great measure to those special preparations which, as already described in par. 5, it became our duty to make for the reception and treatment of the prisoners committed under the "Protection of Person and Property Act," and for which, in part owing to the nature of the works, and in part to the pressure as to time under which they had to be undertaken, it was found absolutely necessary to provide by means of special contracts entered into by us either with Dublin or local tradesmen.

Nature of works provided for.

These works consisted for the most part of the boarding, heating, and lighting of cells, the removal of useless buildings, and other provisions for insuring increased security, the exterior lighting of some of the prisons, and preparations for the accommodation of the necessary military patrols, the provision of an increased water supply, the construction of suitable rooms for visitors, the enlargement of yards, and the erection of sheds for the purposes of shelter while at exercise and association, &c., &c.; and it may be observed that though many of these improvements would most probably never have been considered necessary had this special occasion for them not arisen, yet, now that they have been executed, they will undoubtedly be found to add materially to the permanent comfort and security of the particular prisons in which they have been effected, and will in this way go far to compensate for the rather considerable outlay they have involved.

Cork and Maryboro' works.

17. The most extensive and important works hitherto undertaken by us were those connected with the enlargement and improvement of Cork Male Prison and the adaptation in part of the local prison at Maryboro' to the purposes of an invalid convict prison, and for the execution of which, as described in previous reports, provision was made by the employment of parties of convicts temporarily transferred for this purpose from the Public Works Prison of Spike Island.

Maryboro' Invalid Prison.

These several works are now, it may be said, completed, or nearly so, and we contemplate almost immediately availing ourselves of the accommodation so provided at Maryboro' for the purpose of carrying out the important object with a view to which the works there were originally undertaken, viz. the removal thereto of such convicts as may be unfitted, by reason of constitutional delicacy or infirmity, for bearing the discipline and restraints of the ordinary prisons—an arrangement which, while it will tend to greatly improve the general condition of those affected by it, will, at the same time, relieve the Executive in numerous cases from the necessity of releasing prisoners before the expiration of their sentences, merely on the ground that further detention would be likely to prove dangerous to their lives.

Number to be accommodated.

Though provision has been made in this respect for the accommodation of fifty convicts of the class in question, it is probable that this limit will be rarely if ever reached in practice.

Prison Punishments.

18. In referring in our last report, par. 14, to Table X., which, pursuant to the provisions contained in sec. 15, 40 & 41 Vic., chap. 49, furnishes a detail of the various prison punishments, and of the offences for which they were inflicted, we took occasion to observe upon the decrease there shown, as compared with the previous years' returns, in the case of male prisoners, while, as regards females, on the contrary, an increase was exhibited.

This year, however, we have the satisfaction, to call attention under this head, not only to a still larger diminution in the total number punished, but also to the further fact that in the present instance the reduction applies to both male and female prisoners, though in a very much larger proportion, no doubt, in the case of the former than of the latter. Thus we trust showing that with improved prison management the necessity for punishment has decreased.

The following are the figures as to this for each of the three last years respectively, viz.:—

Year.	Number Punished. Males.	Females.	Total.
1881–82, . . .	7,281	1,321	8,602
1880–81, . . .	8,235	1,369	9,604
1879–80, . . .	8,608	1,205	9,813

19. In our last report, par. 15, we explained in detail the nature of the various branches of industrial labour which were at that time pursued in several of our local prisons, and which it was shown, had yielded a total profit payable to the Exchequer for the year 1880–81 of £5,418 10s. 11d., as against only £618 16s. 9d., the amount obtained from the operations of the preceding year, and the following Table will give the comparative results as to this for the years 1881–82 and 1880–81 respectively, viz.:— Industrial labour.

	Year 1881–82. £	s.	d.	Year 1880–81. £	s.	d.
Profit realised on Manufactures, .	4,463	2	9	3,886	10	4
Do. on Farm and Garden, . .	845	5	5	544	10	8
Total profit on productive services,	5,308	8	2	4,431	10	0
Extra receipts, ...	508	4	10	987	0	11
Total payable to the Exchequer, .	5,806	13	0	5,418	10	11

From the foregoing Table it will be seen that the greatly improved results under this head, to which we had last year the satisfaction of adverting, have been fully sustained during the intervening period, notwithstanding that the occupation of some of our principal prisons by the "Suspect" class, necessarily interfered with and interrupted very seriously our ordinary industrial operations during the year just closed, in as much as in several of our prisons no reproductive labour could be carried on. Continued increase of profits.

20. In the Appendix A, Tables VIII. and IX., will be found the usual educational statistics, and which, it will be seen, compare rather favourably, upon the whole, with the returns given in our last report, both as regards the proportion borne by the wholly illiterate prisoners to the total number of committments, and the number of those to whom school instruction was imparted during their period of detention in the larger prisons. Education.

The number of "wholly illiterate" prisoners, as shown last year, was 14,571, out of a total of 38,053, as against this year 13,833, out of a total of 38,968, and the number that received school instruction during the past year was 1,870, as against 1,747 for 1880-81.

Juvenile Offenders.

21. In Table XI. we submit the usual particulars connected with the offences and commitments of juvenile offenders, that is, of prisoners not exceeding sixteen years of age.

It will be observed that the total number of commitments in this class—1,053—is almost identical with that shown by the return for the preceding year—1,052—the only notable difference being that in the present instance an increase is shown in the case of the males, and a decrease as regards the females, whereas last year we had to point attention to the fact that while the males had decreased the female prisoners of this class had remained stationary in number.

The number of persons committed to local prisons during year ended 31st March, 1882, who are known to have been previously in reformatories was:—

Males.	Females.	Total
95	17	112

Visiting Committees under 40 & 41 Vic., cap. 49, sec. 24.

22. In the Prisons Act of 1877, section 24, provision is, it will be seen, made for the appointment, at such time as the Lord Lieutenant may prescribe each year, by the Grand Jury of every county of a visiting committee, "consisting of such number of persons, being Justices of the Peace, as having regard to the locality of such prison and to the class of prisoners to be confined in such prison may from time to time be determined by the Lord Lieutenant"; and section 25 both defines certain duties which are to be performed by the committees, and also enables the Lord Lieutenant to make by rules further provision with respect to the same subject.

Much valuable assistance has been received from time to time from individual members of these committees of justices in attending at the prisons and investigating complaints against prisoners of too serious a complexion to be dealt with by the governors, &c.; but, as a rule, we have regretted to observe that they do not ordinarily appear to visit the several prisons or interest themselves in the details of administration connected with them to the extent we should have desired, or in the manner which was manifestly contemplated both by the framers of the Act and by the rules which, pursuant to the provisions to that effect contained in section 25, were made and published by the Lord Lieutenant on the 22nd March, 1878.

Number of commitments to Prison.

23. We referred in our last report as a subject of congratulation to the fact that, notwithstanding the distress which had prevailed in certain parts of Ireland during the close of 1880, and the beginning of 1881, the prison statistics showed a considerable diminution in the total number of commitments.

This year we are not, we regret to say, in a position to record so favourable a state of things in this respect, but this interruption to the progressive decline previously observed upon has nevertheless not been very considerable during the year just ended.

The following are the figures as to this for each of the four last years, viz. :—

Year.	No. of Commitments to Prison.
1881–82,	41,435
1880–81,	40,192
1879–80,	44,659
1878–79,	45,297

From this return it will be observed that though the commitments for the past year are 1,243 in excess of those for 1880–81, they fall below those for 1879–80 by 3,224, and those for 1878–79 by 3,862.

It is, however, to be noted that the figures given above for the year 1881–82, do not include the 987 committals referred to in par. 12 of this Report.

The operations under the Act 44 Vic., cap. 4, being altogether abnormal and exceptional, the introduction of the number committed by virtue of warrants issued under its provisions by the Lord Lieutenant, would only tend to disarrange our tables and detract from their future value and interest as a record of the comparative statistics of successive years of the criminal classes.

Abstracts.

24. Following up the practice pursued by us in our three previous reports, we here submit three abstracts, the two first dealing with the numbers in custody at certain recurring dates in all the local prisons of Ireland from 1851 to 1882, and the third showing the number of commitments and the daily average number in custody during each year from 1854 to 1882, viz. :—

Numbers in custody on the 1st January in each of the last 32 years.

No. 1.—Number of Prisoners (of all Classes) in County and Borough Gaols on the 1st January in each year.

On 1st January,		1851,	10,064	On 1st January,		1867,	2,332
Do.	do.	1852,	8,803	Do.	do.	1868,	2,463
Do.	do.	1853,	7,604	Do.	do.	1869,	2,024
Do.	do.	1854,	5,755	Do.	do.	1870,	2,029
Do.	do.	1855,	5,060	Do.	do.	1871,	2,161
Do.	do.	1856,	3,561	Do.	do.	1872,	2,098
Do.	do.	1857,	3,419	Do.	do.	1873,	2,477
Do.	do.	1858,	3,265	Do.	do.	1874,	2,609
Do.	do.	1859,	2,644	Do.	do.	1875,	2,517
Do.	do.	1860,	2,538	Do	do.	1876,	2,496
Do.	do.	1861,	2,488	Do.	do.	1877,	2,289
Do.	do.	1862,	2,916	Do.	do.	1878,	2,617
Do.	do.	1863,	3,055	Do.	do.	1879,	2,497
Do.	do.	1864,	3,023	Do	do.	1880,	2,690
Do.	do.	1865,	2,747	Do.	do.	1881,	2,476
Do.	do.	1866,	2,663	Do.	do.	1882,	2,601

[No. 2.

Monthly return of prisoners in custody last 32 years.

No. 2.—RETURN of the NUMBERS (of all Classes) in GAOLS on the 1st day of each Month in the Years—

Year	Jan.	Feb.	March.	April.	May.	June.	July.	August.	Sept.	Oct.	Nov.	Dec.
1851, .	10,084	11,032	11,444	10,689	11,066	12,217	12,223	10,869	9,406	8,436	8,547	8,481
1852, .	8,803	9,187	9,871	8,944	8,890	8,827	8,854	7,821	7,869	7,408	7,104	7,592
1853, .	7,604	8,184	9,141	7,510	7,981	7,924	7,084	6,943	6,039	5,823	5,471	5,781
1854, .	6,745	6,185	6,423	5,978	5,846	5,977	5,810	5,636	5,487	5,230	4,930	5,100
1855, .	5,080	5,773	4,788	4,768	4,680	4,637	4,582	4,385	4,148	3,753	3,747	3,844
1856, .	3,561	3,865	4,022	3,665	3,596	3,686	3,492	3,599	3,495	3,337	3,454	3,318
1857, .	3,419	3,589	3,477	3,298	3,252	3,482	3,373	3,354	3,272	3,224	3,373	3,395
1858, .	3,265	3,323	3,193	2,906	2,939	3,047	2,867	2,910	2,935	2,779	2,787	2,780
1859, .	2,844	2,928	2,847	2,799	2,502	2,806	2,740	2,699	2,631	2,534	2,666	2,585
1860, .	2,535	2,810	2,623	2,533	2,540	2,736	2,742	2,680	2,474	2,439	2,498	2,368
1861, .	2,485	2,636	2,709	2,608	2,708	2,908	3,058	2,899	2,714	2,789	2,835	2,843
1862, .	2,916	2,985	3,182	2,993	3,050	3,149	3,398	3,025	3,049	3,032	3,064	3,031
1863, .	3,065	3,309	3,348	3,308	3,190	3,313	3,418	3,099	3,081	2,950	3,018	3,187
1864, .	3,023	3,036	2,953	2,979	3,035	3,072	3,066	3,018	3,013	2,979	2,829	2,736
1865, .	2,747	2,689	2,788	2,675	2,743	2,885	2,914	2,871	2,918	2,990	2,860	2,784
1866, .	2,683	2,768	3,094	3,170	3,087	2,841	2,934	2,711	2,619	2,311	2,396	2,313
1867, .	2,282	2,200	2,438	2,344	2,040	2,844	2,500	2,722	2,690	2,645	2,570	2,498
1868, .	2,463	2,379	2,398	2,307	2,168	2,158	2,348	2,283	2,344	2,235	2,180	2,098
1869, .	2,044	2,056	2,107	2,160	2,220	2,219	2,336	2,370	2,316	2,282	2,166	2,197
1870, .	2,029	2,166	2,128	2,286	2,428	2,456	2,548	2,502	2,697	2,512	2,359	2,378
1871, .	2,161	2,162	2,316	2,343	2,284	2,409	2,419	2,418	2,361	2,389	2,358	2,310
1872, .	2,098	2,273	2,397	2,081	2,226	2,281	2,363	2,394	2,516	2,536	2,880	2,487
1873, .	2,477	2,465	2,417	2,856	2,513	2,047	2,080	2,867	2,739	2,789	2,832	2,651
1874, .	2,609	2,639	2,490	2,848	2,630	2,648	2,807	2,885	2,971	3,001	2,982	2,818
1875, .	2,517	2,867	2,823	2,714	2,860	2,832	2,837	2,821	2,910	2,851	2,765	2,684
1876, .	2,496	2,612	2,607	2,582	2,632	2,800	2,963	2,931	3,032	3,070	3,194	3,034
1877, .	2,229	3,006	2,911	2,609	2,784	2,911	3,123	3,259	3,246	3,063	3,117	3,032
1878, .	2,817	2,839	2,898	2,809	2,843	2,774	2,987	3,026	3,011	3,041	2,893	2,845
1879, .	2,497	2,580	2,647	2,765	2,815	3,031	3,088	3,069	3,084	3,058	3,282	2,999
1880, .	2,690	2,965	2,875	3,186	3,100	3,258	3,708	3,184	3,281	3,148	3,094	2,702
1881, .	2,478	2,366	2,458	2,238	2,822	2,741	2,924	2,762	2,852	2,749	2,537	2,681
1882, .	2,601	2,712	2,689	–	–	–	–	–	–	–	–	–

Number of commitments, daily averages, &c.

No. 3.—COMMITMENTS (exclusive of Debtors) in the Twenty-eight Years ended 31st March, 1882.

Years.	Number of Commitments.	Daily Average No. of Prisoners.	Years.	Number of Commitments.	Daily Average No. of Prisoners.
1854, .	60,445	5,700·9	1868, .	29,501	2,130·6
1855, .	48,446	4,418·3	1869, .	29,874	2,123·8
1856, .	43,713	3,560·6	1870, .	32,370	2,277·2
1857, .	39,886	3,273·4	1871, .	31,129	2,224·5
1858, .	33,899	2,694·6	1872, .	30,222	2,289
1859, .	32,142	2,605·4	1873, .	33,894	2,578
1860, .	30,712	2,523·8	1874, .	38,586	2,770
1861, .	30,087	2,631·3	1875, .	38,922	2,741
1862, .	32,159	2,895·9	1876, .	41,817	2,828
1863, .	33,840	3,028·7	1877, .	43,841	2,995
1864, .	32,870	2,843·1	1878–79*	45,297	2,825
1865, .	32,731	2,718·8	1879–80*	44,658	2,812
1866, .	29,097	2,559·4	1880–81*	40,192	2,620
1867, .	30,067	2,540·6	1881–82*	41,435	3,111

* To 31st March.

Bridewell statistics.

25. The following Table, which exhibits the number confined in the Bridewells from 1850 to 1882, will show that the progressive

reduction in numbers observed in the returns of previous years still continues, viz.:—

No. confined in bridewells for last 32 years.

No. Confined in Bridewells.

Years.		Years.	
1850	88,899	1866	18,447
1851	85,080	1867	16,964
1852	69,860	1868	14,137
1853	58,563	1869	13,510
1854	48,356	1870	15,801
1855	36,002	1871	10,283
1856	33,534	1872	7,823
1857	31,504	1873	5,732
1858	27,424	1874	6,704
1859	25,298	1875	6,365
1860	22,421	1876	4,889
1861	20,166	1877	5,576
1862	22,064	1878–79*	4,856
1863	21,053	1879–80*	4,247
1864	20 563	1880–81*	3,888
1865	20,556	1881–82*	3,810

*To 31st March.

Separate Reports on Local Prisons. App. A.

26. We beg to refer to the Appendix A for the detailed reports furnished by the respective governors as to the several local prisons, and which show, in regard to each separately, the daily average number of prisoners, employed and unemployed, the description of their employments, the net profit realised on the work done, and the estimated value of the work done for the prisons.

II.—The Convict Prisons.

27. The accommodation afforded for convicts by the four Convict Prisons on the 1st of January, 1882, may be still estimated, as last year, at 1,070, and the number in custody at that date was:—

	Male.	Female.	Total.
In Convict Prisons,	647	110	757
In Local Prisons,	47	–	47
Gross total of Convicts in Custody on 1st January,	694	110	804

28. The number of Convicts sentenced to Penal Servitude during the year ending 31st March, 1882, was:—

	Males.	Females.	Total.
5 years,	131	16	147
7 "	27	5	32
10 "	11	–	11
12 "	1	1	2
14 "	1	–	1
15 "	4	–	4
20 "	1	–	1
25 "	1	–	1
Life,	5	5	10
Gross Total sentenced during year,	182	27	*209

* Eleven of these were military convicts.

Disposal of Convicts during the year ending 31st March, 1882.

I.—No. discharged from Prisons:—

	M.	F.	Total.
On Orders of Licence to be at large,	122	57	179
On Commutation of Sentence.	1	–	1
On Completion of Sentence,	30	8	38
	153	65	218
II.—No. of Females discharged from Refuges:—			
On Orders of Licence to be at large,	–	24	24
No. discharged from Prisons and Refuges during the year,	153	89	242*

Of the above number discharged during the year 18 males and 6 females had previously been released on licence under the same sentences, but had forfeited their licence and been recommitted to Prison.

Forty female convicts were transferred from Prison to Refuges during the year.

The number of female convicts in Refuges during the year ending 31st March, 1882, was 71. Of these 19 had undergone previous sentences of penal servitude, and 14 of them had been previously in Refuges.

29. The Revocations and Forfeitures of Licences in Ireland during the year ended 31st March, 1882, were as follow:—

	Males.	Females.	Total.
Forfeited or revoked for breach of conditions of Licence,	7	3	10
Forfeited or revoked in consequence of a conviction for other offences,	17	9	26
Gross Total,	24	12	36†

30. Subjoined is a table showing the number of Convicts respectively in "Custody," "Convicted," and "Discharged," since the year 1854.

The number of convicts in confinement during 1881–2 known to have been in Reformatories was—males, 61; females, nil.

It will be seen from the above, and also from paragraph 21, p. 10, that a considerable number of males who have had the advantage of being sent to Reformatories return to crime, though the number of females of that class are few, and none are in custody sentenced to penal servitude.

* Four of these were English Convicts.
† Three of these were English Licence Holders.

[Table.

TABLE showing the number of Convicts in "Custody," "Convicted," and "Discharged" since the year 1854, inclusive.

In custody in Convict Prisons, January 1st.	Year.	Convicted.	No. Discharged.
*3,933	1854	710	656
3,427	1855	518	820
3,209	1856	389	1,107
2,614	1857	426	910
2,277	1858	358	946
1,773	1859	822	595
1,631	1860	331	524
1,492	1861	368	561
1,314	1862	592	317
1,575	1863	511	326
1,768	1864	407	391
1,776	1865	299	410
1,637	1866	265	439
1,431	1867	296	330
1,335	1868	246	246
1,325	1869	191	291
1,230	1870	245	253
1,228	1871	219	265
1,196	1872	201	255
1,143	1873	228	250
1,133	1874	221	239
1,133	1875	241	238
1,136	1876	192	196
1,156	1877	188	248
1,114	1878	164	260
†982	1879–80	154	324
†811	1880-81	123	238
‡739	1881–82	‡209	242
‡757	1882		

Condition and working of Prisons.

31. To the Appendix B we beg to refer for the usual reports and returns relating to the four convict prisons of Mountjoy Male, Mountjoy Female, Spike Island, and Lusk respectively, and which will be found to afford full particulars as to the present condition and general working of each of these establishments.

Spike Island.

32. In both our last reports it became our duty to place on record the very strong opinion we have long entertained as to the entire unfitness, owing to its structural arrangements and defects, of Spike Island for the purposes of a convict establishment.

Lord Kimberley's Commission.

33. In our last report, when expressing our full concurrence in the conclusion arrived at by the Commission over which Lord Kimberley presided, as expressed in their report presented to Parliament in 1879, viz., that this prison should "be discontinued," we referred to the fact that, though several communications relating to it had passed between our Board and the Government, no definite conclusion had been up to that time

* In addition to this number there were 345 convicts under detention in the county prisons, and several hundreds in Bermuda and Gibraltar, who were subsequently discharged in Ireland.

† In addition to these numbers, 69, 90, 96 and 47 convicts were in Local Prisons on 1st January, '79, '80, 81, and '82 respectively.

‡ Eleven of these were military convicts.

arrived at on the subject; and we regret to be obliged to add, on the present occasion, that no practical progress towards the solution of the difficulty which has been experienced in devising a suitable substitute for it has been made during the interval.

Departmental Committee of Inquiry.

34. A departmental committee, of which the Chairman of this Board is one of the members, has, however, been engaged in London from time to time for some months past in a general inquiry as to the future disposal of convict labour both in England and Ireland, and we trust that as one result of their deliberations some effective remedy may be suggested for finally discontinuing the use of an institution which has long attracted the special attention and emphatic condemnation not only of this Board but of some of the very highest authorities on the subject.

Opinion of the Roman Catholic Chaplain.

Before finally quitting this subject, for the present, we may be permitted to conclude with the following extract from a report, dated the 2nd May last, from the Roman Catholic Chaplain of that prison, and who, we may observe in passing, enjoys the advantage of being enabled to speak as to its affairs with all the authority which a very lengthened experience of them may be considered to confer. He says:—

"I regret that it is not in my power to give a more favourable report of the religious and moral condition of the Roman Catholic prisoners during the last year than during several previous years, although it was a year of jubilee when the greatest efforts were made to produce a better sense and a better practice among them. I even got a religious mission to be conducted in the prison by six neighbouring clergymen to accomplish that desirable object, but the corrupting influence of the close association of the prisoners here, soon destroyed all the good that was done by the jubilee and by the mission, as well as by the discipline of the prison. And this uncontrollable evil must continue until the prison is reconstructed into proper separate cells, as at Mountjoy prison, and now in all the county gaols in Ireland. It is then much to be regretted that Spike Island Prison, where all the convicts pass most of their penal servitude, and where their chief reformation should be effected, is still left without that essential improvement."

Independent Inspection.

35. In the able Report of the Commissioners appointed in 1878 "to inquire into the working of the Penal Servitude Acts," and to which reference has been just made, in connexion with the subject of Spike Island Prison, it is amongst other things recommended:—

"That arrangements should be made for the independent inspection of Convict Prisons by persons appointed by the Government, but unconnected with the Convict Prisons Department, and unpaid."

36. This recommendation was dissented from by one eminent member of the Commission—Dr. Guy—on the ground, amongst several others enumerated by him, of—

Dr. Guy.

"The adverse view taken by two such experienced administrators as Sir Walter Crofton and Sir Edmund DuCane, supported as that view is by reasons to which I attach importance."

But the proposal appears to have received the support of the remaining five members of the Commission, and was subsequently approved, and acted on by the Government of the day.

37. In Ireland two bodies of such unpaid inspectors were appointed by the Lord Lieutenant in 1880, and re-appointed in 1881, viz: I. For the Dublin Convict Prisons— Inspectors appointed.

The Right Hon. Lord Monck.
The Right Hon. W. H. Cogan, D.L., and
Dr. Lyons, M.P.

And II. for Spike Island—

N. D. Murphy, Esq., D.L.
R. Penrose Fitzgerald, Esq., D.L., and
W. R. Meade, Esq., J.P.

38. These gentlemen, it is unnecessary to point out, are appointed, and are intended to act in every way quite independently of our Board; but we entertain no doubt that the judicious exercise of the important functions entrusted to them may render their appointment of the highest practical value in the execution of the Penal Servitude Acts, and on our own part, we can undertake to say, that any recommendations or suggestions at any time emanating from them shall always command our most respectful consideration and attention.

III. Registration of Criminals.

39. We beg to refer your Excellency to the Appendix C. to this Report for the usual Statistical Tables relating to this particular branch of our administration, brought down from 1870 to the close of 1881, which will speak for themselves and which appear to present no features calling, on the present occasion, for any further special explanatory observations upon our part. Statistical Tables.

40. In our last Report we had the satisfaction of being enabled to announce the completion of the "Alphabetical Register of Habitual Criminals" who have been liberated subject to the penalties prescribed by section 8 of the Habitual Criminals Act of 1869, 32 & 33 V., c. 99, or sections 7 & 8 of the Prevention of Crimes Act, 1871, 34 & 35 V., c. 112. Alphabetical Register of Habitual Criminals.

As already explained by us the preparation of this most important record was commenced in this office as far back as the year 1877, but was soon after suspended, and only resumed in the early part of 1880. See Second Report, p. 16.

Extracts, illustrative of the detailed information the compilation has been designed to supply, in aid of the execution of the Criminal Law in this country, were submitted in our previous report, to which it is therefore only necessary that we should here refer your Excellency. Extracts.

We expressed in our Report of 1880 our intention of making this Register, when completed, available for general use with the least possible delay, and we have now the honour to add, for your Excellency's information, that during the past year 1,700 copies of it were printed and distributed as follows, viz.:—

Distribution of copies.

Department to which supplied.	No. of copies furnished.
Royal Irish Constabulary, ...	1,520
Dublin Metropolitan Police, . . .	30
Director of Criminal Investigation, Scotland Yard,	3
London City Police, ...	12
Edinburgh Police, ...	6
English Criminal Registry, ...	3
Irish Prisons, ...	42
Irish Bridewells, ...	43
General Prisons' Office, ...	41
Total, . .	1,700

and that, in further pursuance of the same object, an extended edition of 2,000 copies, to meet the requirements of the current year, is now in active course of preparation for issue in like manner. We cannot therefore but hope for a good result from this very complete registry of the criminal class.

IV. Departmental Arrangements.

41. No changes in our departmental staff have taken place during the past year.

Architect.

In our Second Report we took occasion to advert to the valuable aid we had experienced from the services of a skilled architect temporarily allowed to us to supervise the various works of reconstruction and repair with which we had from time to time to deal.

Lords Commissioners of Her Majesty's Treasury.

This officer's term of service, as at present limited, will expire before the close of the current year, but so indispensable an addition has he proved to our official staff, that we purpose when the time arrives making application to the Lords Commissioners of Her Majesty's Treasury for the necessary authority to retain him permanently.

V. Appendix.

Appendices.

42. In the Appendices hereto—A, B, C, D and E—will be found the various statistical tables and other information which it has been our practice to submit with each annual report, together with copies of all the important circular letters and instructional memoranda issued from our office during the course of the year.

We have the honour to be,
Your Excellency's obedient, faithful servants,

CHARLES F. BOURKE, *Chairman.*
J. BARLOW, *Vice-Chairman.*
W. P. O'BRIEN.

JOHN LENTAIGNE, *Hon. Member.*

APPENDICES

TO

FOURTH REPORT OF GENERAL PRISONS BOARD IRELAND, FOR THE YEAR 1881-82.

sed by the University of Southampton Library Digitisation Unit

APPENDICES

TO

FOURTH REPORT OF GENERAL PRISONS BOARD IRELAND, FOR THE YEAR 1881–82.

PRISON OFFICERS not to COMMUNICATE with NEWSPAPERS on PRISON MATTERS.

Circular No. 206, 4784.

General Prisons Board, Dublin Castle,
8th April, 1881.

It having been found that prison officers have, without the permission of or authority from the Prisons Board, addressed communications to the public press on prison matters, the Board request that you will inform the several officers, superior and others, attached to the prison under your charge, that as such a practice is subversive of order and discipline, they request that it may not be acted on in the future.

CHARLES F. BOURKE, Chairman.

To the Governors of Prisons.

ACCOUNT for MEDICINES OBTAINED from LOCAL APOTHECARIES.

MEMORANDUM, 3731.

General Prisons Board, Dublin Castle,
8th April, 1881.

SIR,

I am directed by the General Prisons Board to send you the subjoined copy of a memorandum in reference to accounts furnished for medicines, &c., obtained from local apothecaries, under Circular No. 180.

I am, sir, your obedient servant,

RICHARD CLEGG, Chief Clerk.

To Governors of Local Prisons.

MEMORANDUM WITH REFERENCE TO CIRCULAR, No. 180.

"Accounts submitted under above mentioned circular cannot be considered unless copies of prescriptions are attached."

Note.—You will please acknowledge the receipt of this memorandum, and observe the same course with regard to all circulars in future.

DISTINCTIVE DRESSES for PRISONERS ASSAULTING OFFICERS or TEARING their ORDINARY PRISON CLOTHING.

Circular No. 207.

General Prisons Board, Dublin Castle,
12th April, 1881.

With the view to distinguish prisoners who commit themselves in either of the following ways, the General Prisons Board direct that the following instructions shall be carried out, viz. :—

I. That male prisoners who assault an officer shall wear a party coloured dress.

II. That prisoners (male and female) who tear their ordinary prison clothing shall wear special canvas dresses.

A few of each of the respective dresses will be supplied you from Mountjoy Male Prison for the above purposes.

CHARLES F. BOURKE, Chairman.

To Governors of Prisons.

REQUISITIONS for BUILDING MATERIALS.

General Prisons Board, Dublin Castle,
CIRCULAR MEMORANDUM. 28th April, 1881.

As requisitions for building materials will in future be sent direct from this office to the contractors, and not as heretofore through the Board of Public Works, it will be necessary that separate requisitions shall be furnished by you for each contractor, or for each class of articles required, in order to obviate the necessity of dissecting the requisitions in this office, and sending copies of their portions to the various contractors; and the General Prisons Board request you will be so good as to be careful to give effect to their wishes in this respect in the future.

RICHARD CLEGG, Chief Clerk.

To Governors of Prisons.

EXPENSES INCURRED in ESCORTING and CONVEYING PRISONERS to and from the COURT of BANKRUPTCY.

General Prisons Board, Dublin Castle,
CIRCULAR MEMORANDUM. 3rd May, 1881.

In the case of a prisoner brought to the Court of Bankruptcy by order of that Court, the Governor of the Prison should send with the prison officer, who has charge of the prisoner, a written application addressed to the Court for the expenses incurred, in order that on the application the Court may give direction to the proper person to pay the expenses.

CHARLES F. BOURKE, Chairman.

To Governors of Prisons.

MILITARY PRISONERS may MEMORIAL COMMANDING OFFICERS, &c.

General Prisons Board, Dublin Castle,
CIRCULAR MEMORANDUM. 3rd May, 1881.

I am directed by the General Prisons Board to acquaint you that military prisoners—under sentences to imprisonment *only*—may be allowed to address applications for remission or mitigation of such sentences direct to the Commanding Officer, who confirmed such sentence.

The printed forms supplied for the memorials to the Commander-in-Chief, or Lord Lieutenant, are not to be used for this purpose, but they may be submitted on plain paper.

RICHARD CLEGG, Chief Clerk.

To Governors of Prisons.

EXPENSES of REMOVING PRISONERS for TRIAL.

No. 7408.

General Prisons Board, Dublin Castle,
CIRCULAR MEMO. 31st May, 1881.

It has been arranged that in future the Constabulary will provide for the conveyance of prisoners to and from Petty Sessions, or for examination before Magistrates, and will defray the expenses of such conveyance, which will be afterwards recovered by the Constabulary from Grand Juries.

Payments of such expenses will not therefore appear in the Accounts of the Prisons.

You will at once acquaint the officers in charge of minor Prisons and Bridewells, for which you account, if any, with the above arrangement.

You are requested to acknowledge the receipt of this Circular.

J. BARLOW, Vice-Chairman.

The Governors of H. M. Prisons.

COMMUTATION of SUPERANNUATION ALLOWANCES PAYABLE by TREASURY or LOCAL AUTHORITIES.

Circular No. 208.

General Prisons Board, Dublin Castle,
SIR, *1st July*, 1881.

The General Prisons Board have the honour to transmit to you for the consideration of the Grand Jury of the county of   at the ensuing Summer Assizes, the annexed extracts from a communication addressed by the Lords Commissioners of Her Majesty's Treasury to the Chief Secretary for Ireland, drawing attention to the provisions of the Act 41 and 42 Vic., cap. 63, as bearing on the superannuation allowances granted to retiring officers in the Prison service, under the 32nd section of the Prisons (Ireland) Act, 1877, 40 and 41 Vic., cap. 49, where such retiring allowances are payable partly by moneys provided by Parliament and partly by local authorities out of rates.

The Prisons Board request that you will call the special attention of the Grand Jury of the county of   to this matter, and that you may be so good as to report to them, immediately after the Assizes, the decision which the Grand Jury may arrive at, in order that the information shall be at once furnished to the Treasury, in compliance with the desire of their Lordships.

A copy of the Act 41 and 42 Vic., cap. 63, is enclosed herewith.

I have the honour to be, sir, your obedient servant,

CHARLES F. BOURKE, Chairman.

The Secretary of the Grand Jury of the county of ———

EXTRACT from TREASURY LETTER (No. 14,861/81) dated 12th May, 1881.

"The Act 41 & 42 Vic., cap. 63, by Section 2 of which Act it is provided that:—

"'When an annuity granted by way of superannuation allowance to an existing officer of a prison, under the sections of the Prison Acts mentioned in the first schedule to this Act, is apportioned to be paid partly by the Treasury out of moneys provided by Parliament, and partly by the local authority out of rates, the Treasury and the local authority may agree for the commutation of the share of the annuity apportioned to either of them; that is to say, for the payment by that one to the other of them of the capital value of such share ascertained according to the tables contained in the second schedule to this Act.'

"Thus far the statute contemplates a voluntary arrangement which is independent both of the total amount of the pension, and also of the amount of the parts of it paid by the several contributories.

"The rest of the section is limited to annuities of which the Imperial portion is less than £20, and admits of being put into force compulsorily by either of the contributories. This latter part of the section is as independent as the former part of the total amount of the pension.

"My Lords have always been and are ready to entertain any proposal from Prison Authorities for the commutation of either of the parts of pensions under the voluntary provisions of the section.

"Under the compulsory provisions, His Excellency is aware that My Lords have as yet made no general requirement on the local authorities to accept commutation of the Imperial share of the annuities in question, and before My Lords take into consideration the expediency of making such general requirement, they will be glad to learn whether the several local authorities would prefer that the Treasury should not make such compulsory requirement, that is to say, whether they would prefer to take advantage themselves of the compulsory provisions contained in the third paragraph of the section and require the Treasury to accept commutation of the shares apportioned to be paid by the local authorities which may be of any amount.

"Looking both to administrative convenience and to the interest of the Pensioners, it is obvious that it is preferable to pay these pensions from one source rather than from two, and that if the payment from one of the sources is less than £20, the duty of getting rid of such a part payment, by commuting it as soon as power to do so is given, arises as matter of course.

"With this object in view, My Lords request you to move His Excellency to cause a Circular to be issued to the several local authorities embodying the substance of this letter, and requesting replies at the earliest date convenient, stating:—

"1. If the Imperial portion of the annual payment be over £20 per annum whether they desire to make any proposal to the Treasury under the voluntary part of the Section?

"2. If the Imperial portion of the annual payment be under £20 per annum, whether they desire to make any requisition on the Treasury under the compulsory part of the section?

"My Lords will assume after the 31st August next, that any Prison Authority which has not then replied declines to require the Treasury to accept commutation of the part of the pension payable by such authority."

PRISONERS with INFANTS may RECEIVE MILK, &c., DAILY.

General Prisons Board, Dublin Castle,
MEMORANDUM. 18th July, 1881.

The General Prisons Board have to acquaint you that in the event of a female prisoner with an infant being committed to the prison under your charge, you are authorized to issue one quart of milk and half a pound of white bread, or a portion of the above allowance daily, for the use of such child, in case the mother is unable to maintain it.

CHARLES F. BOURKE, Chairman.

To Governors of Prisons.

PRISON OFFICERS on TEMPORARY DUTY in TOWNS where other PRISONS are SITUATED.

Circular No. 310, 11099/81.

General Prisons Board, Dublin Castle,
SIR, 27th July, 1881.

The General Prisons Board direct that when a prison officer is sent on duty out of his or her proper district he or she shall on arrival report him or herself to the Governor or other officer in charge of the prison in the town to which sent, and place him or herself under his orders until returning to the prison to which he or she is attached, which should be done so soon as such officer's services are no longer required.

I am, sir, your obedient servant,

CHARLES F. BOURKE, Chairman.

To Governors of Prisons.

NOTIFICATION of TRANSFER of PRISONERS.

General Prisons Board, Dublin Castle,
CIRCULAR MEMORANDUM. 27th July, 1881.

I am directed by the General Prisons Board to request that on occasions of the removal of a number of prisoners from your custody to another prison you will, by telegram after they have left, inform the Governor of the prison to which they are proceeding, of the number, and of the hour at which he may expect them.

By order,

RICHARD CLEGG, Chief Clerk.

To Governors of Prisons.

UNUSED BUILDINGS to be KEPT LOCKED, &c.

General Prisons Board, Dublin Castle,
CIRCULAR MEMORANDUM. 27th July, 1881.

The Prisons Board request the Governors and other officers in charge of prisons to be very careful in having any portions of the buildings not in daily use always kept locked and inspected occasionally, so as to prevent their being had resort to by unauthorized persons.

By order,

RICHARD CLEGG, Chief Clerk.

ACCOUNTS to be SIGNED in FULL.

General Prisons Board, Dublin Castle,
CIRCULAR MEMORANDUM. 28th July, 1881.

In some cases the receipts furnished for payments made by sub-accounting officers of prisons and charged in their accounts, exhibit only the initials of the firm or person to whom payment is made. The General Prisons Board, at the request of the Audit Department, have to desire that in future all receipts may be signed *in full.*

J. BARLOW.

The Governors, &c., of Prisons.

COUNTY CESS, POOR RATE, &c., NOT PAYABLE BY PRISON OFFICERS.

Circular No. 213.
13400.

General Prisons Board, Dublin Castle,
20th September, 1881.

The General Prisons Board desire to inform you with reference to the demands made on Officers of Local Prisons for payment of County Cess, Poor Rate, &c., that the Lords of Her Majesty's Treasury have decided "that those Officers are not liable to assessment in respect of the apartments which they occupy *ex-officio* in Prisons, but that contributions in respect of Prison property will be given by Her Majesty's Treasury to Local Rates by way of bounty."

J. BARLOW, Vice-Chairman.

To the Governors, &c., of Prisons.

PRIVATE CLOTHING of PRISONERS sentenced to PENAL SERVITUDE to be RETAINED for a YEAR in PRISONS, unless by PERMISSION it be given to PRISONER'S FRIENDS.

13,974
CIRCULAR MEMO.

General Prisons Board, Dublin Castle,
28th September, 1881.

The General Prisons Board request that the private clothing of prisoners sentenced to Penal Servitude shall be retained in the Prison for twelve months after the prisoner's conviction, excepting when the Governor is permitted to give it to the prisoner's friends.

By order,

RICHARD CLEGG, Chief Clerk.

The Governors of H. M. Prisons.

SENTENCES IMPOSED AT ADJOURNED QUARTER SESSIONS TAKE EFFECT from TIME of PRONOUNCEMENT.

Circular No. 214.
13,225.

General Prisons Board, Dublin Castle,
30th September, 1881.

Referring to Circular No. 129, and the Memorandum subsequently issued in relation thereto, dated the 29th January, 1880, the General Prisons Board have to state, for your information and guidance, that doubts having arisen as to the date from which sentences imposed upon prisoners at *adjourned* Quarter Sessions should count, the matter was referred to the Law Officers of the Crown, and the following Opinion has now been received on the subject.

J. BARLOW, Vice-Chairman.

OPINION.

"In our opinion the period of imprisonment in these cases runs from the time of the sentences being pronounced (the Defendants being then in Custody), and not from the original commencement of the Sessions."

Signed, H. LAW.
W. M. JOHNSON.
JOHN NAISH.

GOVERNORS not EMPOWERED to take EVIDENCE on OATH.

Circular No. 215.
15,020.

General Prisons Board, Dublin Castle,
8th October, 1881.

Some Governors of Prisons being under the impression that they have power to take evidence on oath; this power would of course extend to Deputy Governors and others performing their duties in their absences. The Board desire to inform Governors and their substitutes that they have not power to take evidence on oath.

The Board request that any cases in which evidence has been taken on oath by the above mentioned officers may be stated.

By order, RICHARD CLEGG, Chief Clerk.

The Governors, H. M. Prisons.

SOLDIERS CONVICTED by CIVIL POWER and ORDERED to be DISCHARGED from ARMY to be sent on Release to place of Conviction, &c.

15,173.
CIRCULAR MEMO.

General Prisons Board, Dublin Castle,
12th October, 1881.

The Governors of Prisons are reminded that soldiers who have been convicted by the *Civil Power*, and who have been ordered to be discharged from the army, can be sent on their release from Prison only to their places of conviction, or to any other intended places of residence to which the expense of sending them is not greater than to the place of conviction.

These expenses will be charged to the sub-head "Escort and Conveyance of Prisoners."

By order, RICHARD CLEGG, Chief Clerk.

The Governors, H. M. Prisons.

Treatment of Prisoners under Consecutive Sentences.

Circular No. 216.
14,276/81.

General Prisons Board, Dublin Castle,
16th October, 1881.

Sir,

I am directed by the General Prisons Board to send you, for your information and guidance, the subjoined copy of the Opinion of the Law Officers of the Crown, in reference to the treatment of prisoners in custody under sentence to consecutive terms of imprisonment.

I am, sir, your obedient servant,
Richard Clegg, Chief Clerk.

To the Governors of Prisons, &c., &c., &c.

Copy Opinion of Law Officers.

"The question we understand to be whether in point of law sentences of imprisonment for consecutive terms (where authorized) are to be regarded by the Prison Authorities in the application of Prison Rules, as distinct and separate terms of imprisonment, or as one single term equal in duration to the sum of the several consecutive terms. In our opinion they cannot properly be treated as all constituting one single term of imprisonment, but must each during its continuance be considered as a separate term, quite distinct from all which may succeed it, just as if it and it alone were the limit of imprisonment. We think too that this is the legal view of the case, whether the term is absolute or conditional, in default of payment of a fine imposed on the primary punishment."*

(Signed), H. L.
W. M. J.
16/9. 81.

Prison Dietary.

Circular No. 217.
16,103.

General Prisons Board, Dublin Castle,
29th October, 1881.

I am directed by the General Prisons Board to send you the attached copy of the Rules for the Dietaries of the Local Prisons, which are to be gazetted on Tuesday next, the 1st of November, and will therefore come into operation on and after that date.

The Dietaries in Bridewells are set forth on page 4, and a copy of these Rules has been sent to each keeper.

Please procure and forward offers to supply till 31st March next, any articles of Diet mentioned in these Rules not in contract.

Posters:— I. General Rules for Dietaries.
II. Hospital Diet.
III. Dietaries in Bridewells.

will in due course be supplied; please state how many copies of each you will require.

Richard Clegg, Chief Clerk.

To Governors of Prisons and Bridewell Keepers.

The General Prisons (Ireland) Act, 1877.

Rules for the Dietaries of the Local Prisons in Ireland, subject to the General Prisons (Ireland) Act, 1877.

By the General Prisons Board for Ireland.

In pursuance of the General Prisons (Ireland) Act, 1877, the General Prisons Board for Ireland hereby make the following Rules with respect to the Diets of Prisoners confined in ordinary Prisons in Ireland:

* See Circular 234, p. 30, Addenda to Rules, Sections I. and II.

[illegible] for the Dietaries of the Local Prisons in Ireland.

Meals	Class 1.	Men, Women, and Boys under 16 years of age, with and without hard labour.	Class 2.	Men with hard labour.	Men without hard labour, Women, and Boys under 16 years of age.	Class 3.	Men with hard labour.	Men without hard labour, Women, and Boys under 16 years of age.	Class 4. Prisoners awaiting Trial, Misdemeanants of First Division who do not maintain themselves, and Debtors.	
Breakfast,	Daily, Bread,	8 oz.	Daily . Bread, . Cocoa, .	6 oz., . 1 pint,	5 oz. 1 pint.	Daily, Stirabout (consisting of 4½ oz. Oatmeal, and 4½ oz. Indian Meal . New Milk,	1½ pint, 1 pint,	1½ pint. ½ pint.	Daily, . Bread, . Tea or Cocoa, or at option of Prisoner Stirabout, . as in Class 3, New milk, .	8 oz. 1 pint. 1½ pint. ½ pint.
Dinner,	Daily, Stirabout (containing 4 oz. Indian Meal and 4 oz. oatmeal).	1½ pint.	Sunday, and Thursday, . Bread, . Suet Pudding.	6 oz., 6 oz.	5 oz. 5 oz.	Sunday, . Meat soup with 4 oz. of beef without bone . Potatoes, .	1 pint, 16 oz.,	1 pint. 16 oz.	Sunday, Monday, Tuesday, Thursday, Saturday, . Bread, . Potatoes, Cooked Beef without bone	6 oz. 8 oz. 6 oz.
			Wednesday, and Friday, Bread, . Potatoes,	6 oz., . 6 oz., .	5 oz. 5 oz.	Monday, Tuesday, Thursday, Saturday, . Bread, . Vegetable Soup,	16 oz., . 1 pint,	14 oz. 1 pint.	Wednesday, and Friday, . Bread, . Vegetable Soup, .	16 oz. 1 pint.
			Monday, Tuesday, and Saturday, . Bread, . Soup, .	8 oz., . ½ pint,	6 oz. ½ pint.	Wednesday, and Friday, . Bread, . Potatoes, .	6 oz., . 16 oz., .	5 oz. 24 oz.		
Supper, .	Daily, Bread,	4 oz.	Daily Bread, . Cocoa, .	6 oz., . 1 pint.	5 oz. 1 pint.	Daily, Bread, . Cocoa, .	14 oz., 1 pint, .	8 oz. 1 pint.	Daily, . Bread, . Tea or Cocoa, .	8 oz. 1 pint.

The terms to which the first three classes of the above Diets are intended to be severally applied are those set forth in the following Table:—

Term.*	Class 1.	Class 2.	Class 3.
Seven days and under, ...	Whole term.	—	—
More than seven days and not more than one month . .	Seven days. . . .	Remainder of term.	—
More than one month and not more than four months, . .	. . . .	One Month, ...	Remainder of Term.
More than four months, ...	. . . .	. . . .	Whole term.

Note.—2 pints of Buttermilk may be given as an equivalent for 1 pint of New Milk. Bread may be given as an equivalent for stirabout, at the discretion of the Medical Officer in the proportion of 14 and 12 oz. Bread for 8 or 7 oz. meal respectively. In case of a Fast day in the Roman Catholic Church falling on any day other than Wednesday or Friday, the Prisoners of that persuasion may be given on such day the same Diet as on Friday.

* See Chapter 194, [illegible]

DIETARIES IN BRIDEWELLS.

CONVICTED.			UNCONVICTED.		
Breakfast,	Daily, Bread, . .	8 oz.	Breakfast,	Daily, { Bread, . . . Tea or Cocoa. . Or at option of Prisoner, Stirabout consisting of 3½ oz. oatmeal and 3½ oz. Indian meal, . New milk, . .	8 oz. 1 pint. 1¾ pint. ½ pint.
Dinner,	{ Daily, Stirabout consisting of 3 oz. Indian meal and 3 oz. oatmeal. }	1½ pint.	Dinner, .	Daily, { Bread, . . . Milk,* . . .	16 oz. 1 pint.
Supper, .	Daily, Bread, . .	8 oz.	Supper, .	Daily, { Bread, . . . Tea or Cocoa, . .	8 oz. 1 pint.

* Milk to be given warm in cold weather.

INGREDIENTS AND INSTRUCTIONS.

Bread, . . . To be made with whole meal, which is to consist of all the products of grinding the wheaten grain, with the exception of the coarser bran.

Soup, . . . In every pint 4 ounces clod (or shoulder), cheek, neck, leg, or shin of beef; 4 ounces split peas; 2 ounces fresh vegetables; ½ ounce onions; pepper and salt.

Suet pudding, . . 1½ ounce of mutton suet, 8 ounces flour, and about 6½ ounces water to make 1 pound.

Stirabout, . . . Equal parts of Indian meal and oatmeal, with salt. The Indian meal requires more cooking than the oatmeal.

To make 1½ pint stirabout, boil 2¼ pints water, to which a ¼ of an ounce of salt should be added; stir in 3 ounces of Indian meal, and afterwards 3 ounces oatmeal; keep constantly stirring, and when the meals are cooked, the required quantity of 1½ pint stirabout will be produced.†

Cocoa, . . . To every pint, ¾ ounce flaked or Admiralty cocoa. Sweetening:

For flaked cocoa, ¾ ounce molasses or sugar to the pint.

For Admiralty cocoa, ½ ounce molasses or sugar to the pint.

Meat liquor, or broth, . The liquor in which the meat is cooked on Sundays is to be thickened with ¼ ounce flour, and flavoured with ½ ounce onions to each ration, with pepper and salt to taste.

Vegetable soup, . Add to 1 gallon of boiling water 2 oz. pearl barley, 8 oz. oatmeal (blended in a little cold water), 2 lbs. of turnips peeled and sliced, 4 oz. of onions cut small, and pepper and salt to taste; when boiled for one hour the soup is fit for use. Parsnips or carrots may be substituted for turnips. The outer leaves of celery cut fine make an excellent addition to this soup, and where celery is grown it would be well to add them in the proportion of 2 oz. to each gallon.

Tea, . See instructions under Hospital Diets.

TABLE OF SUBSTITUTES FOR COOKED IRISH BEEF.

(All the Meats to be Weighed without bone.)

—	Colonial Beef or Mutton* Preserved by Heat.	Beans† and Fat Bacon (both Weighed after Cooking).	American or other Foreign Beef Preserved by Cold.‡	Cooked Fresh Fish.	Cooked Salt Meat.	Cooked Salt Fish.
	Ounces.		Ounces.	Ounces.	Ounces.	Ounces.
In lieu of 4 oz. cooked Irish beef.	5	Beans, 9 oz., Fat bacon, 1 oz.,	4	8	6	12
In lieu of 3 oz. cooked Irish beef,	3¾	Beans, 7 oz., Fat bacon, ¾ oz.,	3	6	4½	9

* The nutritive properties of this meat are injured by further heating, and it should be served cold.
† Broad or Windsor beans, dried in the green state and decorticated; or Haricot beans.
‡ Weighed after cooking.

TABLE OF SUBSTITUTES FOR POTATOES.

(All Weighed after Cooking.)

—	Cabbage or Turnip Tops.	Parsnips, Turnips, or Carrots.	Preserved (Dried) Potatoes.	Leeks.	Rice Steamed till tender.
	Ounces.	Ounces.	Ounces.	Ounces.	Ounces.
In lieu of 12 oz. potatoes, .	8	12	12	8	12
In lieu of 10 oz. potatoes, .	7	10	10	7	10
In lieu of 8 oz. potatoes, .	6	8	8	6	8
In lieu of 6 oz. potatoes, .	4	6	6	4	6

HOSPITAL DIETS FOR LOCAL PRISONS IN IRELAND.

MEN AND WOMEN.

DIETS.	PER DAY.					
	Bread.	Cooked Mutton without Bone.	New Milk.	Rice Pudding.	Arrow-root made with Milk.	Tea.
	Oz.	*Oz.*	*Oz.*	*Oz.*	*Oz.*	*Oz.*
Ordinary, . . .	16	5	20	8	—	—
Low, . . .	8	—	20*	—	20	15

* Additional to that in arrowroot.

The following Articles may be ordered as Extras or Substitutes in the quantities deemed necessary by the Medical Officer.

Ale.	Corn Flour.	Jelly.	Sago.
Bacon.	Eggs.	Lemonade.	Spirits.
Beef Tea.	Fruit.	Milk.	Stout.
Biscuits.	Greens (or other Vegetables).	Porter.	Sugar.
Butter.	Ice.	Potatoes.	Tea.
Cake.	Jam.	Poultry.	Waters (Mineral).
Cocoa.		Rice (ground).	Wine.
Coffee.			

Instructions.

Rice Pudding, . .	2 ounces rice; 1 pint milk; 1 ounce sugar; 1 egg and nutmeg, to produce 20 ounces.
Arrowroot, . . .	1 ounce arrowroot; 1 pint milk; 1 ounce sugar, to produce 1 pint.
Beef Tea, . . .	16 ounces of the lean parts of the neck of the ox to 1 pint water.
Tea, . . .	¼ ounce tea; ¾ ounce sugar; 2 ounces milk, and water to make up ¾ pint.
Cocoa, ...	¾ ounce flaked or Admiralty cocoa to 1 pint water, sweetened with ¾ ounce molasses or sugar for flaked cocoa, and ½ ounce molasses or sugar for Admiralty cocoa.
Lemonade, . . .	¼ ounce cream of tartar; ½ lemon (sliced); 2 ounces loaf sugar; water 1½ pint. The water to be added hot to the other ingredients, and the whole to be allowed to stand till cold; then strain.
Mutton, . .	To be roast or baked on four days in the week, and boiled on three days. On the days on which the mutton is boiled the meat liquor to be thickened with ¼ ounce flour, and flavoured with ¼ ounce onions per diet

---

Diets for Ill-conducted or Idle Prisoners.

No. 1.—Bread and Water Diet.

Men and Women.

1 lb. Bread per diem, with Water.

This diet to be limited, in the first place, to 3 days; after that, one of the undermentioned diets, according to labour performed, for 3 days before its repetition, when it is again to be limited to 3 days, and a second interval on one of the undermentioned diets is to elapse before it is again repeated. The entire period, including intervals, for which any single term of this diet may be ordered, is not to exceed 15 days. No task of labour is to be enforced on any one of the 9 days on which the bread and water constitute the sole food supplied to the prisoner.

No. 2.—Stirabout Diet.

For Men and Women performing a daily task of any labour not expressly defined as Hard Labour.

Breakfast, . .	Bread, 8 ounces.
Dinner, . . .	1 pint stirabout, containing 2 ounces oatmeal, and 2 ounces Indian meal, with salt. Potatoes, 8 ounces.
Supper, . . .	Bread, 8 ounces.

This diet to be limited, in the first place, to 21 days; after that, the diet of the class to which the prisoner belongs, for 1 week before its repetition, when it is to be limited to 14 days. The entire period, including the interval, for which any single term of this diet may be ordered, is not to exceed 42 days.

No. 3.—For Men performing a daily task of Hard Labour.

Breakfast, .	Daily, .	$1\frac{1}{2}$ pint stirabout, containing $3\frac{1}{2}$ oz. oatmeal, and $3\frac{1}{2}$ oz. Indian meal.
Dinner, .	Sunday, .	1 pint meat soup, with 4 oz. beef without bone. Potatoes, 16 oz.
	Monday, . Tuesday, . Thursday, . Saturday, .	Bread, 16 oz. Vegetable soup, 1 pint.
	Wednesday, Friday, .	Bread, 8 oz. Potatoes, 16 oz.
Supper, .	Daily, .	Bread, 10 oz. Cocoa, 1 pint.

This diet to be limited to 28 days; after that the diet Class 3 shall be resumed for 14 days, before its repetition. The Governor shall have authority to direct this dietary for any period not exceeding 28 days.

The foregoing rules shall apply to the prisoners confined in every ordinary prison, and shall come into operation upon the expiration of forty days after the same having been settled and approved by the Lord Lieutenant or Lords Justices and Privy Council, shall have been laid before Parliament.

Made and executed this 10th day of August, 1881, by "The General Prisons Board for Ireland."

Charles F. Bourke, *Chairman.*

[Seal.]

By the Lord Lieutenant and Privy Council of Ireland.

Cowper.

In pursuance of the General Prisons (Ireland) Act, 1877, We, the Lord Lieutenant-General and General Governor of Ireland, with the approval, advice, and consent of the Privy Council of Ireland, have settled and hereby approve of the foregoing rules made by the General Prisons Board for Ireland, with respect to the diets of the prisoners confined in ordinary prisons in Ireland.

Given at the Council Chamber, Dublin Castle, the 20th day of August, 1881.

O'Hagan, C. Henry Ormsby.

AMENDED RULES as to DISCIPLINE and DIETARY of PRISONERS in CUSTODY, under SENTENCES for CONSECUTIVE TERMS of IMPRISONMENT.

Circular No. 234.

General Prisons Board, Dublin Castle,
2nd May, 1882.

SIR,

I am directed by the General Prisons Board to send you, for your information and guidance, a copy of the amended Rules, and to inform you that His Excellency the Lord Lieutenant, has approved of their being put into operation at once.

Please inform the Medical Officer of these Rules, and as to His Excellency's sanction for their immediate adoption.

I am, sir, your obedient servant,

RICHARD CLEGG, Chief Clerk.

To the Governor, H. M.'s Prisons.

BY the GENERAL PRISONS BOARD for IRELAND.

In pursuance of the General Prisons (Ireland) Act, 1877, the General Prisons Board hereby make the following amended rules for the government of Prisons:—

I. Addenda to Rule 24 (General Rules for the government of Prisons):—"For the purposes of this rule, a prisoner in custody under sentences for consecutive terms of imprisonment, which in the aggregate exceed one month shall be considered as a prisoner whose sentence exceeds one month."

II. Addenda to Rule 38:—"The word 'sentence' in this rule includes the period, or the aggregate of the periods, during which a male prisoner above 16 years of age sentenced to hard labour is to be retained in custody, whether under one, or more than one, committal."

III. Dietaries for Local Prisons:—"The word 'term' in schedule m 'Rules for the Dietaries of Local Prisons in Ireland' shall include the period, or aggregate of the periods, during which a convicted prisoner is to be retained in custody, whether under one, or more than one, committal."

The foregoing rules shall apply to the prisoners confined in every ordinary prison, and shall come into operation upon the expiration of forty days after the same, having been settled and approved by the Lord Lieutenant, or Lords Justices and Privy Council, shall have been laid before Parliament.

Made and executed this 6th day of April, 1882, by "The General Prisons Board for Ireland."

[Seal.] J. BARLOW, Vice-Chairman.

BY the LORD LIEUTENANT and PRIVY COUNCIL of IRELAND.

COWPER.

In pursuance of the General Prisons (Ireland) Act, 1877, We, Francis Thomas De Grey, Earl Cowper, Lord Lieutenant-General and General Governor of Ireland, with the approval, advice, and consent of the Privy Council of Ireland, have settled and hereby approve of the foregoing rules made by the General Prisons Board for Ireland.

Given at the Council Chamber, Dublin Castle, this 20th day of April, 1882.

H. LAW, *C.* LEINSTER. BELMORE. HENRY ORMSBY,

VISITORS to PRISONERS.

General Prisons Board, Dublin Castle,
2nd November, 1881.

I am directed by the General Prisons Board to send you a supply of the accompanying "Order for Visitors to Prisoners," to be issued by you on the occasions of visits to prisoners, and to request that you will call the attention of the officers of the prison to the directions on backs of forms, and take care they are strictly carried out.

RICHARD CLEGG, Chief Clerk.

The Governors, H. M. Prisons.

N.B.—A further supply will be sent when received from printer.

DIETARIES in LOCAL PRISONS.

Circular 218, 16427/81 C.

General Prisons Board, Dublin Castle,
SIR, 3rd November 1881.

The General Prisons Board in sending you a copy of "The Rules for Dietaries in Local Prisons," beg to draw your attention to the annexed extract from the report of the committee upon whose recommendation these dietaries have been approved of by the Lord Lieutenant and Privy Council, and to express the desire of the Prisons Board that you will be guided in your orders for the issue of extra diet to prisoners by the opinion therein expressed.

I am, sir, your obedient servant,

C. F. BOURKE, Chairman.

To the Medical Officers of Local Prisons.

EXTRACT FROM REPORT OF MEDICAL COMMITTEE.

"The amended dietaries which we have prepared have been framed upon a sufficiently liberal basis to render it in our opinion unnecessary for medical officers of prisons to interfere with the suggested scales in the direction of any increase, except under circumstances distinctly connected with the existence of disease in individual prisoners. We, at the same time, recognize the expediency and the necessity of leaving in the hands of medical officers a discretionary power to effect minor alterations such, for instance, as the substitution of an equivalent in the shape of bread for the daily allowance of stirabout, where that article of diet is ascertained on the report of the prison authorities to disagree with a prisoner; but, with such exceptions, we disapprove of any interference with the dietary scales as laid down for healthy prisoners."

ACCOUNTING for EXTRA REMUNERATION by OFFICERS.

General Prisons Board, Dublin Castle,
CIRCULAR MEMO. 7th November 1881.

In accordance with instructions received from the Lords of Her Majesty's Treasury, the General Prisons Board has to desire that you will inform every officer of the prison, and bridewells, if any, for which you account, that he or she will be held responsible for duly apprising the chairman of the General Prisons Board, through you, annually, of all extra remuneration he or she has received out of public funds, or from fees, during the preceding financial year ending on 31st March, in addition to the fixed salary and ordinary emoluments of his or her office, stating *the amount of such extra remuneration, the service for which it was received, and the source from which it was provided.* This rule is intended to apply to all extra remuneration, however casual or variable (including of course remuneration for assessing and collecting income-tax in public departments), and to any pension or compensation allowance in respect of public service that an officer may receive—its object being to bring into one view the whole of his or her official emoluments from whatever source.

You will obtain and furnish to the chairman of the Board yearly on the 1st of May, in the annexed form, the statements of extra remuneration specified in this circular.

If none of the officers of the prison or bridewells for which you account received extra remuneration, a "Nil" return should be furnished by you.

It is requested that statements of extra remuneration for the year ended 31st March, 1881, as directed in this circular, may be obtained and forwarded as soon as possible, and not later than the 15th instant, by you to the chairman for the present staff of the prison and bridewells, if any, and that you will at the same time report that you have informed every officer of the contents of this circular.

C. F. Bourke, Chairman.

The Governor of each Prison.

———

——— Prison.

Return showing the Officers of this Prison who received Extra Remuneration out of Public Funds, in addition to the fixed Salaries and Ordinary Emoluments of their Offices, during the Year ended 31st March, 188 .

Name of Officer.	Rank in Prisons Service.	Service for which extra remuneration was received.	Source from which provided.	Amount.

——— Governor.

Date, ———

COPY WARRANT to be SENT with REPORT of a PRISONER'S LIFE BEING IN DANGER.

Circular No. 220.
19,411. General Prisons Board, Dublin Castle,
SIR, 15th December, 1881.

With reference to Rule 114 and circular No. 44, I am directed by the General Prisons Board to request that, in case of a prisoner whose life is certified to be in immediate danger by further confinement, you will forward with the usual report of the Medical Officer a copy of the rule of court or of the warrant or warrants under which the prisoner is detained, for the information of His Excellency the Lord Lieutenant.

I am, sir, your obedient servant,

RICHARD CLEGG, Chief Clerk.

The Governors, H. M. Prisons.

General Prisons Board, Dublin Castle,
CIRCULAR MEMO. 31st December, 1881.

With reference to the Law Officers' opinion conveyed to you in Circular No. 214, in which it was directed that sentences imposed at adjourned Quarter Sessions should run from the time of their being pronounced :

Inasmuch as there are several cases in which convicts had already been informed in accordance with a previous opinion of the Law Officers, that their sentences would be reckoned from the date of commencement of the sessions at which they were convicted :

I am directed by the General Prisons Board to inform you that in a case of this sort that was recently submitted to the Law Adviser, he, having regard to the fact that the convict had been informed that his sentence would be reckoned from the date of commencement of the sessions, directed that his sentence should be reckoned from that date, not from the date of conviction, and I am to request that you will submit to the Board the case of each such convict for instructions as to whether the sentence is to be reckoned from the date of commencement of the sessions or not, each case to be submitted one month prior to the time when the convict would be eligible for release on licence if his sentence were reckoned from the earlier date.

RICHARD CLEGG, Chief Clerk.

To Governors and Superintendents
of Convict Prisons.

TRAVELLING EXPENSES and PERSONAL ALLOWANCES to PRISON OFFICERS in ATTENDANCE as CROWN WITNESSES at ASSIZES or QUARTER SESSIONS.

757. General Prisons Board, Dublin Castle,
Circular Memo. 10th January, 1882.

The General Prisons Board desire to inform you that Prison Officers are not entitled to travelling expenses or personal allowances from prison funds for attendance at Assizes or Quarter Sessions Courts, as Crown witnesses. The officers receive payment from the Crown or Quarter Sessions Solicitors for such services.

By order,

RICHARD CLEGG, Chief Clerk.

The Governors, H. M. Prisons.

PAYMENT for UNAUTHORIZED WORKS.

Circular No. 222.
1,493/82. General Prisons Board, Dublin Castle,
SIR, 6th February, 1882.

It having been found that in some instances, Governors of Prisons have had without authority works done by contractors in excess of those in their contract, I am directed by the General Prisons Board to inform you that in the future the cost of such unauthorized works will be surcharged to the Governor who permits the carrying out of such works, unless they shall be considered by the Prisons Board to have been of so urgent a nature as to justify the Governor in having them effected without formal authority from them.

I am, sir, your obedient servant,

RICHARD CLEGG, Chief Clerk.

The Governor, H. M. Prison.

CERTIFICATE of BIRTH to ACCOMPANY SUPERANNUATION PAPERS in CERTAIN CASES.

Circular No. 223.
2,437/82. General Prisons Board, Dublin Castle,
SIR, 11th February, 1882.

I am directed by the General Prisons Board to inform you that the Lords Commissioners of Her Majesty's Treasury desire that in the future all applications for superannuation from officers who have not obtained Civil Service Certificates of qualification, shall be accompanied by Legal Certificates of dates of birth, and you are requested to comply with their Lordships' directions in all such cases.

I am, sir, your obedient servant,

RICHARD CLEGG, Chief Clerk.

To the Governors of Local Prisons.

MILITARY PRISONERS' CONVEYANCE, CLOTHING, &c., ON RELEASE.

General Prisons Board, Dublin Castle,
18th February, 1882.

CIRCULAR MEMO.

Referring to Circular 142, dated 30th July, 1879, from this Office, relating to allowances for conveyance, clothing, and subsistence, on release of Military Prisoners who have been discharged from the Army, and which have been hitherto charged in the accounts, under the sub-head " Advances for War Department," the General Prisons Board have to acquaint you that no charge of this nature will be made against the War Department for any Military Prisoners of the class referred to in this Circular, who have been released since the 1st January, 1882, inclusive, or who may hereafter be released.

In future, such prisoners will be treated on release in every respect as prisoners who have been convicted by the Civil Power are treated.

This arrangement will apply also to similar cases of Naval Prisoners.

J. BARLOW.

Governors of Prisons.

EXTRA DIET TO PRISONERS NOT IN HOSPITAL.

Circular No. 224.
3520/82.

General Prisons Board, Dublin Castle,
3rd March, 1882.

SIR,

Having regard to Circular No. 218, 3rd November, 1881—Dietaries in Local Prisons—I am directed by the General Prisons Board to request that you will inform the Medical Officer that they are of opinion that Prisoners, not in Hospital, ordered by him "Extra Diet," should be considered as "Sick Prisoners," to be seen by him daily, and that their names, &c., should be entered in the Medical Officer's Book.

I am, sir, your obedient servant,
RICHARD CLEGG, Chief Clerk.

The Governor, H.M. Prison.

CONVEYANCE of PRISONERS ON RELEASE to PLACE of CONVICTION.

Circular No. 227.
4471/82.

General Prisons Board, Dublin Castle,
6th March, 1882.

SIR,

I am directed by the General Prisons Board to inform you in reference to Circular No. 128, 27th June, 1879, that in cases where you are unable to provide a prisoner with a passage by Railway or other public conveyance the *entire* way to the place of his conviction, you may give the prisoner such a sum of money as will be sufficient to pay for his conveyance for the remainder of his journey, taking care to obtain his receipt for such payment.

This instruction refers to prisoners whether committed direct to the Prison in your charge or transferred thereto from other Gaols.

I am, sir, your obedient servant,
RICHARD CLEGG, Chief Clerk.

The Governor, H. M. Prison.

QUARTERLY REPORT as to CESSPOOLS in PRISONS.

Circular No. 226.
4885/82.

General Prisons Board, Dublin Castle,
7th March, 1882.

SIR,

I am directed by the General Prisons Board to request that you will, within seven days after the commencement of each Quarter, furnish a report to them as to the condition and cleanliness of any cesspools or other receptacles in connection with the sewerage of the Prison under your charge.

I am, sir, your obedient servant,
RICHARD CLEGG, Chief Clerk.

The Governors of H.M. Prisons.

RECEIPT STAMPS to be CANCELLED by WRITING ACROSS THEM.

General Prisons Board, Dublin Castle,
16th March, 1882.

CIRCULAR MEMO.

The Audit Department having called attention to a case in which an adhesive stamp on a receipt was not cancelled, the General Prisons Board have to desire that in future such stamps may in all cases be properly cancelled by the person who gives the receipt, by his writing on or across the stamp his name or initials (or the name or initials of his firm), together with the date of his so writing, so that the stamp may be effectually cancelled.

J. BARLOW, Vice-Chairman.

The Governors and Sub-Accounting Officers of Prisons.

ISSUE of UNIFORM to WARDERS on PROBATION.

Circular No. 228.
B. O. 13/3/81.

General Prisons Board, Dublin Castle,
18th March, 1882.

SIR,

Referring to Circular No. 200, dated 19th January, 1881, I am to inform you that the General Prisons Board direct that the following instructions as to the issue of Uniform to Warders on Probation may be acted on until further orders.

I. Upon receipt of a certificate of an officer's fitness from the Civil Service Commissioners, uniform will be issued immediately.

II. If the officer should not pass probation, the uniform is to be taken up and issued to officer joining subsequently.

I am sir, your obedient servant,

RICHARD CLEGG, Chief Clerk.

The Governor, ——— Gaol.

COPIES of CIRCULARS issued to GOVERNORS of PRISONS in which PRISONERS under the ACT 44 VIC., CAP. 4, are CONFINED.

6,754.

General Prisons Board, Dublin Castle,
9th May, 1881.

SIR,

I am directed by the General Prisons Board to transmit to you the subjoined copy of a ruling, which has been approved of by the Executive, relating to newspaper editors detained in prison under the Lord Lieutenant's warrant.

I am, sir, your obedient servant,

RICHARD CLEGG, Chief Clerk.

The Governor, H. M. Prison.

"Newspaper editors detained in prison under the Lord Lieutenant's "warrant may be allowed in future to continue their employment as "editors, and should be afforded all reasonable facilities accordingly.

"The Governor should not, however, allow them to send out of prison "any leading articles or statements containing any reference to imprison- "ment, or any reflection upon the Government.

"In doubtful cases the Governor should apply directly to the* Chief "Secretary's Office for instructions."—T. H. B., 9/5/81.

* See Order 0393, 30th June, 1881.

General Prisons Board, Dublin Castle,
28th May, 1881.

SIR,

I am directed by the General Prisons Board to forward to you, for your information and guidance, the subjoined copy of an Order from the Executive in reference to letters written by one "Suspect" to another.

I am, sir, your obedient servant,

RICHARD CLEGG, Chief Clerk.

The Governor, H. M. Prison.

"As to letters from one imprisoned "Suspect" to another, they should "not be forwarded unless they are confined to personal matters, having "no connexion with politics or administration."

REGULATION as to VISITS to PRISONERS CONFINED under the ACT for the BETTER PROTECTION of PERSON and PROPERTY, 44 VIC., CAP. 4.

Visitors to prisoners, and prisoners, are informed that in such interviews communications must be confined to personal or business matters, or to representations with regard to personal treatment, and if other matters are introduced the visit will at once cease.

General Prisons Board, Dublin Castle,
4th June, 1881.

8,188. General Prisons Board, Dublin Castle,
9th June, 1881.

SIR,

The General Prisons Board having received representations respecting the conversation of visitors with prisoners and letters to and from prisoners, they direct me to instruct you that the discretion with regard to conversations and letters must rest with the Governors, who will deal with each case upon its merits; but it is desirable that conversations and letters should be confined to business and personal matters, and the Governors will be supported in such instructions.

Should the prisoners complain to their friends, either by word of mouth or in letters, with regard to their personal treatment or the grounds of their detention, the Prisons Board advise the Governor to forward such representations if couched in respectful terms.

I am, sir, your obedient servant,

RICHARD CLEGG, Chief Clerk.

The Governor, —— Prison.

9393. General Prisons Board, Dublin Castle,
30th June, 1881.

SIR,

I am directed by the General Prisons Board to inform you with regard to Rule XIV. of the Special Rules for the treatment of prisoners in confinement under warrant of the Lord Lieutenant, that it is the desire of the Executive that any letters from this class of prisoners you desire to submit to the Chief or Under Secretary, you will in future forward through this department.

I am, sir, your obedient servant,

RICHARD CLEGG, Chief Clerk.

The Governor, H. M. Prison.

Circular No. 209.

9841. General Prisons Board, Dublin Castle, 7th July, 1881.

SIR,

The General Prisons Board have to acquaint you that the Executive has been pleased to direct that whenever the Medical Officer of a prison in which are confined prisoners detained under the Lord Lieutenant's warrant, considers that the health of any such prisoner is seriously impaired, or likely to be impaired, or that his life is endangered, or is likely to be endangered by further confinement, such Medical Officer should at once report the fact to the Under Secretary through this department for the Lord Lieutenant's information.

You are requested to inform the Medical Officer that such reports are to be made *mutatis mutandis* in the same form as the ordinary reports by Surgeons of prisons, hereto annexed.

When any such prisoner is attended by his own medical attendant, a copy of this Order should be handed to such medical attendant for his information and guidance.

I am, sir, your obedient servant,

CHARLES F. BOURKE, Chairman.

The Governor, H. M. Prison.

11307. General Prisons Board, Dublin Castle, 11th August, 1881.

SIR,

I am directed by the Executive to inform you that whenever the medical attendant of a prisoner, confined under the Lord Lieutenant's warrant, requires such patient to undergo a personal examination of a delicate nature, the presence of a Prison Warder is to be dispensed with, if such is the expressed wish of the prisoner in question.

These directions will only be followed on full understanding between the Governor and medical attendant, that no conversation takes place between the prisoner and medical attendant during the absence of the Prison Officer, except directly in reference to the prisoner's health, and that no communications whatever are conveyed to or from the prisoner.

This order applies only to P. P. P. prisoners.

I am, sir, your obedient servant,

CHARLES F. BOURKE, Chairman.

The Governor, H. M. Prison.

Circular. General Prisons Board, Dublin Castle,
22nd October, 1881.

The GOVERNOR, H. M. Prison.

No visits are to be permitted to P. P. P. prisoners, unless between the hours of 10 A.M. and 3.30* P.M., until further notice.

By order of the Board,

RICHARD CLEGG, Chief Clerk.

* Extended until further orders to 5 o'clock, by Memo. dated 20th March, 1882.

15788. General Prisons Board, Dublin Castle,
24th October, 1881.

The GOVERNOR, H. M. Prison.

I am directed by the General Prisons Board to send you the attached copy of instructions as to visits to P. P. P. Prisoners, and to request that you will take care that they are strictly carried out in the Prison under your charge.

By order,

RICHARD CLEGG, Chief Clerk.

"I. As regards visits to any important P. P. P. Prisoner, a Superior Officer should be always present, and accordingly an Officer of this description should always be in readiness during the times set apart for such visits.

"II. As regards the privilege accorded to Prisoners of being attended, if out of health, by their usual medical man, the rule requires that before a Physician (not being the Surgeon to the prison) is admitted to visit a Prisoner, it should appear that the Prisoner is out of health, and that the Physician in question is the usual Medical Attendant of the Prisoner, and before the privilege is accorded, the Governor should be satisfied as to both these points. Where a proper case arises for permitting the privilege, the Physician may see the Prisoner, either in consultation with the Medical Officer of the Prison or any other Medical Officer required by the Governor to attend; or if the Governor thinks fit, either in private or in the presence of the Governor or a superior and confidential officer. The Governor's discretion in such cases should be regulated by the consideration that no abuse of the privilege is to be permitted.

"Any directions by a private medical man as to diet, exercise, &c., should be submitted to the Medical Officer of the Prison, and if he does not think they should be carried out, the matter must be referred to the Governor.

"III. The privilege accorded to Prisoners of seeing their legal adviser must not be abused, and before it is permitted the Governor should be satisfied that the visit is *bona fide* sought for the transaction of private legal affairs.

"Where such a visit is *bona fide* sought, the Clerk, if furnished with the written authority of his principal, should be admitted."

17529. General Prisons Board, Dublin Castle,
SIR, 18th November, 1881.

I am directed by the General Prisons Board to inform you that on receipt of an Order for the removal of a Prisoner confined under the

Act for the better Protection of Person and Property from your custody to another Prison, you will have him examined by the Medical Officer as to his physical fitness for such removal, and if the Surgeon considers such removal inadvisable on medical grounds, you will detain the Prisoner and report the circumstances at once to the Under Secretary to the Lord Lieutenant, and to this Department.

I am, sir, your obedient servant,

RICHARD CLEGG, Chief Clerk.

The Governor, Prison.

20381. General Prisons Board, Dublin Castle, 30th December, 1881.

SIR,

I am directed by the General Prisons Board to state for your information and guidance that His Excellency the Lord Lieutenant approves of Chess and Draughts being permitted to be played by the prisoners detained under His Excellency's warrant.

I am, sir, your obedient servant,

R. CLEGG, Chief Clerk.

The Governor, H. M. Prison.

General Prisons Board, Dublin Castle, 13th May, 1881.

The GOVERNOR H. M. Prison.

I am to inform you that the Executive request that a return in the form annexed may be furnished them every Monday morning through this department.

By order,

RICHARD CLEGG, Chief Clerk.

GENERAL PRISONS BOARD.

* Weekly Return showing number of Persons detained under the Lord Lieutenant's Warrant, 44 Vic., cap. 4, for the Week ending———

Gaol.	Number detained.	Actual Accommodation under existing Arrangements.	Observations.

Signature of Governor, ———

Date, ———

* To be posted so as to reach the General Prisons Board on morning of each succeeding *Monday*.

General Prisons Board, Dublin Castle, 188

SIR,

I am directed by the General Prisons Board to transmit to you forms of list of prisoners detained under the Protection of Person and Property Act, and to request that you will furnish such return to the

Board on the 1st of each month, in the event of your having prisoners of this class in your custody.

You are also to furnish the Board within twenty-four hours of the committal to your custody of a prisoner of this class with the following return:—

Name of Prisoner.	Date of Committal.	Place from whence committed.

I am, sir, your obedient servant,

RICHARD CLEGG,
Chief Clerk.

The Governor, H. M. Prison.

MONTHLY RETURN.

List of all Persons detained in ——— Prison under the Statute 44 Victoria, chapter 4, intituled "An Act for the better Protection of Person and Property in Ireland."

To be laid before each House of Parliament within the first seven days of ——— 188 .

No.	Name of Prisoner.	Ground stated for his Arrest in the Warrant under which he is detained.

Signature of Governor, ———

Date, ——— 188 .

H. M. PRISON AT ———

Nominal Return of Prisoners committed to the above Prison under Warrant of His Excellency the Lord Lieutenant, within the previous Twenty-four hours.

No.	Name.	Date of Committal.	Place from whence committed.

Signature of Governor, ———

Date, ———

The Chairman, General Prisons Board, Dublin Castle.

General Prisons Board, Dublin Castle,
Memo. 7th September, 1881.

The GOVERNOR, H. M. Prison.

I am to request that you will report to this office from time to time the name of any prisoner committed under the Act for the better Protection of Person and Property, who may be discharged by order of the Executive, stating whether the usual undertaking has been signed.

RICHARD CLEGG, Chief Clerk.

H. M. PRISON AT ———

Nominal Return of P. P. P. Prisoners discharged from the above Prison, by order of His Excellency the Lord Lieutenant, within the previous Twenty-four hours.

Name.	Date of Committal.	Place from whence committed.	Conditions upon which released.

Signature of Governor, ———
Date, ———

The Chairman, General Prisons Board, Dublin Castle.

1693. 21st January, 1882.

Prisoners should not be allowed to write to newspapers.

T. H. B., 20/1/82.

To Governors of Prisons for their information.

RICHARD CLEGG,
Chief Clerk, 1/2/82.

7,999/81.

NEWSPAPERS.

The following is the rule as to newspapers to P. P. P. prisoners:—

A prisoner under His Excellency's warrant may receive the papers from his own locality, and also the London daily papers, and the *Graphic* and *Punch*, should they so desire.

Circular No. 225.
4,885/82. General Prisons Board, Dublin Castle,
SIR, 4th March, 1882.

I am directed by the General Prisons Board to request you to inform the Medical Officer that they desire that he will, until further orders, furnish at the commencement of each month a report on the sanitary condition of the prison, and at the same time be good enough to offer any suggestion on the subject he may deem advisable.

I am, sir, your obedient servant,

RICHARD CLEGG, Chief Clerk.

The Governor, H. M. Prison.

Circular No. 229.
6,383.

General Prisons Board, Dublin Castle,
18th March, 1882.

Sir,

I am directed by the General Prisons Board to send you the attached copy of amended rules as to the hours of exercise and association to be allowed to prisoners confined by warrant of the Lord Lieutenant, under the Act for the Protection of Person and Property, and to request that you will immediately carry out these arrangements, and report when such are in force.

I am, sir, your obedient servant,

Richard Clegg, Chief Clerk.

The Governors, H. M. Prisons in which P. P. P. prisoners are confined.

P. P. P. Prisoners' Exercise and Association.

Exercise in Open Air.

Summer.

From 7 to 8 A.M.
" 9.40 to 11.10 A.M.
" 2 to 5 P.M.

Association in Hall.

From 11.10 A.M. to 12.10 P.M.
" 5.30 P.M. to 7 P.M.

In the hours of exercise and association the prisoners may, in future be in the open air or in association hall, as they may select.

"I approve of modification of rules as above, to be carried out as soon as arrangements permit.

"W. E. F., 16/3/82."

6,080/82.
Memo.

General Prisons Board, Dublin Castle,
20th March, 1882.

The following copy of a direction given by the Vice-Chairman to the Governor of Monaghan Prison is sent for your information and guidance:—

"Governor, Monaghan Prison.

"All bottles containing the porter or wine sent in to prisoners should "be opened by a warder.

"J. Barlow.

"March 16/82."

By order,

Richard Clegg, Chief Clerk.

To Governors of Prisons in which P. P. P. prisoners are confined.

Extension of Hours during which Visits to P. P. P. Prisoners may be permitted.

6,613.
General Prisons Board, Dublin Castle,
Memo. 20th March, 1882.

Until further instructions on the subject, the hours during which P. P. P. prisoners may be permitted to receive visits shall be extended to 5 o'clock.

By order,
R. Clegg, Chief Clerk.

To Governors of Prisons in which
P. P. P. prisoners are confined.

6,865.
General Prisons Board, Dublin Castle,
Memo. 22nd March, 1882.

The following Order of the Board is sent for your information and guidance:—

"In all cases where P. P. P. prisoners are in the exercise ground, one "warder will remain in the shed when it is occupied by prisoners."

By order,
A. Newton Brady, *Pro* Chief Clerk.

To Governors of Prisons in which
P. P. P. prisoners are confined.

6,893.
General Prisons Board, Dublin Castle,
Memo. 23rd March, 1882.

I am directed by the General Prisons Board to request that in the event of your receiving any application from the Guardians of a Poor Law Union to be informed as to whether a particular P. P. P. prisoner has been released from custody, that you will afford them the required information.

By order,
A. Newton Brady, *Pro* Chief Clerk.

To Governors of Prisons in which
P. P. P. prisoners are confined.

7,661.
General Prisons Board, Dublin Castle,
Circular Memo. 29th March, 1882.

Where P. P. P. prisoners desire white bread in place of brown, such may be issued if the Medical Officer sees no objection.

J. Barlow, Vice-Chairman.

The Governors, H. M. Prisons.

7,805. General Prisons Board, Dublin Castle,
Circular Memo. 1st April, 1882.

His Excellency the Lord Lieutenant has been pleased to approve of the following Rule, which you will be careful to carry out :—

"Editors of Newspapers confined as 'Suspects' are to be informed that "if they wish to be supplied with unobjectionable Weekly Newspapers "(other than those from their own locality) which may be sent to them for "business purposes, they are at liberty to apply for permission to receive "such papers to the General Prisons Board, who will carefully consider "same."

By order,

RICHARD CLEGG, Chief Clerk.

The Governors, H. M. Prisons, where
P. P. P. prisoners are confined.

GAMES not PERMITTED on SUNDAYS.

General Prisons Board, Dublin Castle,
10th May, 1882.

SIR,

I am directed by the General Prisons Board to instruct you that no games are to be permitted to be played by the prisoners on Sundays.

I am sir, your obedient servant,

RICHARD CLEGG, Chief Clerk.

The Governors, H. M. Prisons in which
P. P. P. prisoners are confined.

Table I.—Number of Commitments to Local Prisons

Names of Prisons.	Convicted. At Assizes and Quarter Sessions. Found Guilty. M.	F.	Found Insane. M.	F.	Summarily. Offences under Larceny Act. M.	F.	Misdemeanants. M.	F.	Under Revenue Laws. M.	F.	Under Poor Law Act. M.	F.	By Courts-Martial. M.	Deserters. M.	Under Vagrancy Act. M.	F.	Drunkards. M.	F.
Armagh,	63	8	–	–	61	37	248	59	2	–	–	–	2	7	20	14	297	106
Belfast,	68	12	1	–	248	130	1,440	934	4	6	3	–	18	32	58	75	1,888	878
Carlow,	9	3	–	–	5	3	18	7	–	–	–	–	–	–	2	1	67	8
Carrick-on-Shannon,	20	6	–	–	2	–	51	4	–	–	8	–	10	1	4	2	40	10
Castlebar,	24	2	–	–	27	10	176	60	5	2	9	3	–	3	–	4	100	43
Cavan,	–	–	–	–	1	–	27	8	–	–	–	–	–	8	–	–	71	17
Clonmel,	25	5	1	–	31	13	327	58	–	–	1	–	4	6	18	–	385	41
Cork, Male,	154	–	–	–	132	–	848	–	–	–	21	–	83	13	60	–	942	–
Cork, Female,	–	35	–	3	–	59	–	503	–	–	–	18	–	–	–	–	–	808
Downpatrick,	42	8	–	1	6	9	48	8	–	–	1	–	2	1	26	2	80	41
Drogheda,	–	4	–	1	–	14	–	52	–	–	–	1	–	–	–	6	–	127
Dundalk,	24	–	–	–	73	–	223	–	1	–	16	–	2	7	23	–	150	–
Ennis,	–	–	–	–	2	2	38	4	1	–	1	–	–	–	12	1	66	12
Enniskillen,	4	–	–	–	–	3	11	5	–	–	–	–	–	–	–	1	124	31
Galway,	63	6	–	–	11	9	467	104	10	2	6	2	58	–	11	3	285	132
Grangegorman,	11	86	1	–	[illegible]	117	1,091	2,017	2	–	–	–	6	–	36	76	1,891	3,006
Kilkenny,	94	18	–	–	17	6	106	48	–	–	–	–	58	4	61	8	136	44
Kilmainham,	35	1	–	–	117	6	640	20	–	–	7	–	10	2	38	4	498	30
Lifford,	–	–	–	–	1	1	11	–	2	–	1	–	2	–	1	–	14	3
Limerick, Male,	44	–	95	–	–	–	643	–	–	–	25	–	19	17	83	–	387	–
Limerick, Female,	–	17	–	–	–	42	–	405	–	–	–	–	–	–	–	9	–	130
Londonderry,	80	16	1	2	66	20	309	95	16	12	4	1	81	5	10	19	236	192
Longford,	–	–	–	–	4	5	21	10	–	–	1	–	–	–	1	–	80	19
Maryboro',	29	1	–	–	2	1	66	11	–	–	10	1	88	6	11	–	107	10
Monaghan,	4	–	–	–	3	–	14	3	1	–	–	–	2	–	–	–	55	24
Mullingar,	91	6	–	–	38	15	406	112	6	–	14	14	25	1	4	–	242	86
Naas,	17	1	–	–	28	6	117	37	–	–	4	1	36	–	22	6	258	52
Nenagh,	27	–	–	–	6	1	107	9	–	–	7	–	2	–	8	–	142	9
Omagh,	52	10	–	–	16	8	126	9	13	–	–	–	17	3	4	8	98	64
Richmond,	464	–	4	–	244	–	704	–	1	–	9	–	4	36	4	–	55	–
Roscommon,	3	2	–	–	2	1	45	12	–	–	–	–	–	2	2	–	61	12
Sligo,	81	14	1	–	18	6	282	50	10	7	22	2	1	–	4	–	121	76
Tralee,	32	2	1	–	48	5	368	70	1	–	8	–	–	1	3	–	221	48
Trim,	18	3	–	–	18	4	46	9	–	–	4	3	–	1	15	–	47	6
Tullamore,	19	4	–	–	–	5	2	149	82	–	–	1	102	–	6	1	126	41
Waterford,	96	3	1	–	38	28	321	115	–	–	11	–	9	12	1	5	864	144
Wexford,	28	4	–	–	67	19	97	24	–	–	12	4	–	2	8	1	60	5
Wicklow,	–	–	–	–	9	4	30	8	1	–	1	3	–	6	–	–	94	14
Total, Males,	1682	–	79	–	1391	–	10086	–	110	–	200	–	546	171	585	–	9,183	–
Total, Females,	–	235	–	7	–	604	–	5,096	–	30	–	54	–	–	–	251	–	9,274
Total, M. and F.,	1,917		86		1,973		15,182		140		254		717		836		18,457	

Note.—The prisoners committed under the Act for the Better Protection of Person and

from 1st April, 1881, to 31st March, 1882.

Trial.		Not Convicted.						Untried Prisoners in Custody on 31st March, 1882.		Total Commitments.			Names of Prisons.
		Acquitted on Trial.		For Further Examination, Remanded, and Discharged.		Total.							
M.	F.	M.	F.	M.	F.	M.	F.	M.	F.	M.	F.	M. & F.	
706	217	14	6	44	5	60	9	2	–	764	226	990	Armagh.
5,204	2,018	47	14	585	88	870	102	21	4	6,601	2,141	8,742	Belfast.
101	22	–	–	61	14	61	14	–	–	102	66	168	Carlow.
136	26	–	–	50	9	50	9	–	–	186	31	217	Carrick-on-Shan.
342	121	23	1	101	9	124	10	4	–	471	131	602	Castlebar.
102	24	–	–	31	7	31	7	–	–	133	32	165	Cavan.
748	113	10	–	60	7	70	7	4	–	822	122	944	Clonmel.
2,193	–	81	–	127	–	208	–	61	–	2,462	–	2,462	Cork, Male.
–	1,426	–	8	–	26	–	34	–	8	–	1,468	1,468	Cork, Female.
212	75	9	5	26	2	35	7	6	1	253	83	336	Downpatrick
–	208	–	7	–	7	–	14	–	1	–	223	223	Drogheda.
518	–	7	–	48	–	55	–	3	–	576	–	576	Dundalk.
118	15	–	–	187	20	187	20	3	–	258	39	297	Ennis.
136	40	1	–	54	12	55	13	–	2	194	55	249	Enniskillen.
912	653	64	8	168	6	232	14	8	1	1,152	670	1,822	Galway.
2,663	6,304	–	46	–	148	–	197	–	2	2,663	6,503	9,166	Grangegorman.
467	116	12	11	65	6	77	17	4	–	548	135	683	Kilkenny.
1,346	63	2	–	46	1	48	1	11	–	1,406	67	1,473	Kilmainham.
38	4	–	–	26	2	26	2	2	–	60	6	66	Lifford.
1,298	–	86	–	207	–	330	–	4	–	1,632	–	1,632	Limerick, Male.
–	603	–	4	–	137	–	141	–	2	–	746	746	Limerick, Female.
814	603	21	13	58	9	79	22	10	4	903	629	1,297	Londonderry.
116	46	–	–	27	5	27	6	5	–	148	46	194	Longford.
326	24	4	1	17	1	21	2	13	3	360	29	389	Maryboro'.
78	29	–	–	45	12	48	12	–	–	121	41	162	Monaghan.
820	228	17	8	83	4	100	12	4	1	936	248	1,184	Mullingar.
482	106	17	–	25	2	42	2	–	–	524	108	632	Naas.
291	19	7	–	12	2	19	2	–	–	310	21	331	Nenagh.
330	108	18	8	17	2	35	10	6	–	371	110	481	Omagh.
1,575	–	104	–	548	–	652	–	69	–	2,296	–	2,296	Richmond.
102	27	8	4	39	2	47	6	2	–	151	33	184	Roscommon.
540	154	7	2	86	8	93	10	7	1	640	165	805	Sligo.
678	125	41	–	96	10	137	10	45	–	860	135	995	Tralee.
146	25	3	2	17	3	20	5	1	–	167	30	197	Trim.
410	81	18	3	31	2	49	5	5	–	465	86	551	Tullamore.
782	808	12	6	40	10	55	16	1	2	838	326	1,164	Waterford.
268	57	–	–	12	1	12	1	4	1	284	59	343	Wexford.
141	24	16	6	–	–	18	6	2	–	161	30	191	Wicklow.
24,103	–	607	–	2,828	–	3,420	–	306	–	27,834	–	–	Total, Males.
–	12,469	–	161	–	590	–	747	–	35	–	13,254	–	Total, Females.
36,572		768		3,418		4,173		343		–	–	41,088	Total, M. and F.

Property in Ireland, 44 Vic., cap. 4, are not included in this or the following Tables.

D 2

TABLE II.—NUMBER of PRISONERS in each of the LOCAL PRISONS on the First

PRISONS.	1st April, 1881.			1st May, 1881.			1st June, 1881.			1st July, 1881.			1st August, 1881.			1st September, 1881.		
	M.	F.	Tot.	M.	F.	Tot.	M.	F.	Tot.	M.	F.	Tot.	M.	F.	Tot.	M.	F.	Tot.
Armagh, . .	78	28	106	71	18	89	58	26	84	65	23	88	73	29	102	61	60	[illegible]
Belfast, . . .	283	138	421	253	179	432	317	181	498	268	152	420	250	169	419	240	150	390
Carlow, . . .	–	–	–	1	–	1	–	1	1	3	1	4	–	–	–	2	–	2
Car.-on-Shannon, .	–	–	–	–	–	–	–	–	–	8	–	8	3	3	6	1	–	1
Castlebar, . .	35	12	47	24	8	32	28	3	31	26	16	42	36	12	48	48	17	65
Cavan, . . .	4	–	4	–	2	2	3	1	4	7	–	7	4	1	5	1	–	1
Clonmel, . .	50	20	70	61	21	82	69	22	91	98	14	112	109	20	129	90	20	110
Cork, Male, . .	180	–	180	182	–	182	201	–	201	266	–	266	308	–	308	258	–	258
Cork, Female, .	–	77	77	–	72	72	–	64	64	–	60	60	–	60	60	–	64	64
Downpatrick, .	39	5	44	56	6	62	43	7	50	60	38	98	81	30	111	66	12	78
Drogheda, . .	–	12	12	–	10	10	–	14	14	–	15	15	–	13	13	–	18	18
Dundalk, . .	64	–	64	91	–	91	98	–	98	84	–	84	88	–	88	65	–	65
Ennis, . . .	–	–	–	2	1	3	4	1	5	5	–	5	3	2	5	4	1	5
Enniskillen, . .	2	–	2	4	–	4	3	1	4	4	1	5	2	–	2	2	–	2
Galway, . .	69	14	83	48	18	66	67	17	84	94	13	107	112	28	140	98	21	119
Grangegorman, .	103	115	218	111	122	233	130	180	310	146	206	352	82	185	267	87	172	259
Kilkenny, . .	24	9	33	37	12	49	52	11	63	80	7	87	76	7	83	93	11	104
Kilmainham, .	62	13	75	86	19	105	95	–	95	108	–	108	109	–	109	92	–	92
Lifford, . . .	2	–	2	1	1	2	1	–	1	–	–	–	2	1	3	–	–	–
Limerick, Male, .	89	–	89	101	–	101	90	–	90	117	–	117	101	–	101	118	–	118
Limerick, Female,	–	21	21	–	30	30	–	31	31	–	41	41	–	41	41	–	41	41
Londonderry, .	45	26	71	101	22	123	97	23	120	103	26	129	73	17	90	72	16	88
Longford, . .	5	2	7	12	3	15	4	1	5	–	–	–	3	–	3	1	–	1
Maryboro', . .	53	1	54	76	4	80	59	–	59	97	1	98	100	1	101	73	2	75
Monaghan, . .	1	–	1	1	–	1	2	1	3	–	1	1	–	–	–	1	2	3
Mullingar, . .	52	13	65	55	16	71	68	14	82	90	16	106	95	11	106	83	12	95
Naas, . . .	67	14	81	89	17	106	56	14	70	70	–	70	87	–	87	80	–	80
Nenagh, . .	32	5	37	29	7	36	52	11	63	54	5	59	56	–	56	80	–	80
Omagh, . . .	49	3	52	42	13	55	40	12	52	53	26	79	59	17	76	72	20	92
Richmond, . .	281	–	281	262	–	262	258	–	258	264	–	264	246	–	246	246	–	246
Roscommon, . .	2	–	2	1	–	1	4	2	6	1	–	1	–	4	4	3	–	3
Sligo, . . .	48	9	57	51	9	60	35	14	49	50	6	56	67	13	80	62	16	78
Tralee, . . .	84	3	87	52	6	58	45	7	52	55	3	58	44	2	40	41	6	47
Trim, . . .	1	–	1	1	1	2	1	–	1	1	–	1	2	–	2	–	–	–
Tullamore, . .	37	6	43	37	6	43	73	5	78	65	12	77	86	6	92	93	–	93
Waterford, . .	18	17	35	22	16	38	38	19	57	51	20	71	67	12	79	78	19	[illegible]
Wexford, . .	16	4	20	14	1	15	16	2	18	45	6	51	58	6	64	56	2	58
Wicklow, . . .	5	–	5	6	5	11	3	–	3	3	2	5	3	1	4	7	1	8
Convict Prisons*—																		
Mountjoy, Male,	177	–	177	164	–	164	207	–	207	201	–	201	196	–	196	204	–	204
Mountjoy, Fem.,	–	58	58	–	56	56	–	66	66	–	38	38	–	52	52	–	60	60
Total, 1881–82,	1893	668	2561	2134	687	2821	2812	769	3101	2659	786	3445	2642	745	3267	2567	752	[illegible]
Total, 1880–81,	2310	845	3155	2333	687	3100	2816	940	[illegible]	2347	861	3208	2289	845	3134	2304	967	[illegible]

* County Prisoners.

Day of each Month during the Year ended 31st March, 1882.

1st October, 1881.			1st November, 1881.			1st December, 1881.			1st January, 1882.			1st February, 1882.			1st March, 1882.			Prisons.
M.	F.	Tot.	M.	F.	Tot.	M.	F.	Tot.	M.	F.	Tot.	M.	F.	Tot.	M.	F.	Tot.	
57	32	89	70	13	83	97	–	97	74	–	74	97	–	97	107	–	107	Armagh.
228	168	481	290	175	455	250	149	400	283	137	450	297	139	536	291	153	386	Belfast.
–	–	–	1	–	1	3	2	5	6	1	7	–	1	1	8	–	9	Carlow.
5	–	5	5	–	6	2	–	2	1	–	1	3	–	3	9	–	6	Car.-on-Shannon.
29	13	42	51	12	63	42	13	55	31	6	37	46	7	53	42	11	93	Castlebar.
3	–	3	3	2	5	–	–	–	8	6	14	5	–	5	–	1	1	Cavan.
62	26	88	59	31	86	97	–	97	142	–	142	181	–	191	199	–	133	Clonmel.
190	–	222	199	–	109	212	–	212	218	–	210	255	–	252	215	–	215	Cork, Male.
–	194	194	–	91	91	–	86	86	–	70	70	–	78	78	–	66	66	Cork, Female.
34	14	48	33	13	46	38	8	46	36	4	40	32	8	43	33	5	38	Downpatrick.
–	12	12	–	29	33	–	24	24	–	20	20	–	26	26	–	35	35	Drogheda.
43	–	43	85	–	85	92	–	92	104	–	104	95	–	95	105	–	105	Dundalk.
3	1	4	6	2	8	6	1	7	3	–	3	31	–	81	91	–	81	Ennis.
1	2	3	–	–	–	1	1	2	2	1	3	5	–	5	13	–	13	Enniskillen.
86	22	108	90	7	78	101	7	108	128	12	140	177	14	191	118	18	136	Galway.
92	205	297	72	178	250	101	185	286	102	147	249	104	191	295	121	163	284	Grangegorman.
84	17	94	88	12	85	47	8	95	99	7	73	00	4	84	101	–	101	Kilkenny.
86	–	86	94	–	99	98	–	96	144	–	144	154	–	134	126	–	126	Kilmainham.
1	–	1	–	–	–	1	–	1	–	–	–	1	–	1	1	–	1	Lifford.
191	–	191	119	–	118	147	–	147	128	–	128	131	–	131	111	–	111	Limerick, Male.
–	42	42	–	46	46	–	73	73	–	49	49	–	64	64	–	48	48	Limerick, Female.
58	36	98	55	21	76	58	30	88	78	91	167	09	98	105	88	38	97	Londonderry.
3	1	4	6	1	8	9	–	9	5	1	6	6	3	9	12	–	12	Longford.
74	1	75	72	1	73	112	3	113	90	–	90	104	1	105	109	4	113	Maryboro'.
1	–	1	2	–	2	–	–	–	3	–	3	28	2	30	96	2	66	Monaghan.
132	19	151	92	16	98	94	14	108	99	0	107	09	17	110	89	16	96	Mullingar.
40	–	40	89	–	83	92	–	92	102	–	102	107	–	107	112	–	112	Naas.
87	–	87	52	–	52	59	–	59	90	–	90	51	–	61	68	–	88	Nenagh.
88	22	95	65	25	87	57	14	71	56	–	38	77	–	77	78	–	78	Omagh.
232	–	200	250	–	252	294	–	204	307	–	303	276	–	275	292	–	292	Richmond.
2	1	3	1	–	1	2	–	2	5	1	6	5	–	5	–	–	–	Roscommon.
48	8	56	34	8	42	46	18	69	89	19	97	42	12	81	61	12	73	Sligo.
47	8	55	50	7	57	45	5	50	33	5	38	47	5	52	43	5	48	Tralee.
1	–	1	4	–	4	2	–	2	5	–	5	4	1	5	4	–	4	Trim.
70	5	76	83	7	90	82	7	89	80	3	83	84	8	92	60	5	55	Tullamore.
42	12	56	45	11	56	46	27	72	53	20	73	48	19	67	50	21	71	Waterford.
38	3	41	35	1	36	45	3	48	39	5	44	45	7	50	38	8	40	Wexford.
3	–	3	9	–	9	2	4	6	9	–	9	1	3	4	2	–	2	Wicklow.
																		Convict Prisons—
200	–	200	208	–	208	193	–	193	193	–	193	184	–	184	181	–	181	Mountjoy, Male.
–	48	48	–	53	53	–	58	58	..	90	90	–	55	55	–	52	52	Mountjoy, Fem.
2282	918	3282	2334	758	3066	2551	791	3283	2725	616	3341	2859	958	3518	2645	987	3566	Total, 1881–82.
2166	984	3148	1912	779	2894	2032	797	2756	1695	941	2676	1780	580	2359	1794	994	2456	Total, 1880–81.

TABLE III.—DAILY AVERAGE NUMBER of PRISONERS in CUSTODY, &c., &c., from 1st April, 1881, to 31st March, 1882.

NAMES OF PRISONS.	Daily Average Number of Prisoners.			Highest Number confined at any one time (both Sexes).		Lowest Number confined at any one time (both Sexes).		Highest Number of Male Prisoners confined at any one time.		Highest Number of Female Prisoners confined at any one time.		Lowest Number of Male Prisoners confined at any one time.		Lowest Number of Female Prisoners confined at any one time.	
	M.	F.	Total.	No.	Date.	No.	Date.	No.	Date.	No.	Date.	No.	Date.	No.	Date.
Armagh,	72	24	96	112	16:2	58	23:5	116	21:2	47	16:16	45	29:10	12	8:11
Belfast,	295	166	461	562	20:4	348	10:3	328	17:7	211	13:5	304	1:6	118	2:9
Carlow,	2	1	3	7	31:12	–	–	8	31:12	3	17:11	–	–	–	–
Carrick-on-Shan.,	6	1	7	107	18:3	–	–	88	18:12	18	16:12	–	–	–	–
Castlebar,	35	9	44	77	9:2	34	15:6	67	9:9	36	6:9	17	16:6	4	26:12
Cavan,	3	–	3	35	4:1	–	–	13	18:3	7	4:3	–	–	–	–
Clonmel,	56	12	68	163	11:2	48	8:4	118	22:7	25	21:4	47	4:4	–	8:11
Cork, Male,	190	–	190	246	9:12	–	–	246	9:12	–	–	19	11:4	–	–
Cork, Female,	–	80	80	–	–	–	–	–	–	114	7:10	–	–	52	30:2
Downpatrick,	45	12	57	112	31:7	25	7:6	83	31:7	66	16:1	16	7:8	8	7:3
Drogheda,	–	20	20	46	17:11	2	17:8	–	–	46	17:11	–	–	8	17:11
Dundalk,	75	–	73	–	–	–	–	183	17:3	–	–	43	9:1	–	–
Ennis,	10	–	10	78	20:2	–	16:4	73	30:2	4	14:3	–	16:4	–	19:4
Enniskillen,	6	1	7	50	11:3	7	18:4	88	11:3	8	16:4	3	18:4	–	–
Galway,	92	14	106	191	31:1	68	24:4	177	31:1	29	26:7	36	24:4	8	6:12
Grangegorman,	89	170	259	376	6:6	165	6:5	170	6:3	237	17:10	61	6:11	165	10:6
Kilkenny,	68	9	77	146	24:3	90	8:4	146	24:3	17	8:12	20	8:4	3	6:7
Kilmainham,	104	17	121	147	18:6	73	3:4	120	10:6	56	3:5	23	19:15	4	21:6
Lifford,	2	1	3	19	17:7	–	–	16	16:7	3	18:7	–	–	–	–
Limerick, Male,	111	–	111	–	–	–	–	152	8:9	–	–	58	8:4	–	–
Limerick, Female,	–	46	46	–	–	–	–	–	–	73	30:11	–		18	19:4
Londonderry,	79	18	97	141	2:7	86	6:18	117	2:7	38	18:6	43	6:10	19	14:6
Longford,	6	1	6	75	3:3	–	6:6	25	3:3	3	28:6	–	6:6	–	6:6
Maryborough,	42	1	50	76	12:6	4	1:4	75	17:3	8	26:4	6	1:4	–	12:6
Monaghan,	11	–	11	77	14:3	–	18:10	76	14:2	3	14:3	–	18:16	–	18:10
Mullingar,	84	13	97	183	8:10	63	23:4	126	8:10	22	26:1	45	22:4	8	6:11
Naas,	76	6	72	118	28:4	41	15:6	117	22:3	23	4:3	29	14:6	7	7:6
Nenagh,	82	7	89	91	7:7	26	1:4	79	16:3	11	3:6	80	1:4	1	14:7
Omagh,	53	15	68	111	13:10	15	16:3	86	11:2	30	12:10	7	27:3	1	16:3
Richmond,	271	–	271	92	–	–	–	321	16:8	–	–	223	3:9	–	–
Roscommon,	3	–	3	20	{24:10, 18:1, 16:1}	–	–	20	24:16	6	15:7	–	–	–	–
Sligo,	50	11	61	92	24:12	40	23:1	74	13:7	23	8:3	30	12:12	3	10:23
Tralee,	46	0	51	84	22:6	35	26:3	88	22:3	15	16:10	34	28:3	1	1:4
Trim,	3	–	3	13	21:4	–	–	10	21:4	3	26:3	–	–	–	–
Tullamore,	73	5	78	110	23:3	34	20:4	110	23:3	14	10:3	30	20:6	–	–
Waterford,	48	20	68	90	21:6	38	19:4	73	12:3	31	21:6	15	1:4	3	2:11
Wexford,	39	4	43	70	25:7	14	23:4	63	22:7	8	7:3	19	23:4	1	1:12
Wicklow,	4	1	5	18	25:3	–	13:6	12	25:9	9	30:3	–	13:3	–	13:6
County Prisoners in—															
Mountjoy, Male,	184	–	184	–	–	–	–	216	26:9	–	–	181	8:6	–	–
" Fem.,	–	84	84	–	–	–	–	–	–	68	1:3	–	–	68	1:10
Total, 1881-82,	2,369	742	3,111	–	–	–	–	–	–	–	–	–	–	–	–
Total, 1880-81,	1,896	727	2,623	–	–	–	–	–	–	–	–	–	–	–	–

TABLE IV.—DEATHS in LOCAL PRISONS and their CAUSES from 1st April, 1881, to 31st March, 1882.

NAMES OF PRISONS.	No.	Initials of Name.	Sex.	Age.	Crime, &c., for which Convicted or charged.	Date of Committal.	Date of Death.	Disease, &c., which caused Death.
Belfast, . .	1	B. M.	F.	44	Drunkenness, .	11:4:81,	19:4:81,	Bronchitis and debility.
	2	A. M.	F.	50	Vagrancy, .	–	–	Chronic bronchitis.
Clonmel, .	3	P. B.	M.	–	Assault, . .	9:4:81,	28:4:81,	Epilepsy.
Cork, Male, .	4	M. B.	M.	–	Drunkenness, .	23:3:81,	3:4:81,	Liver disease.
	5	P. M.	M.	–	Assault & robbery	10:1:81	30:11:81	Consumption.
	6	J. K.	M.	–	Stealing Calves,	10:1:82,	30:1:82,	Pneumonia.
" Female.	7	B. C.*	F.	44	Drunkenness, .	8:4:81,	2:7:81,	Consumption.
Kilkenny, .	8	E. W.	F.	28	Destroying prison property.	13:10:81,	12:12:81,	Apoplexy.
Limerick, .	9	J. B.	M.	60	Maliciously setting on fire and burning a dwelling house.	8:11:81,	9:2:82,	Chronic bronchitis and asthma.
Maryboro' .	10	G. M.	M.	70	Robbery, . .	21:6:81,	24:6:81,	Committed suicide.
Nenagh, .	11	M. C.	M.	23	Riot and assault,	28:12:81,	30:6:82,	Endocarditis.
Roscommon, .	12	P. L.	M.	29	Larceny, . .	17:11:81,	25:12:81,	Consumption.
Sligo, . .	13	B. K.	M.	49	Assault, . .	28:6:81,	2:7:81,	Effusion of blood on brain.
Tralee, . .	14	J. B.	M.	19	" . .	20:6:81,	19:7:81,	Injuries received by throwing himself off a height and coming in contact with flags while labouring under temporary suicidal impulsive mania.
" . . .	15	M. T.	F.	41	Drunkenness, .	24:8:81,	29:8:81,	Epileptic seizure.
Tullamore, .	16	J. D.	M.	24	Assault bodily harm.	13:6:81,	23:12:81,	Cerebral affection.
" . . .	17	K. C.	M.	75	Rape, . .	14:12:81,	23:12:81,	Acute bronchitis.
Mountjoy, Male,	18	M. D.	M.	32	Larceny, . .	22:11:80	21:7:81,	Heart disease.

* NOTE.—This woman's sentence had expired at the time of her death, but she was unable to leave the Prison Hospital.

TABLE V.—ESCAPES from LOCAL PRISONS and BRIDEWELLS from 1st April, 1881, to 31st March, 1882.

PRISONS.	Initials of Name.	Sex.	Age.	Date	Offence of which convicted or charged.	Tried or Untried.	Whether confined separately or with others.	Whether retaken or not.
Dundalk, . . .	J. C.	M.	23	14:1:82	Illegal fishing, .	Tried, .	Separately, .	Yes.
Kilmainham, . .	S. H.	M.	25	30:9:81	Burglary, . .	Untried,	Separately, .	Yes.
Londonderry, . .	P. J.	M.	27	31:1:82	Military, . .	Tried, .	Separately, .	No.
Maryboro' . . .	W. B.	M.	23	2:8:81	Burglary, . .	Tried, .	Separately, .	Yes.

TABLE VI.—NUMBER of INDIVIDUALS, exclusive of DEBTORS, committed to the
them who were not known to have been in Prison before that year, and the
from their *first* Commitment in *any year*,—to 31st March, 1882.

PRISONS.	Number of Commitments.		Number of Individuals Committed.		Number of them who had not been in Prison before 1st April, 1881.		Number					
							Once only.		Twice.		Thrice.	
	M.	F.	M.	F.	M.	F.	M.	F.	M.	F.	M.	F.
Armagh,	754	226	505	140	401	88	348	80	64	14	22	9
Belfast,	3,601	2,141	2,800	1,078	1,114	597	1,404	491	354	168	96	112
Castlebar,	471	131	331	98	298	40	317	70	29	14	13	5
Clonmel,	822	122	734	77	520	56	351	34	25	6	85	6
Cork, Male,	2,452	–	1,908	–	1,344	–	1,160	–	251	–	114	–
Cork, Female,	–	1,400	–	737	–	388	–	334	–	116	–	23
Downpatrick	252	88	216	67	162	40	161	34	16	11	21	2
Drogheda,	–	220	–	187	–	77	–	64	–	26	–	14
Dundalk,	570	–	481	–	351	–	301	–	60	–	20	–
Galway,	1,162	670	716	229	389	107	356	144	99	21	65	18
Grangegorman,	3,625	5,508	2,521	2,078	1,615	1,082	1,505	982	227	164	161	144
Kilkenny,	548	136	445	89	349	63	320	45	66	14	12	6
Kilmainham,	1,403	67	1,256	61	1,024	26	994	23	23	6	30	1
Limerick, Male,	1,622	–	1,121	–	872	–	575	–	244	–	98	–
Limerick, Female,	–	746	–	510	–	289	–	284	–	129	–	23
Londonderry,	803	638	691	156	496	74	406	58	85	17	53	6
Maryborough,	360	26	323	24	319	12	295	15	17	5	7	1
Mullingar,	985	245	815	136	792	178	759	154	14	10	9	8
Naas,	524	1[illegible]	394	36	109	24	225	18	53	8	30	1
Nenagh,	317	21	236	17	147	6	197	2	42	2	16	1
Omagh,	371	110	324	76	258	86	246	36	42	13	16	16
Richmond,	2,222	–	1,922	–	1,191	–	1,046	–	606	–	112	–
Sligo,	640	169	489	90	394	61	368	62	40	8	58	4
Tralee,	360	135	302	95	377	48	366	50	102	19	38	5
Tullamore,	455	36	392	64	316	32	257	28	50	9	23	2
Waterford,	832	322	540	157	220	53	225	69	76	21	41	16
Wexford,	284	59	221	64	145	25	101	26	25	8	14	4
Total, Males,	26,062	–	20,062	–	13,720	–	12,334	–	2,578	–	1,128	–
Total, Females,	–	12,875	–	6,305	–	3,272	–	3,115	–	808	–	434
Total, M. and F.,	38,968		26,367		17,001		15,450		3,386		1,562	

undermentioned PRISONS from 1st April, 1881, to 31st March, 1882; Number of Number of them who had undergone One, Two, Three, &c., &c., Commitments

…HAD BEEN UP TO THE 31ST MARCH, 1882, COMMITTED—

Four times.		Five times.		Six times.		Seven to Eleven times.		Twelve to Sixteen times.		Seventeen to Twenty times.		Twenty-one times and upwards.		Number of Imprisonments known to have been undergone by the Individuals committed up to 31st March, 1882. (Column No. 2.)		PRISONS.
M.	F.	M.	F.	M.	F.	M.	F.	M.	F.	M.	F.	M.	F.	M.	F.	
23	6	13	2	11	7	33	13	10	8	7	2	10	4	1,965	602	Armagh.
96	65	72	36	60	29	181	71	111	34	78	16	202	66	14,648	6,626	Belfast.
3	2	4	–	5	1	6	1	2	1	–	–	2	2	717	287	Castlebar.
50	4	21	3	16	3	46	16	4	2	1	3	13	8	2,364	772	Clonmel.
91	–	46	–	65	–	147	–	51	–	10	–	16	–	5,766	–	Cork, Male.
–	33	–	21	–	14	–	55	–	24	–	17	–	87	–	6,202	Cork, Female.
12	1	5	1	2	2	4	5	–	1	–	2	5	4	506	403	Downpatrick.
–	9	–	4	–	4	–	11	–	3	–	2	–	1	–	446	Drogheda.
10	–	6	–	2	–	14	–	11	–	2	–	5	–	1,175	–	Dundalk.
36	3	27	4	15	6	72	3	21	2	5	–	11	11	2,589	909	Galway.
172	110	132	68	96	56	170	10[illegible]	42	114	19	67	8	239	6,770	15,816	Grangegorman.
12	4	8	–	7	–	9	8	8	4	1	1	4	6	926	453	Kilkenny.
31	2	20	–	13	1	37	5	15	1	5	2	20	18	2,817	1,357	Kilmainham.
63	–	45	–	3	–	45	–	6	–	3	–	6	–	2,822	–	Limerick, Male.
–	16	–	12	–	12	–	16	–	3	–	1	–	10	–	1,416	Limerick, Fem.
23	10	14	5	12	6	27	7	24	10	13	6	20	66	2,513	1,186	Londonderry.
3	1	–	–	2	–	4	2	2	–	1	–	3	–	636	51	Maryborough.
3	3	10	6	3	3	16	2	2	4	1	5	3	4	1,129	541	Mullingar.
21	2	15	6	7	1	22	5	5	3	5	3	6	15	1,209	1,041	Naas.
12	2	6	–	7	1	11	2	4	–	3	–	8	2	1,131	133	Nenagh.
7	2	2	4	2	2	6	2	2	2	1	–	–	1	–	–	Omagh.
37	–	57	–	34	–	72	–	45	–	3	–	26	–	5,213	–	Richmond.
13	4	5	6	7	4	3	2	13	4	1	1	7	4	1,160	441	Sligo.
12	3	19	1	10	2	21	4	9	3	3	–	10	6	1,597	423	Tralee.
16	1	4	–	6	–	7	5	1	5	1	1	4	2	782	270	Tullamore.
[illegible]	[illegible]	[illegible]	[illegible]	[illegible]	[illegible]	[illegible]	[illegible]	[illegible]	[illegible]	[illegible]	[illegible]	[illegible]	[illegible]	[illegible]	[illegible]	[illegible]

TABLE VII.—SENTENCES OF DEATH, PENAL SERVITUDE, IMPRI-

Prisons.	Death.		Penal Servitude for Life.		Above 15 Years.		15 Years and above 10.		10 Years and above 7.		7 Years.		5 Years.		Imprisonment for 3 Years and above 2.		2 Years and above 18 Months.	
	M.	F.	M.	F.	M.	F.	M.	F.	M.	F.	M.	F.	M.	F.	M.	F.	M.	F.
Armagh,	–	–	–	–	–	–	–	–	–	–	1	–	6	1	–	–	1	–
Belfast,	–	–	–	–	–	–	1	–	–	–	1	–	9	3	–	–	1	–
Carlow,	–	–	–	–	–	–	–	–	–	–	–	–	–	–	–	–	–	–
Carrick-on-Shannon,	–	–	–	1	–	–	1	–	1	1	–	–	2	–	–	–	–	–
Castlebar,	–	–	–	–	–	–	–	–	–	–	–	–	1	1	–	–	–	–
Cavan,	–	–	–	–	–	–	–	–	–	–	–	–	–	–	–	–	–	–
Clonmel,	–	–	–	–	–	–	–	–	–	–	1	–	3	1	–	–	–	–
Cork, Male,	–	–	–	–	–	–	–	–	2	–	6	–	8	–	–	–	8	–
Cork, Female,	–	1	–	–	–	–	–	–	–	–	–	–	–	1	–	–	–	2
Downpatrick,	–	–	–	–	–	–	–	–	–	–	1	–	2	–	–	–	2	–
Drogheda,	–	–	–	–	–	–	–	–	–	–	–	–	–	1	–	–	–	–
Dundalk,	–	–	–	–	–	–	–	–	–	–	1	–	1	–	–	–	–	–
Ennis,	–	–	–	–	–	–	–	–	–	–	–	–	–	–	–	–	–	–
Enniskillen,	–	–	–	–	–	–	–	–	2	–	–	–	–	–	–	–	–	–
Galway,	–	–	–	–	–	–	–	–	–	–	–	–	–	–	–	–	–	–
Grangegorman,	–	–	–	–	–	–	–	–	–	–	–	2	1	6	–	–	–	2
Kilkenny,	–	–	–	–	–	–	–	–	–	–	–	–	5	–	–	–	–	–
Kilmainham,	1	–	–	–	–	–	–	–	–	–	2	–	6	–	–	–	1	–
Lifford,	–	–	–	–	–	–	–	–	–	–	–	–	–	–	–	–	–	–
Limerick, Male,	–	–	–	–	–	–	–	–	–	–	1	–	7	–	–	–	3	–
Limerick, Female,	–	–	–	–	–	–	–	–	–	–	–	–	–	1	–	–	–	–
Londonderry,	–	1	–	–	–	–	–	–	–	–	1	–	3	1	–	–	–	–
Longford,	–	–	–	–	–	–	–	–	–	–	–	–	–	–	–	–	–	–
Maryborough,	–	–	–	–	–	–	–	–	–	–	1	–	4	–	–	–	1	–
Monaghan,	–	–	–	–	–	–	–	–	–	–	–	–	–	–	–	–	–	–
Mullingar,	–	–	–	–	1	–	–	–	–	–	1	1	4	–	–	–	3	–
Naas,	–	–	–	–	–	–	–	–	–	–	–	–	–	–	–	–	4	–
Nenagh,	–	–	–	–	–	–	–	–	–	–	1	–	1	–	–	–	–	–
Omagh,	–	1	–	–	–	–	–	–	–	–	2	–	4	1	–	–	1	–
Richmond,	3	–	1	–	–	–	4	–	1	–	5	–	52	–	1	–	24	–
Roscommon,	–	–	–	–	–	–	–	–	–	–	–	–	–	–	–	–	–	–
Sligo,	–	–	–	–	–	–	–	–	–	–	–	–	–	–	–	–	–	–
Tralee,	–	1	–	–	1	–	2	–	2	–	–	–	7	–	–	–	–	–
Trim,	–	–	–	–	–	–	–	–	–	–	–	–	–	–	–	–	–	–
Tullamore,	–	–	–	–	–	–	–	–	–	–	–	2	–	–	–	–	–	–
Waterford,	–	–	–	–	–	–	1	–	–	–	1	–	2	–	–	–	–	–
Wexford,	–	–	–	–	–	–	–	–	–	–	–	–	1	–	–	–	1	–
Wicklow,	–	–	–	–	–	–	–	–	–	–	–	–	–	–	–	–	–	–
Total, Males,	4	–	1	–	2	–	9	–	8	–	26	–	129	–	1	–	50	–
Total, Females,	–	4	–	1	–	–	–	–	–	1	–	5	–	17	–	–	–	4
Total, M. and F.,	8		2		2		9		9		31		146		1		54	

SONMENT, &c., passed from 1st April, 1881, to 31st March, 1882.

Imprisonment for: 18 Months and above 12		12 Months only.		Under 12 Months and above 9.		9 Months and above 6.		6 Months only.		Under 6 Months and above 3.		Prisons.
M.	F.	M.	F.	M.	F.	M.	F.	M.	F.	M.	F.	
3	–	8	1	1	–	3	1	31	5	12	8	Armagh.
11	–	26	4	5	1	23	0	112	77	56	17	Belfast.
–	–	1	–	–	–	4	2	–	–	1	–	Carlow.
3	–	–	–	–	–	–	–	–	–	–	–	Carrick-on-Shannon.
2	–	3	–	–	–	–	–	4	4	4	1	Castlebar.
–	–	–	–	–	–	–	–	–	–	–	–	Cavan.
–	–	10	–	–	–	4	–	9	–	15	4	Clonmel.
7	–	21	–	2	–	6	–	33	–	21	–	Cork, Male.
–	–	–	6	–	–	–	2	–	21	–	10	Cork, Female.
5	–	4	1	–	–	2	–	7	5	8	–	Downpatrick.
–	–	–	–	–	–	–	2	–	1	–	4	Drogheda.
–	–	8	–	3	–	1	–	16	–	14	–	Dundalk.
–	–	–	–	–	–	–	–	–	–	–	–	Ennis.
–	–	1	–	–	–	–	–	–	–	–	–	Enniskillen.
1	–	2	1	1	–	3	–	18	1	3	–	Galway.
–	3	–	19	2	2	1	4	2	29	1	12	Grangegorman.
4	–	10	3	2	–	9	3	20	2	61	–	Kilkenny.
6	–	–	–	4	–	8	–	40	2	16	–	Kilmainham.
–	–	–	–	–	–	–	–	–	–	–	–	Lifford.
8	–	7	–	–	–	8	–	57	–	11	–	Limerick, Male.
–	–	–	1	–	–	–	2	–	25	–	5	Limerick, Female.
1	–	9	2	–	–	8	3	39	7	27	7	Londonderry.
–	–	–	–	–	–	–	–	–	–	–	–	Longford.
2	–	6	–	18	–	4	–	7	1	19	–	Maryborough.
–	–	–	–	–	–	–	–	–	–	–	–	Monaghan.
–	–	12	1	–	–	0	1	33	2	23	1	Mullingar.
6	–	–	–	2	–	1	–	12	–	10	–	Naas.
–	–	5	–	–	–	11	–	6	1	5	1	Nenagh.
1	–	5	1	2	–	3	1	14	2	2	1	Omagh.
8	–	97	–	–	–	62	–	180	–	87	–	Richmond.
–	–	–	–	–	–	–	–	–	–	–	–	Roscommon.
–	–	5	–	–	–	5	1	9	3	18	1	Sligo.
4	–	–	–	–	1	7	–	11	1	1	–	Tralee.
–	–	5	–	–	–	2	1	2	–	0	1	Trim.
–	–	18	–	1	–	3	1	24	2	24	–	Tullamore.
1	–	–	–	–	–	–	–	12	4	5	–	Waterford.
–	–	1	1	–	–	4	1	7	–	13	–	Wexford.
–	–	–	–	–	–	–	–	–	–	–	–	Wicklow.
63	–	259	–	43	–	172	–	707	–	410	–	Total, Males.
–	8	–	41	–	4	–	34	–	195	–	76	Total, Females.
71		300		47		206		902		486		Total, M. and F.

[continued.

TABLE VII., *concluded*.—SENTENCES of DEATH, PENAL SERVITUDE,

PRISONS.	IMPRISONMENT FOR											
	3 Months only.		Under 3 Months and above 2.		2 Months and above 1.		1 Month and above 14 Days.		14 Days and above 7.		7 Days and above 48 Hours.	
	M.	F.	M.	F.	M.	F.	M.	F.	M.	F.	M.	F.
Armagh,	46	9	28	6	124	88	100	59	102	40	117	28
Belfast,	137	76	60	5	241	125	876	942	674	841	916	425
Carlow,	2	1	–	–	2	–	8	3	2	2	68	9
Carrick-on-Shannon,	–	–	–	–	1	–	2	–	–	–	109	16
Castlebar,	12	1	–	1	19	3	79	23	62	20	117	47
Cavan,	–	–	–	–	–	–	–	–	–	–	66	19
Clonmel,	20	9	3	4	60	6	105	85	149	42	368	8
Cork, Male,	77	–	14	–	171	–	477	–	363	–	878	–
Cork, Female,	–	6	–	11	–	50	–	487	–	287	–	453
Downpatrick,	10	4	2	–	20	5	61	15	26	12	62	25
Drogheda,	–	4	–	–	6	35	–	87	–	21	–	41
Dundalk,	17	–	5	–	27	–	98	–	87	–	188	–
Ennis,	–	–	–	–	–	–	–	–	–	–	80	18
Enniskillen,	1	–	–	–	–	–	–	–	4	–	56	21
Galway,	20	8	–	–	79	0	107	61	149	73	279	142
Grangegorman,	–	69	–	5	3	87	587	381	700	1,059	1,677	2,618
Kilkenny,	26	8	1	–	85	3	68	36	65	26	161	88
Kilmainham,	40	2	10	–	157	6	276	3	272	17	419	29
Lifford,	–	–	–	–	–	–	–	–	–	–	21	3
Limerick, Male,	41	–	12	–	79	–	391	–	228	–	274	–
Limerick, Female,	–	9	–	25	–	28	–	210	–	100	–	150
Londonderry,	66	25	82	14	48	34	169	111	185	67	165	76
Longford,	–	–	–	–	–	–	–	–	2	–	63	22
Maryborough	7	–	18	2	3	–	81	6	2	–	102	6
Monaghan,	–	–	–	–	–	–	–	–	–	–	42	16
Mullingar,	35	11	7	–	70	4	254	112	161	84	179	68
Naas,	16	–	–	2	80	12	64	17	63	18	114	38
Nenagh,	14	–	1	–	25	3	82	4	87	4	81	2
Omagh,	18	9	6	2	49	15	104	88	69	16	31	10
Richmond,	248	–	16	–	396	–	132	–	110	–	75	–
Roscommon,	–	–	–	–	–	–	–	–	8	1	48	22
Sligo,	22	14	–	–	38	8	177	51	100	28	81	46
Tralee,	9	–	–	–	34	2	208	30	145	15	245	67
Trim,	1	2	–	1	11	2	24	1	26	1	65	16
Tullamore,	33	–	–	–	44	5	76	19	49	8	119	46
Waterford,	31	9	1	–	51	9	96	93	62	26	188	73
Wexford,	12	2	23	19	21	5	63	3	30	6	86	17
Wicklow,	–	–	–	–	–	–	–	–	–	–	106	20
Total, Males,	968	–	245	–	1,832	–	4,774	–	3,933	–	7,649	–
Total, Females,	–	260	–	97	–	490	–	2,818	–	2,254	–	4,613
* Total, M. and F.,	1,232		342		2,322		7,587		6,187		12,262	

IMPRISONMENT, &c., passed from 1st April, 1881, to 31st March, 1882.

Imprisonment for 48 Hours.		24 Hours and under.		Fine without any alternative Imprisonment.		Unlimited.		Sentence respited and not passed.		Total Number of Sentences.		Prisons.
M.	F.	M.	F.	M.	F.	M.	F.	M.	F.	M.	F.	
19	14	28	7	–	–	7	–	–	–	706	217	Armagh.
3	5	19	4	–	–	21	1	–	–	8,206	2,038	Belfast.
17	3	1	2	–	–	–	–	–	–	101	22	Carlow.
2	–	1	–	–	–	1	–	13	4	186	22	Carrick-on-Shannon.
27	15	10	5	–	–	8	–	–	–	346	121	Castlebar.
34	6	5	–	–	–	3	–	–	–	102	25	Cavan.
3	6	–	–	–	–	6	–	2	–	748	115	Clonmel.
40	–	20	–	–	–	13	–	26	–	2,193	–	Cork, Male.
–	58	–	56	–	–	–	1	–	5	–	1,420	Cork, Female.
10	2	2	3	–	–	1	1	2	2	312	75	Downpatrick.
–	2	–	1	–	–	–	–	–	–	–	205	Drogheda.
40	–	16	–	–	–	–	–	–	–	519	–	Dundalk.
20	5	10	1	–	–	–	–	–	–	119	19	Ennis.
44	14	61	5	–	–	–	–	–	–	130	40	Enniskillen.
97	44	58	20	–	–	–	–	–	–	912	355	Galway.
530	731	177	283	–	–	1	–	–	–	3,626	5,506	Grangegorman.
26	8	6	1	–	–	4	–	–	–	467	118	Kilkenny.
54	7	41	1	–	–	–	–	1	–	1,365	67	Kilmainham.
3	1	5	–	–	–	–	–	–	–	32	4	Lifford.
24	–	126	–	–	–	17	–	–	–	1,288	–	Limerick, Male.
–	11	–	86	–	–	–	–	–	–	–	603	Limerick, Female.
34	7	18	7	–	–	12	2		–	614	643	Londonderry.
41	10	12	6	–	–	–	–	–	–	118	40	Longford.
32	5	18	4	–	–	6	–	–	–	336	24	Maryborough.
18	7	20	6	–	–	–	–	–	–	78	29	Monaghan.
12	3	23	2	–	–	2	–	–	–	826	285	Mullingar.
49	11	110	7	–	–	1	–	–	–	482	100	Naas.
46	2	26	2	–	–	–	–	–	–	291	19	Nenagh.
11	3	4	–	–	–	3	–	1	–	680	100	Omagh.
22	–	7	–	–	–	40	–	61	–	1,575	–	Richmond.
29	–	11	2	–	–	2	–	9	2	102	27	Roscommon.
48	7	40	1	–	–	1	–	1	–	540	154	Sligo.
2	–	5	2	–	–	1	–	–	–	579	126	Tralee.
3	1	–	–	–	–	1	–	–	–	146	25	Trim.
4	–	15	3	–	–	–	–	–	–	410	61	Tullamore.
155	45	155	46	–	–	13	–	–	–	784	803	Waterford.
5	3	–	–	–	–	2	–	–	–	268	57	Wexford.
25	4	8	–	–	–	6	–	–	–	141	24	Wicklow.
1,549	–	1,012	–	–	–	167	–	106	–	24,116	–	Total, Males.
–	1,015	–	517	–	–	–	5	–	13	–	12,474	Total, Females.
2,564		1,529		–		172		119		36,518		Total, M. and F.

TABLE VIII.—AGES, EDUCATIONAL CONDITION on COMMITMENT, and RELIGIOUS
1st April, 1881, to 31st March,

PRISONS.	Total Number of Commitments.			Ages.									
				Under 12 Years.		12 and not exceeding 16 Years.		Above 16 to 21 Years.		21 to 31 Years.		31 to 41 Years.	
	M.	F.	M. & F.	M.	F.	M.	F.	M.	F.	M.	F.	M.	F.
Armagh, . .	764	226	990	2	-	20	5	160	30	298	72	155	72
Belfast, . . .	3,601	2,141	5,742	11	1	57	9	786	244	1,361	781	727	671
Castlebar, . .	471	131	602	5	-	15	8	115	24	136	38	100	34
Clonmel, . .	822	122	944	3	-	36	3	186	44	197	20	200	40
Cork, Male, . .	2,462	-	2,462	11	-	77	-	575	-	915	-	416	-
Cork, Female, .	-	1,460	1,400	-	-	-	7	-	131	-	496	-	458
Downpatrick, . .	252	83	335	-	-	2	-	39	4	98	30	54	14
Drogheda, . . .	-	220	220	-	-	-	1	-	20	-	78	-	64
Dundalk, . .	570	-	570	1	-	11	-	123	-	243	-	118	-
Galway, . .	1,152	370	1,522	2	-	37	4	340	59	375	125	263	111
Grangegorman, .	3,628	5,508	9,136	-	7	3	82	654	1,246	1,430	2,225	822	1,086
Kilkenny, . .	548	135	683	-	-	10	-	110	18	257	64	91	28
Kilmainham, . .	1,406	67	1,473	4	-	62	1	377	4	556	25	231	27
Limerick, Male, .	1,522	-	1,642	3	-	40	-	397	-	710	-	283	-
Limerick, Female, .	-	746	746	-	-	-	7	-	138	-	291	-	164
Londonderry, . .	908	382	1,297	6	-	28	3	202	85	387	142	127	82
Maryborough, .	300	22	322	2	-	3	-	22	-	164	12	126	11
Mullingar, . .	936	248	1,184	4	1	20	2	216	48	376	84	144	72
Naas, . . .	524	102	626	3	-	10	-	104	10	167	42	123	36
Nenagh, . .	310	21	331	8	-	4	-	53	-	105	4	74	11
Omagh, . . .	371	110	481	1	-	12	-	93	20	130	32	66	32
Richmond, . .	2,298	-	2,298	37	-	201	-	656	-	888	-	284	-
Sligo, . . .	640	166	806	3	1	18	2	122	20	256	52	122	26
Tralee, . . .	860	135	995	4	1	48	5	224	13	302	50	166	57
Tullamore, . .	405	86	551	-	-	4	1	85	10	224	11	63	35
Waterford, . .	838	322	1,160	4	-	15	3	207	28	317	116	173	94
Wexford, . .	284	51	345	-	-	6	-	51	13	117	17	83	19
Total, Males, .	26,093	-	-	115	-	777	-	5,906	-	10,019	-	5 014	-
Total, Females, .	-	12,875	-	-	11	-	138	-	2,210	-	4,843	-	3,257
Total, M. and F., .	-	-	38,968	126		915		8,116		1 862		8,231	

PROFESSIONS of all Persons Committed to the undermentioned Prisons from 1882, exclusive of Debtors.

Ages.				Education on Commitment.													
41 Years and upwards.		Age could not be ascertained.		Read and Write.		Read imperfectly.		Know Spelling.		Know Alphabet.		Wholly illiterate.		Education not ascertained.		Prisons.
M.	F.	M.	F.	M.	F.	M.	F.	M.	F.	M.	F.	M.	F.	M.	F.	
134	46	–	–	290	40	117	51	70	22	83	16	202	95	–	–	Armagh.
529	485	–	–	2,141	728	496	503	–	–	–	–	958	808	4	–	Belfast.
97	57	–	–	128	39	37	5	50	12	61	12	199	60	–	–	Castlebar.
200	16	–	–	426	72	145	8	5	–	–	–	245	84	–	–	Clonmel.
438	–	–	–	1,381	–	316	–	4	–	26	–	783	–	–	–	Cork, Male.
–	354	–	1	–	288	–	494	–	78	–	108	–	510	–	–	Cork, Female.
50	35	–	–	125	90	42	20	–	–	–	–	81	43	–	–	Downpatrick.
–	46	–	–	–	47	–	98	–	2	–	2	–	100	–	–	Drogheda.
80	–	–	–	206	–	64	–	21	–	38	–	250	–	–	–	Dundalk.
133	69	–	–	417	80	97	1	–	–	1	–	714	269	–	–	Galway.
717	709	–	–	1,804	2,801	709	776	–	–	–	–	1,020	2,430	–	–	Grangegorman.
83	16	–	–	356	38	30	14	5	–	1	2	151	86	–	–	Kilkenny.
178	17	–	–	865	40	53	10	–	–	–	–	486	17	–	–	Kilmainham.
189	–	–	–	1,009	–	141	–	25	–	24	–	423	–	–	–	Limerick, Male.
–	119	–	7	–	144	–	100	–	–	–	–	–	504	–	–	Limerick, Female
158	70	–	–	405	44	155	126	47	12	65	27	238	178	–	–	Londonderry.
42	6	–	–	206	7	33	9	11	2	6	–	97	11	–	–	Maryborough.
171	66	–	–	570	133	–	–	–	–	–	–	369	65	–	–	Mullingar.
116	11	–	–	161	11	149	84	2	–	1	–	221	57	–	–	Naas.
66	6	–	–	194	9	29	2	–	–	–	–	58	10	–	–	Nenagh.
84	12	–	–	236	15	47	37	1	–	4	–	97	60	–	–	Omagh.
193	–	32	–	1,512	–	840	–	–	–	108	–	204	–	33	–	Richmond.
115	52	–	–	341	47	56	24	16	–	2	2	216	66	–	–	Sligo.
114	43	–	–	301	50	79	9	4	1	2	–	281	73	–	–	Tralee.
89	22	–	–	274	16	42	17	5	1	45	0	90	45	–	–	Tullamore.
124	83	–	–	282	46	103	42	–	–	–	–	448	234	–	–	Waterford.
25	10	–	–	157	9	38	–	2	3	4	3	63	46	–	–	Wexford.
4,229	–	32	–	14,0[illegible]	–	3,288	–	268	–	477	–	7,991	–	37	–	Total, Males.
–	2,398	–	8	–	4,253	–	2,450	–	140	–	189	–	2,842	–	1	Total, Females.
6,627		41		18,265		5,738		408		666		10,833		38		Total, M. and F.

[*continued.*

TABLE VIII., *concluded*.—AGES, EDUCATIONAL CONDITION on COMMITMENT, and RELIGIOUS PROFESSIONS of all Persons Committed to the undermentioned Prisons from 1st April, 1881, to 31st March, 1882, exclusive of Debtors.

PRISONS.	RELIGIOUS PROFESSIONS.										Total Number of Commitments.		
	Protestant Episcopalians of Ireland.		Presbyterians.		Roman Catholics		Other Religious Professions.		Could not be ascertained.				
	M.	F.	M.	F.	M.	F.	M.	F.	M.	F.	M.	F.	M. & F.
Armagh, . . .	163	61	33	14	562	148	8	2	–	–	764	226	990
Belfast, . . .	786	624	984	363	1,889	1,142	12	1	–	–	3,601	2,141	5,742
Castlebar, . .	20	3	1	–	450	128	–	–	–	–	471	131	602
Clonmel, . . .	26	2	–	–	797	120	–	–	–	–	822	122	944
Cork, Male, . .	122	–	7	–	2,331	–	1	–	–	–	2,462	–	2,462
Cork, Female, . .	–	79	–	–	–	1,377	–	2	–	2	–	1,460	1,460
Downpatrick, . .	85	21	36	11	130	51	1	–	–	–	252	83	335
Drogheda, . .	–	25	–	–	–	195	–	–	–	–	–	220	220
Dundalk, . .	20	–	5	–	351	–	–	–	–	–	376	–	376
Galway, . . .	57	7	3	–	1,092	363	–	–	–	–	1,152	370	1,522
Grangegorman, .	148	202	19	3	3,457	5,296	4	1	–	6	3,628	5,508	9,136
Kilkenny, . .	48	21	–	–	500	114	–	–	–	–	548	135	683
Kilmainham, . .	99	14	2	–	1,278	62	27	1	–	–	1,406	67	1,473
Limerick, Male, .	66	–	6	–	1,560	–	2	–	–	–	1,622	–	1,622
Limerick, Female, .	–	5	–	–	–	741	–	–	–	–	–	746	746
Londonderry, . .	364	103	87	29	457	257	–	–	–	–	908	389	1,297
Maryborough, . .	96	1	–	–	264	28	–	–	–	–	360	29	389
Mullingar, . .	56	16	6	–	874	232	–	–	–	–	936	248	1,184
Naas, . . .	27	4	4	–	482	94	16	–	–	–	524	[illegible]	626
Nenagh, . . .	25	1	–	1	284	19	–	–	1	–	310	21	331
Omagh, . . .	58	35	17	2	302	70	1	–	–	–	371	110	481
Richmond, . .	163	–	2	–	2,096	–	6	–	27	–	2,293	–	2,293
Sligo, . . .	33	1	–	–	607	164	–	–	–	–	640	165	805
Tralee, . . .	5	8	–	–	855	127	–	–	–	–	860	135	995
Tullamore, . .	87	9	3	1	375	78	–	–	–	–	465	86	551
Waterford, . .	4	1	–	–	834	321	–	–	–	–	838	322	1,160
Wexford, . . .	9	2	3	–	272	57	–	–	–	–	284	59	343
Total, Males, .	2,588	–	1196	–	23,251	–	80	–	28	–	36,093	–	–
Total Females, .	–	1,241	–	446	–	11,173	–	7	–	8	–	12,875	–
Total M. and F., .	3,779		1,842		33,424		87		36		38,968		

TABLE IX.—SCHOOLS.—NUMBER of PRISONERS in Attendance, Number of Days Schools were held, Number of Teachers, &c., from 1st April, 1881, to 31st March, 1882, in under-mentioned Prisons.

PRISONS.	Number of Individual Prisoners who attended School.		Number of Days School was held.		Average Daily Number of Pupils.		Number of Teachers.		Number of Hours allotted daily for Instruction of each Prisoner.	
	M.	F.	M.	F.	M.	F.	M.	F.	M.	F.
Armagh, . .	60	24	217	145	9	4	1	1	1	1
Belfast, . . .	220	140	298	288	18	15	1	1	1	1
Castlebar, . .	28	–	198	–	6	–	1	–	8 m.	–
Clonmel, . .	–	–	–	–	–	–	–	–	–	–
Cork, Male, . .	64	–	276	–	15	–	1	–	1	–
Cork, Female, .	–	78	–	266	–	8	–	1	–	2
Downpatrick, . .	40	22	218	289	4	4	1	1	1	1
Drogheda, . .	–	–	–	–	–	–	–	–	–	–
Dundalk, . .	280	–	290	–	15	–	1	–	2	–
Galway, . . .	48	–	48	–	1	–	1	–	15 m.	–
Grangegorman, .	–	174	–	279	–	16	–	1	–	2
Kilkenny, . .	36	–	70	–	8	–	1	–	1	–
Kilmainham, . .	–	–	–	–	–	–	–	–	–	–
Limerick, Male, .	20	–	6	–	4	–	1	–	2	–
Limerick, Female, .	–	–	–	–	–	–	–	–	–	–
Londonderry, . .	80	–	171	–	6	–	1	–	1	–
Maryborough, .	–	–	–	–	–	–	–	–	–	–
Mullingar, . .	–	–	–	–	–	–	–	–	–	–
Naas, . . .	38	–	34	–	28	–	1	–	1	–
Nenagh, . .	40	–	224	–	11	–	1	–	12	–
Omagh, . . .	25	2	118	18	9	2*	1	1	1	1
Richmond, . .	–	–	–	–	–	–	–	–	–	–
Sligo, . . .	100	24	282	282	12	2	1	1	1	1
Tralee, . . .	–	–	–	–	–	–	–	–	–	–
Tullamore, . .	62	–	288	–	6	–	1	–	1	–
Waterford, . .	–	–	–	–	–	–	–	–	–	–
Wexford, . .	9	–	159	–	–	–	1	–	1	–
County prisoners in Mountjoy, Male, .	156	–	281	–	62·76	–	1	–	1	–
Mountjoy, Female,	–	55	–	298	–	26	–	2	–	1
Total, 1881-82, .	1,361	519	3,167	1,810	204·76	76	17	9	–	–
Total, 1880-81, .	1,262	485	3,099	2,189	224·17	80	17	11	–	–

* For thirteen days.

TABLE X.—RETURN of PRISON OFFENCES and PUNISHMENTS in

Prisons.	Total number of Prisoners during the Year.		Irons or Hand-cuffs.		Prison Punishments. Punishment Cells.		Prison Punishments. Dietary Punishment.		Total number of Prisoners punished.		Violence.	
	M.	F.	M.	F.	M.	F.	M.	F.	M.	F.	M.	F.
Armagh,	653	174	–	–	83	14	223	14	223	20	–	2
Belfast,	2,039	1,217	–	–	79	23	1,544	493	1,023	524	23	7
Carlow,	137	33	–	–	–	–	15	1	15	1	–	–
Carrick-on-Shannon,	157	25	–	–	–	–	–	–	–	–	–	–
Castlebar,	416	108	–	–	8	–	121	8	71	6	2	3
Cavan,	117	23	–	–	3	1	2	1	4	1	–	–
Clonmel,	789	97	–	–	88	17	401	11	489	28	–	–
Cork, Male,	2,150	–	–	–	293	–	762	–	714	–	–	–
Cork, Female,	–	814	–	–	–	97	–	300	–	101	–	–
Downpatrick,	956	72	–	–	25	–	245	12	128	9	3	–
Drogheda,	–	149	–	–	–	5	–	33	–	27	–	–
Dundalk,	545	–	–	–	15	–	277	–	188	–	4	–
Ennis,	219	35	–	–	2	–	32	–	22	–	–	–
Enniskillen,	194	51	–	–	–	–	–	–	–	–	–	–
Galway,	731	248	–	–	7	5	49	10	56	15	1	1
Grangegorman,	2,624	2,190	–	–	225	97	417	252	642	349	1	3
Kilkenny,	467	99	–	–	10	4	334	8	179	11	2	–
Kilmainham,	1,312	74	–	–	16	–	142	3	163	3	–	–
Lifford,	61	6	–	–	–	–	–	–	–	–	–	–
Limerick, Male,	1,179	–	–	–	117	–	18	–	135	–	1	–
Limerick, Female,	–	531	–	–	–	29	–	–	–	29	–	–
Londonderry,	726	184	1	–	82	3	766	66	437	79	1	1
Longford,	125	37	–	–	–	–	17	1	17	1	–	–
Maryborough,	378	25	–	–	1	–	106	–	107	–	–	–
Monaghan,	122	41	–	–	–	–	11	2	11	2	–	–
Mullingar,	371	201	–	–	12	8	351	9	363	12	3	–
Naas,	451	79	2	–	3	3	20	4	24	7	1	1
Nenagh,	258	28	–	–	5	–	200	2	100	2	2	–
Omagh,	373	84	–	–	28	3	189	18	217	21	–	–
Richmond,	2,220	–	–	–	171	–	703	–	530	–	25	–
Roscommon,	133	26	–	–	–	–	–	–	–	–	–	–
Sligo,	537	99	–	–	20	7	70	30	88	24	–	–
Tralee,	628	96	–	–	4	1	500	–	277	1	–	–
Trim,	83	24	–	–	–	–	1	–	1	–	–	–
Tullamore,	437	62	–	–	21	–	129	–	150	–	4	–
Waterford,	558	200	–	–	7	6	157	11	164	17	–	–
Wexford,	288	55	2	–	4	–	187	3	92	3	1	–
Wicklow,	187	33	–	–	–	–	2	–	2	–	–	–
*Mountjoy, Male,	431	–	–	–	84	–	201	–	104	–	4	–
* „ Female,	–	135	–	3	–	24	–	19	–	23	–	1
Total, Males,	23,737	–	5	–	1,274	–	8,195	–	7,281	–	77	–
Total, Females,	–	7,343	–	3	–	345	–	1,314	–	1,321	–	19
Total, M. and F.,	31,080		8		1,619		9,509		8,602		96	

* County Prisoners.

LOCAL PRISONS from 1st APRIL, 1881, to the 31st MARCH, 1882.

Prison Offences.								Deprivation of Marks or Stage.		PRISONS.
Escapes and Attempts to Escape.		Idleness.		Other Breaches of Regulations.		Total Offences.				
M.	F.	M.	F.	M.	F.	M.	F.	M.	F.	
–	–	130	3	176	23	306	26	11	–	Armagh.
–	–	741	172	860	845	1,026	524	197	46	Belfast.
–	–	6	1	7	–	15	1	–	–	Carlow.
–	–	–	–	–	–	–	–	–	–	Carrick-on-Shannon.
–	–	40	1	67	4	129	6	7	–	Castlebar.
–	–	–	–	5	2	5	2	–	–	Cavan.
–	–	196	–	231	36	427	36	16	2	Clonmel.
–	–	502	–	1,077	–	1,579	–	129	–	Cork, Male.
–	–	–	12	–	290	–	302	–	2	Cork, Female.
–	–	187	7	130	5	270	12	106	8	Downpatrick.
–	–	–	21	–	15	–	36	–	–	Drogheda.
1	–	101	–	186	–	292	–	107	–	Dundalk.
–	–	5	–	29	–	34	–	1	–	Ennis.
–	–	–	–	–	–	–	–	–	–	Enniskillen.
–	–	–	1	55	13	56	15	–	–	Galway.
–	–	286	86	355	200	342	349	2	4	Grangegorman.
–	–	234	1	166	12	444	13	79	1	Kilkenny.
–	–	72	2	104	1	176	3	–	–	Kilmainham.
–	–	–	–	–	–	–	–	–	–	Lifford.
–	–	21	–	116	–	135	–	2	–	Limerick, Male.
–	–	–	–	–	29	–	29	–	1	Limerick, Female.
1	–	167	38	330	31	799	70	25	–	Londonderry.
–	–	–	–	17	1	17	1	–	–	Longford.
–	–	10	–	123	–	166	–	16	–	Maryborough.
–	–	–	–	11	2	11	2	4	–	Monaghan.
–	–	129	–	231	12	363	12	3	–	Mullingar.
–	–	8	4	20	3	29	7	2	–	Naas.
–	–	33	–	166	3	205	3	18	–	Nenagh.
–	–	59	–	158	21	217	21	62	–	Omagh.
–	–	276	–	571	–	674	–	204	–	Richmond.
–	–	–	–	–	–	–	–	–	–	Roscommon.
–	–	34	5	74	34	108	39	14	2	Sligo.
–	–	171	–	365	1	536	1	32	–	Tralee.
–	–	1	–	–	–	1	–	–	–	Trim.
–	–	51	–	96	–	151	–	23	–	Tullamore.
–	–	27	–	137	17	164	17	1	1	Waterford.
–	–	88	–	104	6	193	3	–	–	Wexford.
–	–	1	–	1	–	2	–	–	–	Wicklow.
–	–	90	–	314	–	408	–	165	–	Mountjoy Male.
–	–	–	–	–	46	–	49	–	14	" Female.
2	–	3,645	–	6,620	–	10,344	–	1,192	–	Total, Males.
–	–	–	354	–	1,206	–	1,579	–	70	Total, Females.
2		3,999		7,826		11,923		1,262		Total, M. and F.

TABLE XI.—OFFENCES and COMMITMENTS of JUVENILES, *i.e.*, PRISONERS included in

PRISONS.	COMMITMENTS.								
	CONVICTED								
	AT ASSIZES AND QUARTER SESSIONS.				SUMMARILY.				BY COURTS MARTIAL, AND DESERTERS.
	Under 12 Years.		12 and not exceeding 16 Years.		Under 12 Years.		12 and not exceeding 16 Years.		12 and not exceeding 16 Years.
	M.	F.	M.	F.	M.	F.	M.	F.	M.
Armagh,	–	–	1	–	2	–	16	5	–
Belfast,	–	–	2	–	10	1	56	7	–
Carlow,	–	–	–	–	–	–	–	–	–
Carrick-on-Shannon,	–	–	–	–	–	–	–	–	–
Castlebar,	–	–	–	1	6	–	13	2	–
Cavan,	–	–	–	–	–	–	–	–	–
Clonmel,	–	–	1	–	3	–	23	–	–
Cork, Male,	1	–	3	–	10	–	66	–	–
Cork, Female,	–	–	–	–	–	–	–	7	–
Downpatrick,	–	–	1	–	–	–	1	–	–
Drogheda,	–	–	–	–	–	–	–	1	–
Dundalk,	–	–	–	–	1	–	10	–	–
Ennis,	–	–	–	–	–	–	–	–	–
Enniskillen,	–	–	–	–	–	–	–	–	–
Galway,	–	–	4	1	2	–	23	2	–
Grangegorman,	–	–	–	–	–	6	3	79	–
Kilkenny,	–	–	–	–	–	–	7	–	–
Kilmainham,	–	–	–	–	2	–	63	1	–
Lifford,	–	–	–	–	–	–	–	–	–
Limerick, Male,	–	–	–	–	3	–	35	–	–
Limerick, Female,	–	–	–	–	–	–	–	6	–
Londonderry,	1	–	3	–	6	–	23	3	–
Longford,	–	–	–	–	–	–	–	–	–
Maryborough,	–	–	1	–	2	–	–	–	–
Monaghan,	–	–	–	–	–	–	–	–	–
Mullingar,	–	–	3	–	4	1	17	2	–
Naas,	–	–	–	–	2	–	9	–	–
Nenagh,	–	–	–	–	3	–	4	–	–
Omagh,	–	–	1	–	1	–	11	–	–
Richmond,	1	–	21	–	27	–	127	–	–
Roscommon,	–	–	–	–	–	–	–	–	–
Sligo,	–	–	–	1	–	1	14	1	–
Tralee,	–	–	–	–	4	–	42	3	–
Trim,	–	–	–	–	–	–	–	–	–
Tullamore,	–	–	–	–	–	–	1	1	–
Waterford,	–	–	4	–	–	2	9	2	–
Wexford,	–	–	6	–	3	–	–	–	–
Wicklow,	–	–	–	–	–	–	–	–	–
Total, 1881–82,	3	–	50	3	93	10	575	122	–
Total, 1880–81,	5	–	40	6	93	16	556	142	1

not exceeding 16 years of age, from 1st April, 1881, to 31st March, 1882, foregoing Tables.

Commitments.												
Total Convicted.				Not Convicted and Untried.				Total Number of Commitments.				Prisons.
Under 12 Years.		12 and not exceeding 16 Years.		Under 12 Years.		12 and not exceeding 16 Years.		Under 12 Years.		12 and not exceeding 16 Years.		
M.	F.	M.	F.	M.	F.	M.	F.	M.	F.	M.	F.	
2	–	20	5	–	–	–	–	2	–	20	5	Armagh.
10	1	58	7	1	–	29	2	11	1	67	9	Belfast.
–	–	–	–	–	–	–	–	–	–	–	–	Carlow.
–	–	–	–	–	–	–	–	–	–	–	–	Carrick-on-Shannon.
6	–	13	3	2	–	2	–	8	–	15	3	Castlebar.
–	–	–	–	–	–	–	–	–	–	–	–	Cavan.
3	–	34	–	–	–	2	3	3	–	36	3	Clonmel.
11	–	68	–	–	–	9	–	11	–	77	–	Cork, Male.
–	–	–	7	–	–	–	–	–	–	–	7	Cork, Female.
–	–	2	–	–	–	–	–	–	–	2	–	Downpatrick.
–	–	–	1	–	–	–	–	–	–	–	1	Drogheda.
1	–	10	–	–	–	1	–	1	–	11	–	Dundalk.
–	–	–	–	–	–	–	–	–	–	–	–	Ennis.
–	–	–	–	–	–	–	–	–	–	–	–	Enniskillen.
2	–	27	3	–	–	10	1	2	–	37	4	Galway.
–	5	3	79	–	2	–	3	–	7	3	82	Grangegorman.
–	–	7	–	–	–	3	–	–	–	10	–	Kilkenny.
2	–	53	1	2	–	9	–	4	–	62	1	Kilmainham.
–	–	–	–	–	–	–	–	–	–	–	–	Lifford.
3	–	35	–	–	–	5	–	3	–	40	–	Limerick, Male.
–	–	–	6	–	–	–	1	–	–	–	7	Limerick, Female.
9	–	26	3	–	–	2	–	9	–	28	3	Londonderry.
–	–	–	–	–	–	–	–	–	–	–	–	Longford.
2	–	1	–	–	–	2	–	2	–	3	–	Maryborough.
–	–	–	–	–	–	–	–	–	–	–	–	Monaghan.
4	1	20	2	–	–	6	–	4	1	25	2	Mullingar.
2	–	9	–	1	–	1	–	3	–	10	–	Naas.
3	–	4	–	–	–	–	–	3	–	4	–	Nenagh.
1	–	12	–	–	–	–	–	1	–	12	–	Omagh.
28	–	148	–	9	–	53	–	37	–	201	–	Richmond.
–	–	–	–	–	–	–	–	–	–	–	–	Roscommon.
–	1	14	2	3	–	4	–	3	1	18	2	Sligo.
4	–	42	3	–	1	6	2	4	1	48	5	Tralee.
–	–	–	–	–	–	–	–	–	–	–	–	Trim.
–	–	1	1	–	–	3	–	–	–	4	1	Tullamore.
–	2	13	2	2	–	2	1	2	2	15	3	Waterford.
3	–	5	–	–	–	–	–	3	–	5	–	Wexford.
–	–	–	–	–	–	–	–	–	–	–	–	Wicklow.
95	10	595	125	20	3	149	13	115	13	774	150	Total, 1881–82.
98	18	507	148	35	3	186	18	133	21	733	166	Total, 1880–81.

TABLE XII.—SENTENCES of PENAL SERVITUDE and IMPRISONMENT passed

PRISONS.	Penal Servitude for 5 Years.		Imprisonment for 3 Years and above 18 Months.		12 Months and upwards.		9 Months and above 6.		6 Months and above 3.		3 Months and above 2.		2 Months and above 1.		1 Month and above 14 Days.	
	M.	F.	M.	F.	M.	F.	M.	F.	M.	F.	M.	F.	M.	F.	M.	F.
Armagh,	-	-	-	-	-	-	-	-	1	-	-	-	2	-	1	-
Belfast,	-	-	-	-	1	-	-	-	6	-	1	-	1	-	24	7
Castlebar,	-	-	-	-	-	-	-	-	-	-	-	-	-	-	2	-
Clonmel,	-	-	-	-	-	-	-	-	1	-	2	-	6	-	12	-
Cork, Male,	-	-	-	-	-	-	1	-	-	-	-	-	2	-	6	-
Cork, Female,	-	-	-	-	-	-	-	-	-	-	-	1	-	-	-	-
Downpatrick,	-	-	-	-	-	-	-	-	-	-	-	-	-	-	-	-
Drogheda,	-	-	-	-	-	-	-	-	-	-	-	-	-	-	-	-
Dundalk,	6	-	-	-	1	-	-	-	-	-	-	-	1	-	-	-
Galway,	-	-	-	-	-	-	-	-	-	-	1	-	1	-	6	1
Grangegorman,	-	-	-	-	-	-	-	-	-	-	-	-	-	-	1	6
Kilkenny,	-	-	-	-	-	-	-	-	-	-	-	-	-	-	2	-
Kilmainham,	-	-	-	-	-	-	-	-	1	-	1	-	-	-	6	-
Limerick, Male,	-	-	-	-	-	-	-	-	-	-	2	-	3	-	10	-
Limerick, Female,	-	-	-	-	-	-	-	-	-	-	-	-	-	-	1	-
Londonderry,	-	-	-	-	-	-	-	-	-	-	2	-	1	-	6	1
Maryborough,	-	-	-	-	-	-	-	-	-	-	1	-	-	-	2	-
Mullingar,	-	-	-	-	-	-	-	-	1	-	1	-	1	-	5	1
Naas,	-	-	-	-	-	-	-	-	-	-	-	-	-	-	1	-
Nenagh,	-	-	-	-	-	-	-	-	-	-	-	-	-	-	-	-
Omagh,	1	-	-	-	2	-	-	-	-	-	-	-	4	-	3	-
Richmond,	-	-	-	-	-	-	-	-	5	-	2	-	21	-	27	-
Sligo,	-	-	-	-	-	-	-	-	-	-	-	-	1	-	2	-
Tralee,	-	-	-	-	-	-	-	-	-	-	-	-	1	-	8	-
Tullamore,	-	-	-	-	-	-	-	-	-	-	-	-	-	-	1	1
Waterford,	-	-	-	-	-	-	-	-	-	-	-	-	-	-	1	-
Wexford,	-	-	-	-	-	-	-	-	-	-	-	-	-	-	1	-
Total, Males,	6	-	-	-	4	-	1	-	14	-	13	-	44	-	127	-
Total, Females,	-	-	-	-	-	-	-	-	-	-	-	1	-	-	-	17
Total, M. and F.	6		-		4		1		14		14		44		144	

on Juvenile Prisoners from the 1st April, 1881, to 31st March, 1882.

Imprisonment for — 14 Days and above 7. M.	F.	7 Days and above 48 Hours. M.	F.	48 Hours. M.	F.	24 Hours. M.	F.	Unlimited. M.	F.	Sentence respited and not passed. M.	F.	Total. M.	F.	Prisons.
10	5	7	-	1	-	-	-	-	-	-	-	23	5	Armagh.
22	1	11	-	-	-	3	-	-	-	-	-	36	3	Belfast.
3	3	5	-	-	-	-	-	4	-	-	-	19	3	Castlebar.
9	-	3	-	-	-	-	-	-	-	-	-	37	-	Clonmel.
36	-	25	-	5	-	4	-	1	-	-	-	79	-	Cork, Male.
-	4	-	2	-	-	-	-	-	-	-	-	-	7	Cork, Female.
-	-	-	-	-	-	-	-	-	-	-	-	-	-	Downpatrick.
-	-	-	-	-	-	-	-	-	-	-	-	-	-	Drogheda.
-	-	1	-	8	-	-	-	-	-	-	-	11	-	Dundalk.
3	-	6	2	2	-	5	-	-	-	-	-	29	3	Galway.
-	26	2	33	-	9	-	10	-	-	-	-	3	84	Grangegorman.
3	-	1	-	1	-	-	-	-	-	-	-	7	-	Kilkenny.
29	1	14	-	-	-	4	-	-	-	-	-	55	1	Kilmainham.
15	-	3	-	-	-	5	-	-	-	-	-	38	-	Limerick, Male.
-	5	-	-	-	-	-	-	-	-	-	-	1	5	Limerick, Female.
16	2	7	-	2	-	1	-	-	-	-	-	35	3	Londonderry.
-	-	-	-	-	-	-	-	-	-	-	-	3	-	Maryborough.
10	2	6	-	-	-	-	-	-	-	-	-	24	3	Mullingar.
3	-	3	-	-	-	4	-	-	-	-	-	11	-	Naas.
2	-	3	-	2	-	-	-	-	-	-	-	7	-	Nenagh.
8	-	-	-	-	-	-	-	-	-	-	-	18	-	Omagh.
58	-	39	-	11	-	5	-	-	-	8	-	176	-	Richmond.
6	-	3	1	-	-	2	2	-	-	-	-	14	3	Sligo.
21	-	16	3	-	-	-	-	-	-	-	-	46	3	Tralee.
-	-	-	-	-	-	-	-	-	-	-	-	1	1	Tullamore.
10	1	2	-	-	1	1	-	-	-	1	-	15	2	Waterford.
5	-	1	-	-	-	1	-	-	-	-	-	8	-	Wexford.
274	-	158	-	27	-	33	-	5	-	9	-	729	-	Total, Males.
-	50	-	41	-	10	-	12	-	-	-	-	-	131	Total, Females.
324		204		37		47		5		9		858		Total, M. and F.

TABLE XIII.—CONDITION of JUVENILES as to

Prisons.	Education of											
	Read and Write.				Read Imperfectly.				Knew Spelling.			
	Under 12 years.		12 and not exceeding 16 years.		Under 12 years.		12 and not exceeding 16 years.		Under 12 years.		12 and not exceeding 16 years.	
	M.	F.	M.	F.	M.	F.	M.	F.	M.	F.	M.	F.
Armagh,	–	–	4	2	1	–	5	–	1	–	4	–
Belfast,	6	–	61	6	–	–	–	1	1	1	1	–
Castlebar,	3	–	7	–	–	–	–	–	–	–	1	–
Clonmel,	1	–	16	1	1	–	4	1	1	–	–	–
Cork, Male,	5	–	45	–	2	–	3	–	–	–	3	–
Cork, Female,	–	–	–	2	–	–	–	1	–	–	–	1
Downpatrick,	–	–	1	–	–	–	–	–	–	–	–	–
Drogheda,	–	–	–	–	–	–	–	–	–	–	–	–
Dundalk,	–	–	–	–	1	–	5	–	–	–	–	–
Galway,	–	–	12	2	1	–	4	–	–	–	1	–
Grangegorman,	–	1	1	28	2	–	1	12	–	–	–	–
Kilkenny,	–	–	6	–	–	–	–	–	–	–	–	–
Kilmainham,	1	–	38	1	–	–	4	–	–	–	–	–
Limerick, Male,	2	–	25	–	–	–	2	–	–	–	–	–
Limerick, Female,	–	–	–	2	–	–	–	3	–	–	–	2
Londonderry,	2	–	4	2	3	–	5	1	1	–	3	–
Maryborough,	1	–	2	–	–	–	–	–	–	–	–	–
Mullingar,	3	–	20	–	–	–	–	–	–	–	–	–
Naas,	1	–	5	–	–	–	–	–	1	–	–	–
Nenagh,	3	–	3	–	–	–	–	–	–	–	–	–
Omagh,	1	–	4	–	–	–	–	–	–	–	–	–
Richmond,	7	–	126	–	6	–	31	–	5	–	7	–
Sligo,	–	–	7	–	–	–	–	–	–	–	–	–
Tralee,	4	1	38	5	–	–	2	–	–	–	–	–
Tullamore,	–	–	2	1	–	–	–	–	–	–	–	–
Waterford,	–	–	7	–	–	–	2	–	–	–	1	–
Wexford,	–	–	6	–	–	–	–	–	–	–	–	–
Total, Males,	40	–	440	–	17	–	68	–	10	–	20	–
Total, Females,	–	2	–	52	–	–	–	19	–	1	–	3
Total, M. and F.,	42		492		17		87		11		23	

EDUCATION and RELIGION in 1881–82.

CRIMINAL.

Knew Alphabet.				Wholly Illiterate.				Could not be ascertained.				TOTAL.				PRISONS.
Under 12 years.		12 and not exceeding 16 years.		Under 12 years.		12 and not exceeding 16 years.		Under 12 years.		12 and not exceeding 16 years.		Under 12 years.		12 and not exceeding 16 years.		
M.	F.	M.	F.	M.	F.	M.	F.	M.	F.	M.	F.	M.	F.	M.	F.	
-	-	3	-	-	-	4	3	-	-	-	-	2	-	20	5	Armagh.
-	-	-	-	4	-	26	2	-	-	-	-	11	1	67	9	Belfast.
-	-	-	-	5	-	7	3	-	-	-	-	8	-	15	8	Castlebar.
-	-	-	-	-	-	16	1	-	-	-	-	3	-	88	8	Clonmel.
2	-	10	-	2	-	17	-	-	-	-	-	11	-	77	-	Cork, Male.
-	-	-	1	-	-	-	2	-	-	-	-	-	-	-	7	Cork, Female.
-	-	-	-	-	-	1	-	-	-	-	-	-	-	2	-	Downpatrick.
-	-	-	-	-	-	-	1	-	-	-	-	-	-	-	1	Drogheda.
-	-	-	-	-	-	6	-	-	-	-	-	1	-	11	-	Dundalk.
-	-	1	-	1	-	19	2	-	-	-	-	2	-	37	4	Galway.
-	-	-	-	-	2	1	44	-	-	-	-	2	3	8	84	Grangegorman.
-	-	-	-	-	-	4	-	-	-	-	-	-	-	10	-	Kilkenny.
-	-	-	-	3	-	20	-	-	-	-	-	4	-	62	1	Kilmainham.
1	-	3	-	-	-	10	-	-	-	-	-	8	-	40	-	Limerick, Male.
-	-	-	-	-	-	-	-	-	-	-	-	-	-	-	7	Limerick, Female.
-	-	3	-	16	-	-	-	-	-	-	-	23	-	15	6	Londonderry.
-	-	-	-	1	-	1	-	-	-	-	-	2	-	3	-	Maryborough.
-	-	-	-	1	1	6	2	-	-	-	-	4	1	26	2	Mullingar.
-	-	1	-	1	-	4	-	-	-	-	-	3	-	10	-	Naas.
-	-	-	-	-	-	1	-	-	-	-	-	3	-	4	-	Nenagh.
-	-	5	-	-	-	3	-	-	-	-	-	1	-	12	-	Omagh.
3	-	-	-	18	-	87	-	-	-	-	-	87	-	201	-	Richmond.
-	-	-	-	3	1	11	2	-	-	-	-	8	1	18	2	Sligo.
-	-	-	-	-	-	8	-	-	-	-	-	4	1	48	5	Tralee.
-	-	2	-	-	-	-	-	-	-	-	-	-	-	4	1	Tullamore.
-	-	-	-	4	-	5	3	-	-	-	-	4	-	15	3	Waterford.
-	-	-	-	-	-	2	-	-	-	-	-	-	-	8	-	Wexford.
6	-	28	-	57	-	208	-	-	-	-	-	180	-	764	-	Total, Males.
-	-	-	1	-	4	-	65	-	-	-	-	-	7	-	140	Total, Females.
6		29		61		278		-		-		187		904		Total, M. & F.

[*continued.*

TABLE XIII. *concluded.*—CONDITION of JUVENILES

PRISONS.	RELIGION.											
	Protestant Episcopalians of Ireland.				Presbyterian.				Roman Catholic.			
	Under 12 years.		12 and not exceeding 16 years.		Under 12 years.		12 and not exceeding 16 years.		Under 12 years.		12 and not exceeding 16 years.	
	M.	F.	M.	F.	M.	F.	M.	F.	M.	F.	M.	F.
Armagh, . . .	–	–	8	–	1	–	2	–	1	–	10	4
Belfast, . . .	3	–	29	2	3	–	12	2	6	1	45	5
Castlebar, . . .	–	–	–	–	–	–	–	–	8	–	15	3
Clonmel, . . .	–	–	–	–	–	–	–	–	3	–	36	3
Cork, Male, . .	–	–	–	–	–	–	–	–	11	–	77	–
Cork, Female, . .	–	–	–	1	–	–	–	–	–	–	–	6
Downpatrick, . .	–	–	2	–	–	–	–	–	–	–	–	–
Drogheda, . . .	–	–	–	1	–	–	–	–	–	–	–	–
Dundalk, . . .	–	–	–	–	–	–	–	–	1	–	11	–
Galway, . . .	–	–	–	–	–	–	–	–	2	–	37	4
Grangegorman, . .	–	–	–	6	–	–	–	–	–	5	3	73
Kilkenny, . . .	–	–	–	–	–	–	–	–	–	–	10	–
Kilmainham, . .	–	–	3	–	–	–	–	1	4	–	59	–
Limerick, Male, . .	–	–	3	–	–	–	–	–	3	–	37	–
Limerick, Female, .	–	–	–	–	–	–	–	–	–	–	–	7
Londonderry, . .	1	–	2	2	–	–	–	–	8	–	26	1
Maryborough, . .	–	–	–	–	–	–	–	–	2	–	3	–
Mullingar, . . .	–	–	2	–	–	–	–	–	4	1	24	2
Naas, . . .	–	–	3	–	–	–	–	–	3	–	7	–
Nenagh, . . .	–	–	–	–	–	–	–	–	3	–	4	–
Omagh, . . .	–	–	–	–	–	–	1	–	1	–	11	–
Richmond, . . .	2	–	18	–	–	–	–	–	35	–	183	–
Sligo, . . .	–	–	–	–	–	–	–	–	8	1	18	2
Tralee, . . .	–	–	1	–	–	–	–	–	4	1	47	5
Tullamore, . .	–	–	–	–	–	–	–	–	–	–	4	1
Waterford, . . .	–	–	–	–	–	–	–	–	4	–	15	3
Wexford, . . .	–	–	–	–	–	–	–	–	–	–	8	–
Total, Males, .	6	–	71	–	4	–	15	–	105	–	690	–
Total, Females, . .	–	–	–	12	–	–	–	3	–	9	–	124
Total, M. and F.	6		83		4		18		114		814	

as to Education and Religion in 1881–82.

Religion.												Prisons.
Other Religions.				Could not be ascertained.				Total.				
Under 12 years.		12 and not exceeding 16 years.		Under 12 years.		12 and not exceeding 16 years.		Under 12 years.		12 and not exceeding 16 years.		
M.	F.	M.	F.	M.	F.	M.	F.	M.	F.	M.	F.	
-	-	-	1	-	-	-	-	2	-	20	5	Armagh.
-	-	1	-	-	-	-	-	11	1	67	9	Belfast.
-	-	-	-	-	-	-	-	6	-	15	3	Castlebar.
-	-	-	-	-	-	-	-	3	-	36	3	Clonmel.
-	-	-	-	-	-	-	-	11	-	77	-	Cork, Male.
-	-	-	-	-	-	-	-	-	-	-	7	Cork, Female.
-	-	-	-	-	-	-	-	-	-	2	-	Downpatrick.
-	-	-	-	-	-	-	-	-	-	-	1	Drogheda.
-	-	-	-	-	-	-	-	1	-	11	-	Dundalk.
-	-	-	-	-	-	-	-	2	-	37	4	Galway.
-	-	-	-	-	-	-	-	-	5	8	84	Grangegorman.
-	-	-	-	-	-	-	-	-	-	10	-	Kilkenny.
-	-	-	-	-	-	-	-	4	-	62	1	Kilmainham.
-	-	-	-	-	-	-	-	3	-	40	-	Limerick, Male.
-	-	-	-	-	-	-	-	-	-	-	7	Limerick, Female.
-	-	-	-	-	-	-	-	9	-	28	3	Londonderry.
-	-	-	-	-	-	-	-	2	-	3	-	Maryborough.
-	-	-	-	-	-	-	-	4	1	26	2	Mullingar.
-	-	-	-	-	-	-	-	8	-	10	-	Naas.
-	-	-	-	-	-	-	-	3	-	4	-	Nenagh.
-	-	-	-	-	-	-	-	1	-	12	-	Omagh.
-	-	-	-	-	-	-	-	37	-	201	-	Richmond.
-	-	-	-	-	-	-	-	3	1	18	2	Sligo.
-	-	-	-	-	-	-	-	4	1	48	5	Tralee.
-	-	-	-	-	-	-	-	-	-	4	1	Tullamore.
-	-	-	-	-	-	-	-	4	-	15	3	Waterford.
-	-	-	-	-	-	-	-	-	-	3	-	Wexford.
-	-	1	-	-	-	-	-	115	-	777	-	Total, Males.
-	-	-	1	-	-	-	-	-	9	-	140	Total, Females.
-		2		-		-		124		917		Total, M. and F.

TABLE XIV.—No. of CONVICTED PRISONERS in Custody in the following Prisons on

PRISONS.	Death.	3 Years Penal Servitude and upwards.		2 Years and above 18 Months.		18 Months and above 12.		12 Months only.		Under 12 Months and above 9.		9 Months and above 6.	
	F.	M.	F.	M.	F.	M.	F.	M.	F.	M.	F.	M.	F.
Armagh,	–	–	–	–	–	2	–	5	–	1	–	1	–
Belfast,	–	–	–	–	–	–	–	16	3	1	–	16	8
Castlebar,	–	–	–	–	–	–	–	–	–	–	–	–	–
Clonmel,	–	–	–	–	–	–	–	4	–	–	–	1	–
Cork, Male,	–	–	–	2	–	3	–	22	–	–	–	–	–
Cork, Female,	–	–	1	–	–	–	–	–	3	–	–	–	1
Downpatrick,	–	–	–	–	–	–	–	4	–	–	–	2	–
Drogheda,	–	–	–	–	–	–	–	–	–	–	–	–	–
Dundalk,	–	–	–	–	–	–	–	6	–	–	–	2	–
Galway,	–	–	–	–	–	–	–	–	–	–	–	1	–
Grangegorman,	–	–	–	1	2	4	1	1	2	3	–	–	–
Kilkenny,	–	–	–	–	–	–	–	6	–	–	–	5	–
Kilmainham,	–	–	–	–	–	–	–	–	–	–	–	–	–
Limerick, Male,	–	–	–	–	–	–	–	3	–	–	–	4	–
Limerick, Female,	–	–	–	–	–	–	–	–	1	–	–	–	2
Londonderry,	1	1	–	1	–	2	–	8	1	–	–	8	3
Maryborough,	–	–	–	–	–	–	–	14	–	18	–	5	–
Mullingar,	–	–	–	–	–	–	–	14	–	–	–	4	1
Naas,	–	–	–	–	–	1	–	4	–	–	–	2	–
Nenagh,	–	–	–	–	–	–	–	8	–	–	–	8	–
Omagh,	–	–	–	–	–	–	–	–	–	–	–	–	–
Richmond,	–	–	–	–	–	1	–	25	–	–	–	29	–
Sligo,	–	–	–	–	–	–	–	8	–	–	–	1	1
Tralee,	–	–	–	–	–	–	–	–	–	2	–	–	–
Tullamore,	–	–	–	1	–	–	–	11	–	1	–	4	–
Waterford,	–	–	–	–	–	1	–	1	–	1	–	–	–
Wexford,	–	–	–	–	–	–	–	–	–	–	–	2	2
Total, Males,	–	1	–	5	–	14	–	160	–	28	–	95	–
Total, Females,	1	–	1	–	2	–	1	–	10	–	–	–	18
Total, M. and F.	1	2		7		15		170		28		108	

M.	F.	M.	F.	M.	F.	M.	F.	M.	F.	
4	–	2	–	8	–	16	–	12	–	Armagh.
19	7	25	13	4	–	33	10	39	105	Belfast.
1	1	1	–	–	–	5	1	10	1	Castlebar.
–	–	2	–	–	–	6	–	25	–	Clonmel.
10	–	8	–	5	–	27	–	50	–	Cork, Male.
–	8	–	4	–	–	–	4	–	65	Cork, Female.
–	–	2	1	–	–	2	–	19	5	Downpatrick.
–	8	–	1	–	5	–	4	–	4	Drogheda.
5	–	4	–	4	–	2	–	44	–	Dundalk.
3	–	4	1	–	–	2	1	27	7	Galway.
3	3	7	10	–	5	5	13	74	87	Grangegorman.
25	–	9	–	–	–	4	–	10	–	Kilkenny.
2	–	2	–	–	–	7	–	25	–	Kilmainham.
–	–	7	–	5	–	6	–	33	–	Limerick, Male.
–	2	–	18	–	9	–	–	–	17	Limerick, Female.
7	–	5	4	–	–	16	7	30	18	Londonderry.
13	–	1	–	17	–	11	2	7	–	Maryborough.
4	–	9	5	1	1	17	–	16	7	Mullingar.
–	–	1	–	–	–	–	–	–	–	Naas.
1	–	8	–	2	–	2	–	8	–	Nenagh.
–	–	–	–	–	–	3	–	5	–	Omagh.
9	–	27	–	4	–	45	–	18	–	Richmond.
14	–	4	4	–	–	2	–	11	4	Sligo.
3	–	5	–	1	–	2	–	10	3	Tralee.
13	1	12	1	3	–	14	–	13	2	Tullamore.
1	–	3	2	1	–	5	6	7	8	Waterford.
2	1	2	–	2	–	7	1	19	2	Wexford.
135	–	150	–	52	–	239	–	530	–	Total, Males.
–	21	–	59	–	18	–	49	–	335	Total, Females.
156		209		70		288		865		Total, M. and F.

TABLE XV.—RETURN of COMMITTALS, &c., to BRIDEWELLS

BRIDEWELLS.	COUNTY.	Number of Direct Committals.		Number received from other Bridewells on way to County Gaol.		Number otherwise received.		Total in Bridewell.		Number of Drunkards committed from 1st April, 1881, to 31st March, 1882.	
		M.	F.	M.	F.	M.	F.	M.	F.	M.	F.
Bailieborough, . .	Cavan, . .	85	10	–	–	3	–	88	10	18	1
Ballina, . . .	Mayo, . .	14	9	–	–	26	6	40	8	8	1
Ballinasloe, . .	Galway, . .	196	36	57	22	4	–	256	58	60	15
Ballinrobe, . .	Mayo, . .	90	6	–	–	6	–	96	6	16	–
Ballymena, . .	Antrim, . .	107	10	–	–	1	1	108	11	58	3
Baltinglass, . .	Wicklow, .	6	4	–	–	–	–	6	4	–	–
Bantry, . . .	Cork, . .	91	13	–	–	–	–	91	13	5	–
Cahirsiveen, . .	Kerry, . .	40	4	–	–	–	–	40	4	4	–
Clifden, . . .	Galway, . .	74	13	–	–	–	–	74	13	34	3
Clonakilty, . .	Cork, . .	60	3	–	–	15	6	54	19	–	–
Coleraine, . .	Londonderry, .	56	37	–	–	13	5	68	83	13	7
Dingle, . . .	Kerry, . .	21	5	–	–	–	–	21	5	3	1
Donegal, . .	Donegal, .	58	7	–	–	12	2	70	9	93	6
Dungannon, . .	Tyrone, . .	121	25	–	–	11	3	183	28	78	15
Dungarvan, . .	Waterford, .	96	13	–	–	45	9	141	85	60	3
Fermoy, . . .	Cork, . .	98	18	–	–	–	–	96	19	87	7
Killarney, . . .	Kerry, . .	56	3	5	–	3	–	68	3	1	–
Kilrush, . . .	Clare, . .	36	4	–	–	18	3	54	7	3	1
Letterkenny, . .	Donegal, . .	88	18	–	–	18	2	106	18	76	15
Listowel, . . .	Kerry, . .	42	6	–	–	–	–	42	8	28	5
Loughrea, . . .	Galway, . .	115	10	–	–	–	–	115	10	32	1
Lurgan, . . .	Armagh, . .	114	24	–	–	–	–	114	24	41	3
Mallow, . . .	Cork, . .	176	20	–	–	–	–	176	20	7	3
Mitchelstown, . .	Cork, . .	14	3	–	–	61	3	75	3	14	8
Navan, . . .	Meath, . .	19	–	–	–	35	7	54	7	17	–
New Ross, . .	Wexford, .	8	2	1	1	52	9	68	12	8	2
Newry, . . .	Down, . .	278	94	–	–	21	3	299	96	178	70
Parsonstown, . .	King's, . .	91	28	–	–	65	22	155	50	43	14
Queenstown, . .	Cork, . .	101	8	–	–	–	–	101	8	–	–
Rathkeale, . .	Limerick, .	81	8	–	–	1	–	82	3	–	–
Thurles, . . .	Tipperary, .	86	7	–	–	4	–	90	7	92	4
Tipperary, . .	Tipperary, .	155	29	–	–	42	11	197	40	17	8
Tuam, . . .	Galway, . .	85	17	–	–	78	10	161	27	86	11
Youghal, . . .	Cork, . .	40	13	–	–	–	–	40	13	8	2
	Total, Males, .	2,600	–	58	–	588	–	3,191	–	878	–
	Total, Females,	–	495	–	32	–	101	–	619	–	186
	Total, M. & F.	3,095		88		629		3,810		1,061	

from 1st April, 1881, to 31st March, 1882.

Sentences carried out during the above Period.								Greatest No. of Males and Females in custody at any one time during above period.		BRIDEWELLS.
24 Hours and under.		48 Hours and above 24 Hours.		7 Days and above 48 Hours.		Above 7 Days.				
M.	F.	M.	F.	M.	F.	M.	F.	M.	F.	
3	-	3	2	-	-	-	-	3	2	Bailieborough.
-	-	1	-	-	-	-	-	6	1	Ballina.
37	4	18	9	-	-	-	-	8	3	Ballinasloe.
8	-	8	-	-	-	-	-	8	3	Ballinrobe.
45	4	10	2	-	-	-	-	6	2	Ballymena.
-	-	-	1	-	-	-	-	2	3	Baltinglass.
-	-	-	-	-	-	-	-	7	3	Bantry.
-	-	4	-	-	-	-	-	8	1	Cahirsiveen.
1	-	22	-	-	-	-	-	5	2	Clifden.
-	-	4	-	-	-	-	-	3	2	Clonakilty.
3	5	8	2	-	-	-	-	5	3	Coleraine.
1	1	9	-	-	-	-	-	2	3	Dingle.
6	1	17	3	-	-	-	-	6	1	Donegal.
16	3	28	4	48	11	1	-	7	3	Dungannon.
14	4	14	4	68	6	12	3	3	2	Dungarvan.
10	4	17	3	-	-	-	-	7	2	Fermoy.
14	1	14	-	-	-	-	-	7	1	Killarney.
3	-	3	-	-	-	-	-	8	1	Kilrush.
54	9	72	6	-	-	-	-	5	1	Letterkenny.
13	3	13	2	-	-	-	-	6	1	Listowel.
3	1	19	-	-	-	-	-	16	3	Loughrea.
3	1	10	1	-	-	-	-	10	3	Lurgan.
2	1	5	1	-	-	-	-	16	1	Mallow.
8	-	9	2	-	-	-	-	5	1	Mitchelstown.
1	-	15	-	-	-	-	-	7	3	Navan.
8	2	-	-	-	-	-	-	6	2	New Ross.
111	38	37	48	-	-	-	-	7	2	Newry.
15	1	14	8	30	17	2	2	8	4	Parsonstown.
-	-	-	-	-	-	-	-	14	3	Queenstown.
-	-	-	-	-	-	-	-	3	6	Rathkeale.
4	3	13	1	-	-	-	-	5	3	Thurles.
13	2	1	3	34	13	3	-	23	6	Tipperary.
1	-	37	11	-	-	-	-	14	4	Tuam.
8	3	3	3	-	-	-	-	11	2	Youghal.
380	-	393	-	200	-	18	-	260	-	Total, Males.
-	90	-	109	-	46	-	5	-	75	Total, Females.
470		503		246		23		335		Total, M. and F.

TABLE XVI.—Cases of SICKNESS and LUNACY, from 1st April, 1881, to 31st March, 1882, in the under-mentioned Prisons.

PRISONS.	Number in Prison Hospital.		Daily average Number in Hospital.		Number of Cases of Illness or Disease prescribed for out of Hospital.		Number of Lunatics in Custody during the above period.		Number of Days passed by Lunatics in Gaol.		Greatest Number Sick at any one time in and out of Hospital, including Lunatics.	
	M.	F.	M.	F.	M.	F.	M.	F.	M.	F.	M.	F.
Armagh, . .	20	9	2·	2·	885	72	–	–	–	–	12	7
Belfast, . .	72	60	4·	2·	3,184	1,882	11	1	61	8	18	18
Castlebar, . .	8	3	·14	·05	189	67	3	1	27	15	7	4
Clonmel, . .	101	18	2·	5·	1,581	220	2	–	20	–	10	8
Cork, Male, . .	51	–	1·	–	1,944	–	6	–	01	–	4	–
Cork, Female, .	–	89	–	2·	–	1,040	–	8	–	10	–	22
Downpatrick, . .	–	–	–	–	608	87	–	1	–	22	3	6
Drogheda, . .	–	–	–	–	–	23	–	1	–	8	–	4
Dundalk, . . .	1	–	–		20	–	3	–	18	–	4	–
Galway, . .	186	58	1·	–	565	83	–	1	–	1	7	8
Grangegorman, .	148	330	5·	10·	2,987	3,014	3	8	158	60	31	52
Kilkenny, . .	–	–	–	–	701	59	1	1	7	10	16	8
Kilmainham, .	70	–	10·		964	–	–	–	–	–	10	–
Limerick, Male, .	28	–	1·	–	1,382	–	3	–	88	–	5	–
Limerick, Female,	–	3	–	–	–	327	–	2	–	16	–	10
Londonderry, .	62	8	1·	·12	207	54	2	2	22	14	4	1
Maryborough, .	7	1	1·	·5	287	5	–	–	–	–	5	1
Mullingar, . .	12	4	1·	–	168	81	5	1	145	10	4	6
Naas, . . .	–	–	–	–	25	4	1	–	18	–	8	8
Nenagh, . .	1	–	–	–	540	8	1	1	3	4	6	2
Omagh, . .	10	2	·6	–	228	27	1	1	7	10	6	4
Richmond, . .	685	–	24·	–	8,155	–	9	–	130	–	110	–
Sligo, . . .	26	3	2·	·05	400	90	2	–	16	–	10	1
Tralee, . .	1	2	–	–	228	79	2	–	16	–	4	6
Tullamore, . .	10	2	–	–	848	63	1	–	8	–	18	–
Waterford, . .	5	2	·16	·06	255	72	7	1	58	5	4	2
Wexford, . .	5	–	–	–	215	81	1	–	38	–	2	1
County Prisoners in Mountjoy, Male, .	–	–	3·7	–	1,085	–	2	–	23	–	29	–
Mountjoy, Female,	–	54	–	3·61	–	545	–	3	–	30	–	15
Total, Males, .	1,480	–	62·60	–	27,586	–	71	–	909	–	326	–
Total, Females, .	–	841	–	25·38	–	8,202	–	23	–	280	–	160
Total, M. and F.,	2,121		87·98		35,798		94		1,189		486	

TABLE XVII.—RETURN of the ACTUAL STAFF of the under-mentioned PRISONS on 31st March, 1881.

PRISONS.	Governors or Deputy Governors and Female Superintendents.		Head or Chief Warders.	Chaplains.	Surgeons and Apothecaries.	Clerks, Schoolmasters, and Schoolmistresses.		Matrons.	Warders.	Other Subordinate Officers, including Bridewell Keepers.		Total.	
	M.	F.				M.	F.			M.	F.	M.	F.
Armagh,	1	–	1	3	1	1	1	1	6	1	1	14	3
Belfast,	2	1a	1	2	1	2	1	7	31	1	2b	39	11
Carlow,	–	–	1	–	1	–	–	1	1	–	–	3	1
Carrick-on-Shannon,	–	–	1	–	–	–	–	1	1	–	–	2	1
Castlebar,	1	–	1	2	1	–	–	2	6	2	–	13	2
Cavan,	–	–	1	–	–	–	–	–	1	1	1	3	1
Clonmel,	1	–	1	2	1	1	–	3	9	1	1	16	4
Cork, Male,	2	–	1	2	1	2	–	–	24	16	8	48	8
Cork, Female,	1	–	–	2	1	–	1	10	3	–	–	7	11
Downpatrick,	2	–	–	3	1	–	–	3	6	1	1	13	4
Drogheda,	1	–	–	2	1	1	–	1	–	–	2	5	3
Dundalk,	1	–	3	2	1	–	–	–	9	1	–	17	–
Ennis,	–	–	1	–	–	–	–	1	1	1	1	3	2
Enniskillen,	–	–	1	–	–	–	–	1	1	–	–	2	1
Galway,	1	–	1	2	1	2	–	3	7	4	–	18	3
Grangegorman,	1	1	1	2	1	2	–	16	11	1	3	28	20
Kilkenny,	1	–	1	2	1	1	–	2	4	–	–	10	2
Kilmainham,	–	–	–	–	–	–	–	–	–	–	–	–	–
Lifford,	–	–	1	–	–	–	–	1	1	–	–	2	1
Limerick, Male,	1	–	1	2	2	2	–	–	12	4	3	24	3
Limerick, Female,	1	1	–	2	1	–	–	4	2	1	–	6	6
Londonderry,	2	–	1	2	1	1	–	3	9	6	5	22	8
Longford,	–	–	1	–	–	–	–	1	1	–	–	2	1
Maryborough,	1	–	1	2	1	1	–	1	4	–	–	10	1
Monaghan,	–	–	1	–	–	–	–	–	1	–	1	2	1
Mullingar,	1	–	1	1c	1	1	–	2	8	2	–	15	2
Naas,	1	–	1	2	1	1	–	2	8	–	–	14	2
Nenagh,	1	–	1	2	1	–	–	–	7	1	1	13	1
Omagh,	1	–	1	2	1	1	–	3	8	1	1	14	4
Richmond,	2	–	1	2	1	3	–	–	23	2	1	34	1
Roscommon,	–	–	1	–	–	–	–	1	1	–	–	2	1
Sligo,	1	–	–	2	1	1	–	1	5	–	1	10	2
Tralee,	1	–	1	2	1	–	–	1	8	4	1	17	2
Trim,	–	–	1	–	–	–	–	1	1	–	–	2	1
Tullamore,	1	–	1	2	1	1	–	1	8	1	2	15	3
Waterford,	1	–	1	2	1	–	–	1	7	2	3	14	4
Wexford,	1	–	1	2	1	–	–	2	5	1	1	11	3
Wicklow,	–	–	1	–	–	–	–	–	1	–	1	2	1
Mountjoy, Male,	1	–	1	–	–	1	–	–	7	–	–	9	–
Mountjoy, Female,	–	–	1d	4	1	–	–	1	1	–	3	7	4
Total,	29	3	35	52	29	26	3	75	226	48	44	467	129

a. Matron included as Superintendent. b. "Servant," as other Subordinate Officer. c. 1 vacant.
d. Including one Steward and three Principal Warders.

TABLE XVIII.—RETURN of the ACTUAL STAFF of the under-mentioned PRISONS on 31st March, 1882.

PRISONS.	Governors or Deputy Governors and Female Superintendents.		Head or Chief Warders.	Chaplains.	Surgeons and Apothecaries.	Clerks, Schoolmasters, and Schoolmistresses.		Matrons.	Warders.	Other Subordinate Officers, including Bridewell Keepers.		Total.	
	M.	F.				M.	F.			M.	F.	M.	F.
Armagh, . . .	1	–	2	3	1	1	–	–	10	1	–	18	–
Belfast, . . .	1	–	2	3	1	3	1	10	22	3	2	35	13
Carlow, . . .	–	–	–	1	–	–	–	1	1	–	–	2	1
Carrick-on-Shannon,	–	–	1	–	–	–	–	1	1	–	–	2	1
Castlebar, . .	1	–	1	3	1	–	–	2	5	2	–	13	2
Cavan, . . .	–	–	1	–	–	–	–	–	1	1	1	3	1
Clonmel, . . .	1	–	2	2	1	–	–	–	21	1	1	28	1
Cork, Male, . .	2	–	1	2	1	2	–	–	20	7	7	41	7
Cork, Female, .	1	–	–	2	1	–	1	11	3	–	–	7	12
Downpatrick, . .	2	–	–	3	1	–	–	1	7	1	3	14	4
Drogheda, . .	1	–	–	2	1	–	–	1	2	–	3	6	4
Dundalk, . .	1	–	3	3	1	–	–	1	13	1	–	22	1
Ennis, . . .	1	–	1	1	1	–	–	1	4	1	–	9	1
Enniskillen, . .	1	–	2	1	1	1	–	1	12	–	–	18	1
Galway, . . .	1	–	3	2	1	1	–	3	14	4	–	26	3
Grangegorman, .	1	1	2	2	1	2	1	17	18	1	4	27	23
Kilkenny, . .	1	–	2	2	1	2	–	–	18	–	–	26	–
Kilmainham, . .	2	–	2	2	1	–	–	–	36	1	–	44	–
Lifford, . . .	–	–	1	–	–	–	–	1	1	–	–	2	1
Limerick, Male, .	1	–	2	2	2	2	–	–	19	2	2	30	2
Limerick, Female, .	1	–	–	2	1	–	–	7	2	–	1	6	8
Londonderry, . .	1	–	1	3	1	–	–	3	9	4	4	19	7
Longford, . .	–	–	1	–	–	–	–	1	1	–	–	2	1
Maryborough, . .	1	–	1	2	1	1	–	1	7	–	1	13	2
Monaghan, . .	–	–	2	1	1	1	–	1	9	–	–	14	1
Mullingar, . .	1	–	1	2	1	1	–	2	9	2	–	17	2
Naas, . . .	1	–	2	2	1	1	–	1	13	3	–	23	1
Nenagh, . . .	1	–	1	2	1	–	–	–	8	1	–	14	–
Omagh, . . .	1	–	1	3	1	1	–	–	7	1	1	15	1
Richmond, . .	2	–	1	2	1	3	–	–	25	3	1	37	1
Roscommon, . .	–	–	1	–	–	–	–	1	1	–	–	2	1
Sligo, . . .	1	–	–	2	1	1	–	2	5	–	1	10	3
Tralee, . . .	1	–	1	2	1	1	–	2	7	4	1	17	3
Trim, . . .	–	–	1	–	–	–	–	1	1	–	–	2	1
Tullamore, . .	1	–	1	2	1	1	–	1	8	1	2	15	3
Waterford, . .	1	–	2	2	1	–	–	4	7	2	1	15	5
Wexford, . .	1	–	2	2	1	1	–	2	7	1	1	15	3
Wicklow, . .	–	–	1	–	–	–	–	1	1	–	–	2	1
Mountjoy, Male, .	1	–	1	3	2	1	–	–	8	–	–	16	–
Mountjoy, Female, .	–	1	–	3	2	–	–	5	1	–	3	6	9
Total, . .	34	2	49	71	35	28	3	80	386	48	40	631	131

TABLE XIX.—WORKS of RECONSTRUCTION, REPAIRS, &c., during the Year ended 31st March, 1882, done by CONTRACT or other than PRISON LABOUR.

PRISONS.	WORKS.
Armagh, . . .	Extensive works in fitting prison for prisoners confined under Act for Better Protection of Person and Property in Ireland, visiting cells, recreation shed, boarding floors in hospital, erection of check-gates, &c., &c. New iron staircase in male prison, and formation of cells in old staircase, &c., &c.
Belfast, . . .	Enclosing ground outside stone yard; new gate, &c. Erection of hospital and officers' quarters in female prison; erection of two new heating boilers for prison; constructing quarters for deputy governor.
Carlow, . . .	—
Carrick-on-Shannon, .	Pointing with cement all ridge tiles on male and female prisons; also repairs of stone sheds and W.-C's.; repairing cell windows; painting and repairing skylights on workshop; repairing roof of hospital and kitchen, and windows in female prison damaged by storm.
Castlebar, . . .	Papering and painting governor's house and matron's quarters; new sewer from hospital.
Cavan, . . .	—
Clonmel, . . .	Extensive works in fitting prison for persons confined under the Act for the Better Protection of Person and Property in Ireland, association rooms, recreation shed, visiting rooms, improving chapel, additional gas lamps; hydraulic brake for tread-wheel.
Cork, Male, . .	Water tank, pipes, &c.; entrance-gate lined with iron; staircase to inspection gallery; repairs to tread-wheel; connecting prison sewers with Corporation main.
Cork, Female, .	General painting inside and outside; repairs to roof, window sashes, cell doors, and bolts, laundry stove, gas pipes, water pipes.
Downpatrick, .	Repairs of gas pipes and fittings, clocks, heating apparatus, locks and keys; drying closet in laundry. Newry Bridewell.—Bell at gate; glazing; repairs of water pipes, roof, and locks.
Drogheda, . . .	Putting up new boilers for heating prison; new entrance-gate to prison yard; gaslight into chapel and gas fittings generally; whitewashing and painting interior of prison; repairs to gongs, laundry boiler, prison roof, and glazing.
Dundalk, . . .	Laying hot water pipes; introducing gas into hospital and putting up bells; cleaning gas pipes; putting up exterior lamps; new steam boiler; erecting shed for P.P.P. prisoners; earth closets; putting up crank-pump; two large stoves.
Ennis, ...	Refitting wing which had been closed; re-arrangement of water supply, and various repairs.
Enniskillen, . . .	Extensive works in fitting prison for prisoners confined under the Act for the Better Protection of Person and Property in Ireland; flooring cells; lighting exterior of prison; new cooking apparatus; visiting rooms, recreation shed, &c., &c.

TABLE XIX.—WORKS OF RECONSTRUCTION, REPAIRS, &c.—*continued.*

Prisons.	Works.
Galway, . . .	Alterations and erecting a new partition in chapel and two visiting rooms; repairing W-C's., and alterations in sewer pipes and supply pipes to baths; repairs to laundry, roof of prison, boiler of heating pipes, punishment cell, cooking stove, locks, keys, windows, lead gutter in governor's house; erecting portable registers for recording clocks; erecting a large timber-shed for P.P.P. Prisoners; new stove in governor's house; repairs and alterations in gas-pipes and fixtures.
Grangegorman, . .	Renewing hot water-pipes; repairing and re-setting boilers, repairs to roof, papering superintendent's quarters; kitchen range for superintendent's quarters; sundry works in fitting prison for prisoners confined under the Act for the Better Protection of Person and Property in Ireland, fitting association rooms, visiting rooms, recreation shed, improving exercise yard, &c.
Kilkenny, . . .	Extensive works in fitting prison for prisoners confined under the Act for the Better Protection of Person and Property in Ireland; boarding cell floors, lighting cells and exterior of prison, association rooms, recreation shed, visiting-rooms, &c.; repairs of boundary walls, reconstruction of sewers, new brake for tread-wheel, &c.
Kilmainham, . .	Extensive works in fitting prison for prisoners confined under the Act for the Better Protection of Person and Property in Ireland; removing objectionable buildings and other provisions for security, lighting exterior of prison and preparing for military patrol, making new entrance, introducing additional water supply, erection of visiting rooms, recreation shed, &c.; improving and enlarging exercise yards, providing additional cooking apparatus, &c., &c.; painting and papering governor's house, erecting new kitchen range in governor's house, &c., &c.
Lifford, ...	Repairing water pipes, cleaning spouting; repairing roof after storm.
Limerick, Male, . .	Fitting prison for prisoners confined under the Act for the Better Protection of Person and Property in Ireland, forming association rooms, recreation sheds, &c.; completion of new cells, and heating and lighting them; improvement of Roman Catholic chapel.
Limerick, Female, . .	New heating boiler and reconstruction of heating arrangements; general repairs of pumps, closet, roof, &c.
Londonderry, . .	New heating boiler, hot-water cauldron in female prison. two new W.C.'s in male prison; alterations in water supply to steam boilers, plumbing and gasfitting, erecting a new store, alterations in old store, coping boundary wall, erecting fumigating room, repairing locks, keys, and mangle.
Longford, . . .	Repairs of roof and windows, &c.
Maryborough, . .	Gasfitting in chapel vestry-room, and governor's house; fitting up bells, W.C.'s and heating arrangements in chapel, repairing cistern, alterations, and erecting clock.
Monaghan, . . .	Extensive works in fitting prison for prisoners confined under the Act for the Better Protection of Person and Property in Ireland, fitting association rooms, recreation sheds, closets, &c.; fitting up new kitchen, papering and painting governor's house, quarters for chief warder, external lamps, guard rooms, &c.
Mullingar, . . .	Heating and lighting new cells, and various repairs.
Naas, . . .	Erection of shed in exercise yard for prisoners confined under the Act for the Better Protection of Person and Property in Ireland; erection of horse gear for crank pump; repairs of W.C.'s, boilers, roof of prison, &c.; cleaning gas machine, and putting up new ropes.
Nenagh, ...	General repairs to hot water pipes. lighting female prison, erection of bells, &c., in female prison.

TABLE XIX.—WORKS of RECONSTRUCTION, REPAIRS, &c.—*continued.*

PRISONS.	Works.
Omagh, ...	Supplying new heating boiler to female prison, and overhauling boiler in male prison; repairs to office chimney and roof, and roof of female prison; alterations, repairs, &c., to governor's house, rebuilding a portion of wall in governor's yard; introducing gas to male and female prison, laying hot water-pipe to female bath, supplying and fitting new lamps and sundry repairs, timber for washing troughs, trap hinges and window sashes, fitting female prison for prisoners confined under the Act for the Better Protection of Person and Property in Ireland, recreation shed, improvement of exercise yard, &c.
Richmond, . . .	Sundry works in repairs and alterations on windows; repairs of cooking apparatus; altering and repairing heating apparatus, with sundry repairs to water works.
Roscommon, . . .	Various repairs.
Sligo, ...	Lighting cells with gas; new gas meter; repairs of roof of prison, &c.; roofing and slating stonebreakers' shed; new baths; repairs of locks and keys.
Tralee, ...	Fitting up new offices for governor, &c.; connecting galleries in prison by a bridge.
Trim, ...	Repairs to building damaged by late fire; repairs of slating to the several blocks of buildings; glazing.
Tullamore, . . .	Plumbing; repairs to pump, crank-pump, water-closets, and bells and gongs.
Waterford, . . .	Fitting up store-rooms, and sundry repairs and alterations on laundry; flooring and repairing cells of P. P. P.; repairing locks and keys, water pipes and pumps, and roof of prison; saddle boilers supplied; repairing boiler and putting up hot water pipes.
Wexford, . . .	Supplying water-troughs, plumbing, &c.; supplying and fitting up wooden troughs and other wood work in laundry; repairing pump; removing old buildings; boarding 66 cells; removing doors of same; plastering and general alterations and erection of shed for prisoners confined under the Act for the Better Protection of Person and Property in Ireland; alterations in chapel; painting; building piers to hospital yard; bell-hanging, &c. gasfitting.
Wicklow, . .	Repairing furnace in male prison, water-closets, eve-shoots, &c.
Mountjoy, Male, . .	Hospital heated by hot water.
Mountjoy, Female, .	Repairs to roof of prison, slating, glazing, painting, &c.; drying-closet in laundry; repairs to gas governor and gas engine.
Spike Island, . . .	Gas fitting in chapel, vestry-room, and governor's house; fitting up bells and water-closets; repairing cistern; fitting up heating arrangements in chapel; alterations in and erecting clock.
Lusk, ...	—

TABLE XX.—INDUSTRIAL and TRADES PURSUITS by

PRISONS.	Lime-burning.	Stone-breaking.	Oakum and Fibre Picking.	Mat-making.	Brush-making.	Washing.	Whitewashing.	Weaving.	Sewing.	Knitting.	Tailoring.	Painting.	Carpentering.	Shoemaking and Shoemending.	Clog-making.	Tinkering and Plumbing.	Masons' and Bricklayers' Work.	Glazing.	Plaiting Yarn.	Bobbin-winding.
Armagh,	–	1	1	–	1	1	1	1	1	1	1	1	1	1	–	1	1	1	–	1
Belfast,	–	1	1	1	1	1	1	1	1	1	1	1	1	1	–	1	1	1	1	1
Carlow,	–	–	1	–	–	1	1	–	1	1	–	–	–	–	–	–	–	–	–	–
Carrick-on-Shannon,	–	–	1	–	–	1	1	–	–	–	–	–	–	–	–	–	–	–	–	–
Castlebar,	–	–	1	–	–	1	1	–	1	1	1	1	1	1	–	–	–	1	–	–
Cavan,	–	1	1	–	–	1	1	–	–	1	–	–	–	–	–	–	–	–	–	–
Clonmel,	–	–	–	–	–	1	1	–	–	–	–	1	1	1	–	–	1	1	–	–
Cork, Male,	1	1	1	1	–	1	1	–	–	–	1	1	1	1	–	–	1	1	–	–
Cork, Female,	–	–	1	–	–	1	1	–	–	1	–	–	1	1	–	–	–	–	–	–
Downpatrick,	–	1	1	–	–	1	1	–	1	1	1	1	1	1	–	1	1	1	–	–
Drogheda,	–	–	1	–	–	1	1	–	1	1	–	–	–	–	–	–	–	–	–	–
Dundalk,	–	1	1	1	–	1	1	–	–	–	1	–	–	1	–	1	–	–	–	–
Ennis,	–	1	1	–	–	1	1	–	1	1	1	–	–	–	–	–	–	–	–	–
Enniskillen,	–	1	–	–	–	1	1	–	–	–	1	–	–	1	–	–	–	–	–	–
Galway,	–	1	1	1	–	–	1	–	1	1	1	–	–	1	–	–	–	–	–	–
Grangegorman,	–	1	1	–	–	1	–	–	1	1	–	–	1	1	–	–	–	–	1	–
Kilkenny,	–	1	1	1	1	1	1	–	1	1	1	1	–	1	–	1	–	–	1	–
Kilmainham,	–	–	1	–	–	1	1	–	1	–	1	1	1	1	–	–	–	–	–	–
Lifford,	–	–	–	–	–	–	1	–	–	–	–	–	–	–	–	–	–	–	–	–
Limerick, Male,	–	1	1	1	–	1	1	–	–	–	1	1	1	1	–	–	1	1	–	–
Limerick, Female,	–	–	–	–	–	1	–	–	–	1	–	–	–	–	–	–	–	–	–	–
Londonderry,	–	1	1	1	–	1	1	–	–	1	1	1	1	–	–	1	–	–	–	–
Longford,	–	–	1	–	–	1	1	–	–	–	–	–	–	–	–	–	–	–	–	–
Maryborough,	–	1	1	–	–	–	–	–	–	–	1	1	1	1	–	–	1	1	–	–
Monaghan,	–	–	–	–	–	–	–	–	–	–	–	–	–	–	–	–	–	–	–	–
Mullingar,	–	1	–	–	–	1	–	–	–	1	–	–	–	–	–	–	–	–	–	–
Naas,	–	–	1	1	1	1	–	1	1	1	1	1	1	1	–	–	1	1	1	–
Nenagh,	–	–	–	1	–	–	–	–	1	1	1	–	1	1	–	1	1	–	–	–
Omagh,	–	1	1	1	–	1	–	–	1	1	1	1	1	1	–	1	1	1	–	–
Richmond,	1	1	1	1	–	–	1	1	–	–	1	1	1	1	–	1	–	–	1	–
Roscommon,	–	–	1	–	–	1	1	–	1	1	1	–	–	–	–	–	–	–	–	–
Sligo,	–	1	1	–	–	1	1	–	1	1	1	1	1	1	–	–	–	1	–	–
Tralee,	–	1	1	1	–	1	1	–	–	–	1	1	1	1	–	1	–	1	–	–
Trim,	–	1	–	–	–	1	–	–	–	–	–	–	–	–	–	–	–	–	–	–
Tullamore,	–	–	1	–	–	1	–	–	1	1	1	1	1	1	–	–	–	–	–	–
Waterford,	–	1	1	1	–	1	1	–	1	1	1	–	1	1	–	1	–	–	1	–
Wexford,	–	1	1	1	–	1	1	–	1	1	–	–	1	–	–	–	–	–	1	–
Wicklow,	–	–	1	–	–	1	–	–	–	–	–	–	–	–	–	–	–	–	–	–
Prisoners not Convicts—																				
Mountjoy, Male,	–	–	1	1	1	–	–	–	–	–	1	1	1	1	–	1	1	–	–	–
Mountjoy, Female,	–	–	–	–	–	1	–	–	1	1	1	–	–	–	–	–	–	–	–	–

Prisoners during the year ended 31st March, 1882.

Hair-teasing.	Smith Work.	Cooking.	Sack-making and mending.	Quarrying Stone.	Plastering.	Net-making.	Gasfitting, Bell-hanging, &c.	Garden Work.	Grinding Meal and Baking Bread.	Making Lace.	Quilting.	Making & Repairing Bedding and Clothing.	Stone-cutting.	Slating.	Cutting Linen.	Carpet Cleaning.	Making Firewood.	Coopering.	Prisons.
–	1	–	–	–	1	–	1	1	–	–	–	1	–	–	–	–	–	–	Armagh.
1	1	–	–	–	1	–	1	1	–	–	–	–	–	–	1	1	1	–	Belfast.
–	–	–	–	–	–	–	–	–	–	–	–	–	–	–	–	–	–	–	Carlow.
–	–	1	–	–	–	–	–	–	–	–	–	1	–	–	–	–	–	–	Carrick-on-Shannon.
–	–	1	–	–	–	–	–	–	–	–	–	–	–	–	–	–	–	–	Castlebar.
–	–	–	–	–	–	–	–	1	–	–	–	1	–	–	–	–	1	–	Cavan.
–	–	–	–	–	–	–	–	–	–	–	–	1	–	–	–	–	1	–	Clonmel.
–	1	–	–	–	–	–	–	1	–	–	–	1	1	–	–	–	1	–	Cork, Male.
–	–	1	–	–	–	–	–	1	–	–	1	1	–	–	–	–	–	–	Cork, Female.
–	–	–	–	–	–	–	–	–	1	–	–	1	–	–	–	–	–	–	Downpatrick.
–	–	1	–	–	–	–	–	–	–	–	–	–	–	–	–	–	–	–	Drogheda.
–	–	1	–	–	–	–	–	–	–	–	–	1	–	–	–	–	–	–	Dundalk.
–	–	–	–	–	–	–	–	–	–	–	–	–	–	–	–	–	1	–	Ennis.
–	–	1	–	–	–	–	–	–	–	–	–	–	–	–	–	–	1	–	Enniskillen.
–	–	–	–	–	–	–	–	–	–	–	–	–	–	–	–	–	–	–	Galway.
–	–	–	–	–	–	–	–	–	–	–	–	–	–	–	–	–	–	–	Grangegorman.
–	–	–	–	–	–	–	–	–	–	–	–	–	–	–	–	–	1	–	Kilkenny.
–	–	–	–	–	–	–	–	–	–	–	–	–	–	–	–	–	–	–	Kilmainham.
–	–	–	–	–	–	–	–	–	–	–	–	–	–	–	–	–	–	–	Lifford.
–	–	–	–	–	1	1	–	1	–	–	–	1	1	–	–	–	1	–	Limerick, Male.
–	–	–	–	–	–	–	–	–	1	1	1	1	–	–	–	–	–	–	Limerick, Female.
–	–	–	–	–	–	–	–	–	–	–	–	1	–	–	–	–	–	–	Londonderry.
–	–	–	–	–	–	–	–	1	–	–	–	1	–	–	–	–	–	–	Longford.
–	1	–	–	–	1	–	–	–	–	–	–	–	1	–	–	–	–	1	Maryborough.
–	–	–	–	–	–	–	–	–	–	–	–	–	–	–	–	–	–	–	Monaghan.
–	–	–	1	–	–	1	–	–	1	–	–	1	–	–	–	–	–	–	Mullingar.
–	1	–	1	–	–	–	–	–	–	–	–	1	1	1	–	–	–	–	Naas.
–	–	–	–	–	–	–	–	–	–	–	–	1	–	–	–	–	–	1	Nenagh.
–	1	–	–	–	–	–	–	–	–	–	–	–	–	–	–	–	–	–	Omagh.
–	–	1	–	–	–	–	–	1	–	–	–	1	–	1	–	–	–	–	Richmond.
–	–	–	–	–	–	–	–	1	–	–	–	–	–	–	–	–	–	–	Roscommon.
–	–	1	–	–	–	–	–	–	–	–	–	–	–	–	–	–	1	–	Sligo.
–	1	–	–	1	–	–	–	1	–	–	–	1	–	–	–	–	1	–	Tralee.
–	–	–	–	–	–	–	–	1	–	–	–	–	–	–	–	–	–	–	Trim.
–	1	–	1	–	–	–	–	–	–	–	–	–	–	–	–	–	–	1	Tullamore.
–	–	1	–	–	–	–	–	–	–	–	–	–	–	–	–	–	1	–	Waterford.
–	–	–	–	–	–	–	–	–	–	–	–	–	–	–	–	–	–	–	Wexford.
–	–	–	–	–	–	–	–	–	–	–	–	–	–	–	–	–	–	–	Wicklow.
																			Prisoners not Convicts—
–	1	–	–	–	–	1	–	1	–	–	–	1	–	–	–	–	1	–	Mountjoy, Male.
–	–	1	–	–	–	–	–	–	–	–	–	–	–	–	–	–	–	–	Mountjoy Female.

TABLE XXI.—COMPARATIVE TABLE, showing the Number of Prisoners committed to Local Prisons from the 1st April, 1880, to 31st March, 1881, and from that date to the 31st March, 1882, distinguishing the Sexes and Classes.

CLASS OF OFFENDERS.	To 31st March, 1881.			To 31st March, 1882.		
	Males.	Females.	Total.	Males.	Females.	Total.
CONVICTED.						
At Assizes and Quarter Sessions, .	1,425	323	1,748	1,632	285	1,917
Criminal Lunatics, . . .	11	7	18	79	7	86
Summarily :—						
Offenders under Larceny Acts, .	1,178	563	1,741	1,381	592	1,973
Misdemeanants, . . .	8,910	4,791	13,701	10,086	5,096	15,182
Under Revenue Laws, . .	73	19	92	110	30	140
Under Poor Law Acts, . .	177	53	230	200	54	254
By Courts-martial, . .	674	.	674	546	.	546
Deserters, ...	283	.	283	171	.	171
Under Vagrant Acts, . .	569	245	814	585	251	836
Drunkards, . . .	9,712	7,351	17,063	9,193	6,274	15,467
TOTAL, . .	23,012	13,352	36,364	24,103	12,469	36,572
NOT CONVICTED.						
Acquitted, ... No Bills, or no Prosecution, .	591	131	722	597	161	758
For further Examination & Discharged	2,388	484	2,872	2,829	586	3,415
TOTAL, . .	2,979	615	3,594	3,426	747	4,173
In Custody for Trial on 31st March, .	202	32	234	305	38	343
GENERAL TOTAL, .	26,193	13,999	40,192	27,834	13,254	41,088

[REPORTS.

REPORTS BY THE GOVERNORS AND CHIEF WARDERS ON EACH OF THE LOCAL PRISONS.

ARMAGH PRISON.

RETURN by the GOVERNOR, showing how Prisoners have been employed during the year ending 31st March, 1882, and the Earnings of those engaged in such Employment; also showing the average daily number of Unemployed from Sickness and other reasons.

Description of Employment.	Daily Average Number of Prisoners employed, unemployed, &c.			Net profit on Work done by Prisoners.	Estimated Value of the Work done for the Prison.	Total.
	Males.	Females.	Total.	£ s. d.	£ s. d.	£ s. d.
Gardening,				—	4 8 3	4 8 3
Tailors,				0 5 0	38 8 8	38 11 9
Shoemakers,				—	17 4 5	17 4 5
Carpenters,				—	38 8 6	38 8 6
Bricklayers and labourers,	11	—	11	—	49 5 8	49 5 8
Painters and glaziers,				—	19 0 0	19 0 0
Tinsmiths,				—	8 8 8	8 8 8
Blacksmiths,				—	15 0 0	15 0 0
Whitewashers,				—	7 10 0	7 10 0
Service of prison,	6	2	8	—	137 0 0	137 0 0
Washing clothing and bedding,				1 14 4	108 8 6	110 2 10
Making bedding and clothing,	5	6	11	—	78 5 0	78 5 0
Repairing bedding and clothing,				—	46 10 0	44 10 0
Stone-breaking,	12	—	12	20 14 7	—	20 14 7
Weaving linen,				1 10 1	—	1 10 1
Picking rope junk,	16	8	24	—	98 6 10	98 6 10
Knitting,	—	7	7	8 6 7	16 5 4	24 11 11
Mangling,				0 6 3	8 6 8	8 12 11
Sick,	2	2	4	—	—	—
Unemployed,	16	5	21	—	—	—
Total,	73	25	98	33 16 10	690 12 6	723 9 4

[BELFAST PRISON.

RETURN by the GOVERNORS, showing how Prisoners have been employed during the year ending 31st March, 1882, and the Earnings of those engaged in such Employment; also showing the average daily number of Unemployed from Sickness and other reasons.

BELFAST PRISON.

Description of Employment.	Daily Average Number of Prisoners employed, unemployed, &c.			Net Profit on Work done by Prisoners.	Estimated Value of the Work done for the Prison.	Total.
	Males.	Females.	Total.			
				£ s. d.	£ s. d.	£ s. d.
Scrub-brush and mat-making, picking coir and plaiting, .	24	—	24	34 2 8	2 6 4	36 10 0
Gardening, ...	2	—	2	—	25 16 11	25 16 11
Tailors, ...	8	—	8	1 16 0	223 5 0	225 0 0
Shoemakers, ...	5	—	5	—	150 0 0	150 0 0
Carpenters, ...	2	—	2	—	75 0 0	75 0 0
Labourers, ...	10	—	10	—	150 0 0	150 0 0
Painters and glaziers, . .	1	—	1	—	37 10 0	37 10 0
Tinsmiths, gas-fitters, and blacksmiths, . . .	2	—	2	—	75 0 0	75 0 0
Whitewashers and bricklayers,	2	—	2	—	60 0 0	60 0 0
Weaving and winding, . .	2	1	3	—	20 0 0	20 0 0
Cleaning carpets, . . .	8	—	8	126 8 0	—	126 5 0
Service of prison, . . .	13	6	19	—	142 10 0	142 10 0
Cooking, ...	5	—	5	—	75 0 0	75 0 0
Washing clothing and bedding, ...	—	13	13	21 1 0	271 7 0	292 10 0
Making bedding and clothing, repairing bedding and clothing, knitting and sewing, .	—	55	55	58 10 3	216 9 9	275 0 0
Stone-breaking, ...	71	—	71	140 14 0	4 16 10	145 10 10
Rope, hair and fibre-picking,	56	56	112	40 17 8	—	40 17 8
Linen cutting, ...	—	3	3	11 2 3	—	11 2 3
Making firewood, . . .	3	—	3	31 12 10	1 10 0	33 2 10
Sick, ... } Unemployed, ... }	40	33	73	—	—	—
Total, . . .	261	160	421	466 0 0	1,350 14 4	2,016 15 1

Trades, &c.—Regular tradesmen are charged at one-half ordinary rates, learners, one-fourth, viz.:—2*s.* 6*d.* and 1*s.* 3*d.* per day, respectively. Whitewashers, 1*s.* 6*d.*; washers (female), 1*s.* 0*d.*; labourers and cooks, 1*s.*; cleaners, 6*d.*; females making and repairing clothing, knitting, and sewing, 4*d.*

Shirt and drawers making for public has been extended. This description of work, with training necessary to its proper execution, is such as is hoped may develop habits of industry, while affording sufficient and fairly remunerative labour for female prisoners.

Carpet cleaning continues to prove a profitable source of industrial labour.

Linen-weaving by hand-looms is in operation, but owing to competition with power-looms, and the high price of yarns as compared with the rates ruling for manufactured article, the profit is not such as might be fairly anticipated from a class of labour admirably suited for prison employment.

The manufacture of firewood has been introduced, and although supply is restricted to public departments, the return has been very satisfactory.

Work done for other prisons is included in "estimated value column."

The unemployed are represented by the untried, bail (unwilling to work), the physically unfit, and those discharged during labour hours.

Excepting in manufacture of material, the prison is generally self-supplying.

Calculations are made on year of 300 working days.

[CARLOW PRISON.

RETURN by the CHIEF WARDERS, showing how Prisoners have been employed during the year ending 31st March, 1882, and the Earnings of those engaged in such Employment; also showing the average daily number of Unemployed from Sickness and other reasons.

CARLOW PRISON.

Description of Employment.	Daily average Number of Prisoners employed, unemployed, &c.			Net Profit on Work done by Prisoners, per day.	Estimated Value of the Work done for the Prison.	Total.
	Males.	Females.	Total.			
				£ s. d.	£ s. d.	£ s. d.
Picking oakum,	206	—	206	—	—	—
Gardening,	19	—	19	—	—	—
Whitewashers,	19	—	19	—	—	—
Service of prison (cleaning),	19	—	19	—	—	—
Washing clothing and bedding,	—	14	14	—	—	—
Knitting,	—	13	13	—	—	—
In punishment,	15	1	16	—	—	—
Nursing,	—	3	3	—	—	—
Sewing,	—	1	1	—	—	—
Sick,	14	4	18	—	—	—
Unemployed,	320	79	399	—	—	—
Total,	612	115	727	—	—	—

In the above table I am unable to show the daily average number of prisoners, as I would not have one whole number for each day. I cannot form a *correct* estimate of the earnings of those employed, as I do not know the prices of material bought or sold.

CARRICK-ON-SHANNON PRISON.

Description of Employment.	Daily Average Number of Prisoners employed, unemployed, &c.			Net Profit on Work done by Prisoners.	Estimated Value of the Work done for the *Prison*.	Total.
	Males.	Females.	Total.			
				£ s. d.	£ s. d.	£ s. d.
Whitewashers,	·25	·008	·318	—	4 5 10	4 5 10
Treadwheel,	·23	—	·23	—	3 10 0	3 10 0
Pumping water,	·24	—	·24	—	3 13 4	3 13 4
Service of prison,	·35	·26	·61	—	5 17 6	5 17 6
Washing clothing and bedding,	—	·19	·19	—	2 6 4	2 6 4
Repairing bedding and clothing,	·054	·055	·109	—	1 13 4	1 13 4
Picking oakum,	·16	—	·16	—	1 10 0	1 10 0
Cooking,	·33	—	·38	—	4 13 4	4 13 4
Sick,	·027	·027	·054	—	—	—
Unemployed,	4·72	·505	—	—	—	—
Total,	6·411	1·05	7·516	—	—	30 9 8

The number of convicted prisoners represented in the above were engaged in the different works opposite their number. It takes a good number of prisoners to keep this prison in order without showing any profits for prison labour. The large number of unemployed represented in the above is accounted for by the number of prisoners for trial at the late winter assizes.

RETURN by the GOVERNORS, showing how Prisoners have been employed during the year ending 31st March, 1882, and the Earnings of those engaged in such Employment; also showing the average daily number of Unemployed from Sickness and other reasons.

CASTLEBAR PRISON.

Description of Employment.	Daily Average Number of Prisoners employed, unemployed, &c.			Net Profit on Work done by Prisoners.	Estimated Value of the Work done for the Prison.	Total.
	Males.	Females.	Total.	£ s. d.	£ s. d.	£ s. d.
Shoemakers, repairs,	1	—	1	—	15 3 0	15 3 0
Carpenters,	1	—	1	—	15 3 0	15 3 0
Bricklayers and labourers,	6	—	6	—	60 12 0	60 12 0
Painters and glaziers,	1	—	1	—	22 14 6	22 14 6
Whitewashers,	1	—	1	—	15 8 0	15 8 0
Pumping water,	3	—	3	—	22 18 0	22 18 0
Service of prison,	2	1	3	—	30 6 6	30 6 6
Washing clothing and bedding,	—	2	2	—	15 3 0	15 3 0
Repairing bedding and clothing,	1	1	2	—	20 4 6	20 4 6
Knitting and sewing,	—	3	3	—	11 7 3	11 7 3
Picking rope junk,	10	—	10	—	—	—
Sick,	1	1	2	—	—	—
Unemployed,	8	1	9	—	—	—
Total,	35	9	44	—	228 3 8	226 6 8

During the three months that I have been here most of the convicted have been "short sentence prisoners." The state of the weather has, to a great degree, prevented their breaking stones, and they have been employed picking oakum, which appears to yield no profit. The needs of the prison have obliged me to employ all prisoners out of probation, in cleaning, cooking, repairs, &c., and often the number of such prisoners has been found inadequate.

CLONMEL PRISON.

Description of Employment.	Males.	Females.	Total.	Net Profit on Work done by Prisoners.	Estimated Value of the Work done for the Prison.	Total.
				£ s. d.	£ s. d.	£ s. d.
Mat-making, picking coir, &c.,	—	—	—	2 6 6	—	2 6 6
Shoemakers,	1	—	1	—	31 4 0	31 4 0
Carpenters,	1	—	1	—	12 7 8	12 7 8
Bricklayers and labourers,	4	—	4	—	9 16 2	9 16 2
Painters and glaziers,	—	—	—	—	6 13 4	6 13 4
Whitewashers,	1	—	1	—	5 0 4	5 0
Treadwheel, Pumping water,	5	—	5	—	—	—
Service of prison,	8	1	9	—	—	—
Washing clothing and bedding,	10	8	18	135 3 6	72 17 8	208 1 1
Making bedding and clothing,	—	2	2	—	12 11 10	12 11 10
Repairing bedding and clothing,	1	1	2	—	18 11 11	18 11 11
Cutting timber,	3	—	3	3 16 2	—	3 16 2
Picking rope junk,	5	—	5	—	—	—
Teasing oakum and curled hair,	1	—	1	0 1 8	—	0 1 8
Sick,	2	—	2	—	—	—
Unemployed,	40	—	40	—	—	—
Total,	85	13	97	141 0 10	169 8 0	310 13 10

RETURN by the GOVERNORS or CHIEF WARDERS, showing how Prisoners have been employed during the year ending 31st March, 1882, and the Earnings of those engaged in such Employment; also showing the average daily number of Unemployed from Sickness and other reasons.

CAVAN PRISON.

Description of Employment.	Daily Average Number of Prisoners employed, unemployed, &c.			Net Profit on Work done by Prisoners.			Estimated Value of the Work done for the Prison.			Total.		
	Males.	Females.	Total.	£	s.	d.	£	s.	d.	£	s.	d.
Gardening, stone-breaking and pumping water,	1	—	1	0	7	1½	4	10	10½	5	0	0
Whitewashers, cleaning and picking oakum,	1	—	1	—			5	0	0	5	0	0
Cleaning, washing and knitting,	—	72	72	0	3	0	0	9	8	0	12	0
Sick and unemployed,	1	—	1	—			—			—		
Total,	9	72	75	0	10	1½	12	1	10½	10	12	0

I allowed 4*d*. per head per diem for 300 days for all employment.

CORK (MALE) PRISON.

Description of Employment.	Males.	Females.	Total.	£	s.	d.	£	s.	d.	£	s.	d.
Mat-making, picking coir, &c.,	10	—	10	40	16	8	—			40	15	8
Stonecutting,	5	—	5	—			152	0	0	152	0	0
Gardening,	1	—	1	—			22	10	0	20	18	0
Tailors,	5	—	5	—			152	0	0	152	5	0
Shoemakers,	5	—	5	—			152	0	0	152	0	0
Carpenters,	8	—	8	—			126	16	0	138	18	0
Bricklayers and labourers,	29½	—	29½	—			517	10	0	517	16	8
Painters and glaziers,	1	—	1	—			00	8	0	38	8	8
Tinsmiths,	½	—	½	—			15	4	0	15	4	8
Blacksmiths,	1	—	1	—			45	10	0	45	12	0
Whitewashers,	1	—	1	—			15	4	0	15	4	8
Treadwheel, flushing sewers, Shot-drill and rope-picking,	55	—	55	40	7	9	—			40	7	0
Service of prison,	9	—	9	—			130	16	0	135	10	0
Debtors,	½	—	½	—			—			—		
Washing clothing and bedding,	7	—	7	—			100	0	0	106	8	8
Making bedding & clothing, Repairing bedding and clothing,	1	—	1	—			15	4	0	15	4	0
Stone-breaking,	½	—	½	1	6	2	0	3	10	7	12	0
Chopping firewood,	2	—	2	5	2	8	21	5	2	36	8	8
Making wooden skewers,	½	—	½	1	10	0	5	12	8	7	12	0
Lime-burning,	1	—	1	14	0	4	23	0	0	37	8	4
Flax picking,	½	—	½	5	9	1	—			5	9	1
Cooking,	3	—	3	—			45	12	0	45	12	0
Sick,	1	—	1	—			—			—		
Unemployed,	47	—	47	—			—			—		
Total,	020	—	226	118	7	0	1560	17	10	1710	4	10

New Work.—An office in reception ward erected; shed raised over treadmill machinery; iron bars made and fitted to eight large windows in hospital; one water-closet in work yard, and 500 superficial feet of snow boards made.

Reconstructed.—A detached block, and connected by a newly built corridor three stories in height, with inspection hall of prison; accommodation gained being twenty-one cells and three water-closets and bath-rooms; stone stairs to basement removed and rebuilt; these foregoing works of reconstruction were of a difficult and heavy nature. Large shed in work yard taken down and reconstructed; two punishment cells and cook-house partly altered, and six old cells converted into two workshops; general and extensive repairs to roofs.

RETURN by the GOVERNORS, showing how Prisoners have been employed during the year ending 31st March, 1882, and the Earnings of those engaged in such Employment; also showing the average daily number of Unemployed from Sickness and other reasons.

CORK (FEMALE) PRISON.

Description of Employment.	Daily Average Number of Prisoners employed, unemployed, &c.			Net Profit on Work done by Prisoners.	Estimated Value of the Work done for the Prison.	Total.
	Males.	Females.	Total.			
				£ s. d.	£ s. d.	£ s. d.
Grinding corn, picking coir, oakum, wool, &c.,	—	5	5	4 11 6	5 1 0	9 12 6
Gardening,*	—	—	—	1 7 10	5 5 0	6 12 10
Shoemakers, repairs,	—	0 88/365	—	—	4 7 9	4 7 9
Attending furnaces,	—	1	1	—	11 10 0	11 10 0
Whitewashers,	—	1	1	—	15 3 0	15 3 0
Cooking,	—	1	1	—	18 5 0	18 5 0
Service of prison,	—	3	3	—	45 9 0	45 9 0
Washing clothing and bedding,	—	4	4	2 18 5	139 3 10	142 2 3
Making bedding & clothing, Repairing bedding and clothing,	—	15	15	—	75 15 0	75 15 0
Quilting,	—	5	5	0 18 0	38 2 6	39 0 6
Knitting, Making Slippers,	—	30 2	30 2	30 6 0	151 10 0	181 10 0
Nursing,	—	2	2	—	—	—
Punishment,	—	1	1	—	—	—
Sick,	—	3	3	—	—	—
Unemployed,	—	7	7	—	—	—
Total,	—	80	80	29 15 9	509 12 1	549 7 10

* The prisoners', work in garden during exercise hours has supplied potatoes for prisoners', use from July, 1881, and the remainder on hands will be sufficient until the new crop becomes ripe for use.

The value of prisoners' work for the prison is calculated at the following rates per day:—Shoemakers, 2*s.* 3*d.*; cooks, 1*s.*; whitewashers, 1*s.*; cleaners, 1*s.*; quilting, 6*d.*; sewing and knitting, 4*d.*

DROGHEDA PRISON.

Description of Employment.	Daily Average Number of Prisoners employed, unemployed, &c.			Net Profit on Work done by Prisoners.	Estimated Value of the Work done for the Prison.	Total.
	Males.	Females.	Total.			
				£ s. d.	£ s. d.	£ s. d.
Gardening,	—	—	—	—	4 0 0	4 0 0
Whitewashers,	—	—	—	—	0 11 0	0 11 0
Service of prison,	—	9	9	—	28 7 0	28 7 0
Washing clothing and bedding,	—	1	1	—	11 5 0	11 5 0
Making bedding and clothing, Repairing bedding and clothing,	—	3	3	10 0 0	5 2 4	15 2 4
Knitting,	—	8	8	38 16 2	2 0 0	40 16 2
Picking oakum,	—	4	4	0 15 0	—	0 15 0
Sick,	—	1	1	—	—	—
Unemployed,	—	4	4	—	—	—
Total,	—	23	23	49 11 2	51 5 4	100 16 6

RETURN by the GOVERNORS, showing how Prisoners have been employed during the year ending 31st March, 1882, and the Earnings of those engaged in such Employment; also showing the average daily number of Unemployed from Sickness and other reasons.

DOWNPATRICK PRISON.

				£ s. d.	£ s. d.	£ s. d.
Tailors,	0·50	—	0·50	—	—	—
Shoemakers,	0·50	—	0·50	—	—	—
Carpenters,	0·00	—	0·60	—	34 3 8	34 8 6
Bricklayers and labourers,	0·40	—	0·40	—	21 10 0	21 10 0
Painters and glaziers,	0 50	—	0·50	—	5 3 0	5 8 0
Tinsmiths,	0·50	—	0·60	—	2 12 8	2 12 0
Whitewashers,	1	—	1	—	7 10 0	7 10 0
Pumping water,	1	—	1	—	10 0 0	10 0 0
Service of prison,	3	1	4	—	29 13 0	39 13 0
Debtors,	1	—	1	—	—	—
Washing clothing and bedding,	—	4	4	—	30 8 0	30 5 0
Making bedding and clothing,	—	—	—	—	0 13 9	0 13 9
Repairing bedding and clothing,	—	2	2	—	31 8 0	31 8 0
Stone-breaking,	17	—	17	10 13 4	—	10 13 4
Rope picking,	12	4	16	11 5 0	—	11 5 0
Baking bread,	1	—	1	—	15 0 0	15 0 0
Knitting work,	—	—	—	0 5 6	0 7 4	0 12 10
Labouring work,	1	—	1	—	10 0 0	10 0 0
Sick,	1	—	1	—	—	—
Unemployed,	4	1	5	—	—	—
Total,	45	12	57	22 3 10	198 9 1	220 12 11

The tailors and shoemakers were employed solely in repairing; the value of their work is credited in repairs of bedding and clothing.

Knitting.—Average, a small fraction; not entered.

Picking Rope.—The cash was received for picking junk rope for a contractor. No profit was realised on account of the oakum sold, viz., on 46 cwts. to the Anglo-American Company at £17 10s. per ton, with 5 per cent. discount off.

DUNDALK PRISON.

				£ s. d.	£ s. d.	£ s. d.
Mat-making, picking coir, &c.,	6	—	6	27 6 0	—	27 6 0
Tailors,	1	—	1	—	19 11 8	19 11 8
Shoemakers,	1	—	1	—	31 6 0	31 6 0
Bricklayers and labourers,	8	—	8	—	104 6 8	104 6 8
Tinsmiths,	1	—	1	—	11 14 0	11 14 0
Whitewashers,	1	—	1	—	17 18 0	17 18 0
Pumping water,	4	—	4	—	70 12 0	70 12 0
Service of prison,	8	—	8	—	62 12 0	62 12 0
Debtors,	1	—	1	—	—	—
Washing clothing and bedding,	3	—	3	—	54 15 6	54 15 6
Repairing bedding and clothing,	1	—	1	—	11 14 9	11 14 9
Picking oakum,	20	—	20	8 13 4	—	8 13 4
Stone-breaking,	15	—	15	30 1 3	—	30 1 0
Cooking,	1	—	1	—	—	—
Unemployed,	2	—	2	—	—	—
Total,	78	—	78	75 0 7	384 5 11	459 6 6

[ENNIS PRISON.

RETURN by the GOVERNORS or CHIEF WARDERS, showing how Prisoners have been employed during the year ending 31st March, 1882, and the Earnings of those engaged in such Employment; also showing the average daily number of Unemployed from Sickness and other reasons.

ENNIS PRISON.

Description of Employment.	Daily Average Number of Prisoners employed, unemployed, &c.			Net Profit on Work done by Prisoners.	Estimated Value of the Work done for the Prison.	Total.
	Males.	Females.	Total.			
				£ s. d.	£ s. d.	£ s. d.
Tailors,	0·04	—	0·04	—	1 8 0	1 8 0
Bricklayers and labourers,	0·20	—	0·20	—	8 0 0	8 0 0
Painters and glaziers,	0·05	—	0·05	—	1 2 6	1 2 6
Tinsmiths,	0·02	—	0·02	—	0 6 0	0 6 0
Whitewashers,	0·21	—	0·21	—	4 10 0	4 10 0
Pumping water,	1·	—	1·	—	22 10 0	22 10 0
Service of prison,	0·71	0·01	0·72	—	8 15 0	8 15 0
Washing clothing and bedding,	0·17	0·04	0·21	—	8 5 0	8 5 0
Making bedding and clothing,	—	0·10	0·10	—	1 5 0	1 5 0
Stone-breaking,	3·10	—	3·10	8 5 9	—	8 5 9
Wood chopping,	0·10	—	0·10	—	1 5 0	1 5 0
Cooking,	0·32	—	0·32	—	6 1 0	6 1 0
Sick,	—	0·02	0·02	—	—	—
Unemployed,	4·	0·32	4·32	—	—	—
Total,	9·92	0·49	10·41	8 5 9	56 7 6	64 13 3

ENNISKILLEN PRISON.

Description of Employment.	Males.	Females.	Total.	Net Profit on Work done by Prisoners.	Estimated Value of the Work done for the Prison.	Total.
				£ s. d.	£ s. d.	£ s. d.
Tailors,	1	—	1	—	0 15 9	0 15 9
Shoemakers,	1	—	1	—	1 1 4	1 1 4
Whitewashers,	1	—	1	—	2 5 0	2 5 0
Service of prison,	1	—	1	—	—	—
Washing clothing and bedding,	1	—	1	—	2 15 3	2 15 3
Repairing bedding and clothing,	—	1	1	—	0 8 0	0 8 0
Wood chopping,	1	—	1	—	1 6 0	1 5 0
Freestone breaking,	1	—	1	—	1 0 0	1 0 0
Cooking,	1	—	1	—	—	—
Sick,	·02	—	·02	—	—	—
Total,	8	1	9	—	*9 17 3	9 17 3

* This sum represents value of work done by prisoners for month of March only.

GALWAY PRISON.

Description of Employment.	Males.	Females.	Total.	Net Profit on Work done by Prisoners.	Estimated Value of the Work done for the Prison.	Total.
				£ s. d.	£ s. d.	£ s. d.
Mat-making, picking coir, &c.,	1	—	1	3 11 3	0 15 0	4 6 3
Tailors,	1	—	1	—	22 13 0	22 13 0
Shoemakers,	1	—	1	—	22 13 0	22 13 0
Bricklayers and Labourers,	10	—	10	0 19 0	151 0 0	151 19 0
Whitewashers,	2	1	3	—	40 5 4	40 5 4
Service of prison,	6	1	7	—	100 13 4	100 13 4
Washing clothing and bedding,	—	4	4	—	60 8 0	60 8 0
Making bedding and clothing,	—	1	1	—	15 2 0	15 2 0
Repairing bedding and clothing,	—	3	3	—	30 4 0	30 4 0
Oakum picking,	12	1	13	27 12 10	—	27 12 10
Cooking,	3	—	3	—	30 4 0	30 4 0
Knitting,	—	2	2	—	20 2 8	20 2 8
Stone-breaking,	4	—	4	12 0 10	3 15 0	15 15 10
Sick,	1	—	1	—	—	—
Unemployed,	52	1	53	—	—	—
Total,	92	14	106	44 3 11	497 15 4	541 19 3

RETURN by the GOVERNORS, showing how Prisoners have been employed during the year ending 31st March, 1882, and the Earnings of those engaged in such Employment: also showing the average daily number of Unemployed from Sickness and other reasons.

GRANGEGORMAN PRISON.

Description of Employment.	Daily Average Number of Prisoners employed, unemployed, &c.			Net Profit on Work done by Prisoners.	Estimated Value of the Work done for the Prison.	Total.
	Males.	Females.	Total.			
				£ s. d.	£ s. d.	£ s. d.
Shoemakers,	2	—	2	—	60 16 0	60 16 0
Carpenters,	1	—	1	—	30 8 0	30 8 0
Whitewashers,	2	—	2	—	30 8 0	60 8 0
Service of prison,	6	13	19	—	255 17 4	255 17 4
Washing clothing and bedding,	—	92	92	83 17 9	682 14 0	766 11 9
Making bedding and clothing. Repairing bedding and clothing,	1	19	20	—	439 15 3	439 15 3
Stone-breaking,	4	—	4	4 6 11	—	4 6 11
Picking oakum,	53	23	76	4 15 0	—	4 15 0
Knitting,	—	47	47	9 15 9	50 6 2	60 1 11
Nursing,	—	3	3	—	—	—
Plaiting,	3	—	3	—	22 16 0	22 16 0
Sick,	6	14	20	—	—	—
Unemployed,	17	30	47	—	—	—
Total,	89	170	259	104 14 10	1,623 17 3	1,728 12 1

Washing and repairs have been done here during the year for Richmond and Kilmainham Prisons, but no profit shown, as only a nominal sum, sufficient to cover the expenditure in connexion therewith is charged in the annual transfer accounts.

A quantity of oakum was on hands at the close of the year; the picking of which was not paid for by the owners.

KILKENNY PRISON.

Description of Employment.	Males.	Females.	Total.	Net Profit on Work done by Prisoners.	Estimated Value of the Work done for the Prison.	Total.
				£ s. d.	£ s. d.	£ s. d.
Mat-making, picking coir, &c.,	13·67	—	13·67	14 3 7	59 4 5	73 7 0
Shoemakers,	·87	—	·87	—	11 5 0	11 5 0
Carpenters,	·06	—	·06	—	1 7 2	1 7 2
Bricklayers and labourers,	1·28	—	1·28	—	15 11 6	15 11 6
Painters and glaziers,	·08	—	·08	—	1 10 0	1 10 0
Tinsmiths,	·15	—	·15	—	2 5 0	2 5 0
Whitewashers,	·15	—	·15	—	2 5 0	2 5 0
Pumping water,	7·34	—	7·34	—	74 0 0	74 0 0
Service of prison,	5·81	·57	6·38	—	52 0 0	52 0 0
Washing clothing and bedding,	·43	1·34	1·77	—	26 15 0	26 15 0
Making bedding and clothing,	—	2·16	2·16	—	24 8 0	24 8 0
Repairing bedding and clothing,	·54	2·46	3·0	—	22 13 0	22 13 0
Brush-making,	·68	—	·68	—	15 8 0	15 8 0
Stone-breaking,	·39	—	·39	—	2 18 10	2 18 10
Rope picking,	14·42	·05	14·47	—	—	—
Wood for kindling,	1·25	—	1·25	6 7 6	5 0 0	11 7 6
Sick,	·34	·47	·81	—	—	—
Unemployed,	17·21	1·11	18·32	—	—	—
Total,	67·12	8·16	75·28	20 10 1	316 10 11	337 1 0

A very small quantity of mats sold, the net profit consequently is but small; no demand for good quality in Kilkenny. Stones broken were for prison use; no demand. No oakum disposed of during the year; seven tons probably on hand.

RETURN by the GOVERNORS OR CHIEF WARDERS, showing how Prisoners have been employed during the year ending 31st March, 1882, and the Earnings of those engaged in such Employment; also showing the average daily number of Unemployed from Sickness and other reasons.

KILMAINHAM PRISON.

Description of Employment.	Daily Average Number of Prisoners employed, unemployed, &c.			Net Profit on Work done by Prisoners.	Estimated Value of the Work done for the Prison.	Total.
	Males.	Females.	Total.	£ s. d.	£ s. d.	£ s. d.
Tailors,	1	—	1	—	30 10 0	30 10 0
Shoemakers,	1	—	1	—	30 10 0	30 10 0
Carpenters, Bricklayers and labourers, Painters and glaziers,	1	—	1	—	30 10 0	30 10 0
Whitewashers and labourers,	3	—	3	—	68 12 0	68 12 6
Service of prison,	10	—	10	—	244 0 0	244 0 0
Washing clothing and bedding,	1	4	5	0 13 7	11 10 0	12 3 7
Repairing bedding and clothing,	—	3	3	—	6 9 0	0 9 0
Picking oakum,	10	2	12	—	—	—
Sick and unemployed,	17	8	25	—	—	—
Total,	50	17	67	0 13 7	422 1 0	423 15 1

The average for females is only for the months of April and May, as none were in custody since 25th of May, 1881.

LIFFORD PRISON.

Description of Employment.	Males.	Females.	Total.	£ s. d.	£ s. d.	£ s. d.
Service of prison,	1	—	1	—	—	—
Total,	1	—	1	—	—	—

Prisoners employed cleaning prison and yards.

LIMERICK (MALE) PRISON

Description of Employment.	Males.	Females.	Total.	£ s. d.	£ s. d.	£ s. d.
Mat-making, picking coir, &c.,	1	—	1	0 13 2	—	6 13 2
Gardening and labouring,	4	—	4	—	120 8 0	120 8 0
Tailors,	1	—	1	—	22 11 6	22 11 6
Shoemakers,	2	—	2	—	60 4 0	60 4 0
Carpenters,	1	—	1	—	52 13 6	52 13 6
Bricklayers, Painters and glaziers, Tinsmiths, Blacksmiths,	2	—	2	—	105 7 0	105 7 0
Whitewashers,	1	—	1	—	22 11 6	22 11 6
Pumping water,	6	—	6	—	50 3 4	50 3 4
Service of prison,	6	—	6	—	00 6 0	00 6 0
Washing clothing and bedding,	4	—	4	—	80 4 0	00 4 0
Cooking,	2	—	2	—	45 3 0	45 3 0
Rope junk,	14	—	14	14 17 2	—	14 17 2
Stone-breaking,	13	—	13	5 1 11	—	5 1 11
Firewood,	1	—	1	7 11 9	—	7 11 9
Sick,	1	—	1	—	—	—
Unemployed,	50	—	50	—	—	—
Total,	111	—	111	34 4 0	029 11 10	603 15 10

RETURN by the GOVERNORS, showing how Prisoners have been employed during the year ending 31st March, 1882, and the Earnings of those engaged in such Employment; also showing the average daily number of Unemployed from Sickness and other reasons.

LIMERICK (FEMALE) PRISON.

Description of Employment.	Daily Average Number of Prisoners employed, unemployed, &c.			Net Profit on Work done by Prisoners.	Estimated Value of the Work done for the Prison.	Total.
	Males.	Females.	Total.			
				£ s. d.	£ s. d.	£ s. d.
Mat-making, picking coir, &c.,	—	2	2	—	10 0 0	10 0 0
Painters and glaziers,	—	2	2	—	20 0 0	20 0 0
Whitewashers,	—	2	2	—	20 0 0	20 0 0
Pumping water,	—	5	5	—	50 0 0	50 0 0
Service of prison, cooking, &c.	—	3	3	—	30 0 0	30 0 0
Washing clothing and bedding.	—	8	8	—	250 0 0	250 0 0
Repairing bedding and clothing,	—	30	30	—	90 0 0	90 0 0
Quilt making,	—	—	—	—	—	12 16 6
Stocking "	—	—	—	—	—	3 3 0
Lace "	—	—	—	—	—	1 5 0
Total,	—	—	—	—	470 0 0	17 6 6

Washing done in laundry here for Limerick Male and Female Prisons, and for Governors of both prisons.

Repairs.—Prison clothing done for Limerick Male and Female, and for Clonmel Prisons.

LONDONDERRY PRISON.

Description of Employment.	Males.	Females.	Total.	Net Profit on Work done by Prisoners.	Estimated Value of the Work done for the Prison.	Total.
				£ s. d.	£ s. d.	£ s. d.
Mat-making, picking coir, &c.,	7	—	7	85 3 4	—	85 3 4
Tailors,	2	—	2	—	73 0 0	73 0 0
Shoemakers,	1	—	1	—	36 10 0	36 10 0
Carpenters,	1	—	1	—	36 10 0	36 10 0
Bricklayers and labourers,	4	—	4	—	78 0 0	78 0 0
Painters and glaziers,	1	—	1	—	36 10 0	30 10 0
Whitewashers,	2	—	2	—	27 7 8	27 7 8
Service of prison,	6	2	8	—	182 0 0	182 0 0
Debtors,	2	—	2	—	—	—
Washing clothing and bedding.	—	2	2	—	36 10 0	36 10 0
Making bedding and clothing,	—	6	6	—	111 10 0	111 10 0
Repairing bedding and clothing,	—	2	2	—	38 10 0	38 10 0
Breaking stones,	15	—	15	63 0 0	—	63 0 0
Oakum picking,	20	2	22	4 10 0	—	4 10 0
Knitting stockings,	—	8	8	—	132 0 0	132 0 0
Wood splitting,	3	—	3	7 10 0	28 10 0	36 0 0
Sick,	1	—	1	—	—	—
Unemployed,	8	3	11	—	—	—
Total,	72	25	97	159 3 4	809 17 8	970 0 10

RETURN by the GOVERNORS OF CHIEF WARDERS, showing how Prisoners have been employed during the year ending 31st March, 1882, and the Earnings of those engaged in such Employment; also showing the average daily number of Unemployed from Sickness and other reasons.

LONGFORD PRISON.

Description of Employment.	Daily Average Number of Prisoners employed, unemployed, &c. — Males.	Females.	Total.	Net Profit on Work done by Prisoners.	Estimated Value of the Work done for the Prison.	Total.
				£ s. d.	£ s. d.	£ s. d.
Gardening,	0·70	—	0·70	4 0 0	—	4 0 0
Whitewashers,	0·09	—	0·00	—	0 14 6	0 14 6
Service of prison,	1·00	0·21	1·21	—	0 11 0	0 11 0
Washing clothing and bedding,	—	0·10	0·10	—	1 10 0	1 10 0
Repairing bedding and clothing,	—	0·21	0·21	—	1 12 0	1 12 0
Picking oakum,	0·74	—	0·74	2 18 0	—	5 18 0
Unemployed,	1·60	0·51	2·11	—	—	—
Total,	4·13	1·13	5·26	7 18 0	13 7 6	21 5 6

MARYBOROUGH PRISON.

Description of Employment.	Males.	Females.	Total.	Net Profit on Work done by Prisoners.	Estimated Value of the Work done for the Prison.	Total.
				£ s. d.	£ s. d.	£ s. d.
Mat-making, picking coir, &c.,	—	—	—	0 10 0	—	0 10 0
Tailors,	1	—	1	—	38 0 0	38 0 0
Shoemakers,	1	—	1	—	08 0 0	38 0 0
Carpenters,	8	—	8	—	304 0 0	304 0 0
Bricklayers and labourers,	15	—	15	—	273 0 0	273 0 0
Painters and glaziers,	3	—	3	—	70 0 0	75 0 0
Blacksmiths,	1	—	1	—	30 10 0	35 10 0
Whitewashers,	2	—	2	—	30 10 0	36 10 0
Treadwheel,	2	—	2	—	—	—
Service of prison,	0	—	0	—	109 10 0	100 10 0
Washing clothing and bedding,	2	—	2	—	36 10 0	36 10 0
Repairing bedding and clothing,	—	1	1	—	12 2 0	12 2 6
Sack making,	15	—	18	53 1 0	—	50 1 0
Plasterers,	2	—	2	—	70 0 0	76 0 0
Rope-picking,	10	—	10	—	—	—
Stone-breaking,	4	—	4	24 0 8	—	24 0 8
Coopering,	1	—	1	40 0 0	8 0 0	51 0 0
Stonecutting,	2	—	2	—	87 0 0	87 0 0
Sick,	1	—	1	—	—	—
Unemployed,	12	—	12	—	—	—
Total,	87	1	88	125 17 8	1,068 2 6	1,221 19 2

The extensive alterations of the main building is now complete; this important work has been chiefly done by prison labour. One and a-half ton of oakum was sold during the year for £24 18*s.* 9*d.*; there is no profit on this class of labour.

MONAGHAN PRISON.

Description of Employment.	Males.	Females.	Total.	Net Profit on Work done by Prisoners.	Estimated Value of the Work done for the Prison.	Total.
				£ s. d.	£ s. d.	£ s. d.
Whitewashers,	1	—	1	—	15 10 0	15 10 0
Pumping water,	2	—	2	—	30 15 0	30 18 0
Service of prison,	1	—	1	—	20 15 0	20 18 0
Total,	—	—	—	—	67 0 0	67 0 0

This prison has only been opened on 13th January, for P.P.P. Prisoners. Some fatigue prisoners have been received from other prisons.

RETURN by the GOVERNORS, showing how Prisoners have been employed during the year ending 31st March, 1882, and the Earnings of those engaged in such Employment; also showing the average daily number of Unemployed from Sickness and other reasons.

MULLINGAR PRISON.

Description of Employment.	Daily Average Number of Prisoners employed, unemployed, &c.			Net Profit on Work done by Prisoners.			Estimated Value of the Work done for the Prison.			Total.		
	Males.	Females.	Total.	£	s.	d.	£	s.	d.	£	s.	d.
Grinding corn,	1·	—	1·	5	5	0	—			5	5	0
Tailors,	1·	—	1·	—			22	13	0	22	13	0
Shoemakers,	1·	—	1·	—			41	9	6	41	9	6
Carpenters,	·33	—	·53	—			30	8	0	30	8	0
Bricklayers and labourers,	2·15	—	2·15	—			55	0	0	55	0	0
Painters and glaziers,	·57	—	·57	—			7	10	0	7	10	0
Tinsmiths,	·45	—	·45	—			6	0	0	6	0	0
Blacksmiths,	·55	—	·55	—			7	10	0	7	10	0
Whitewashers,	1·38	—	1·38	—			30	4	0	30	4	0
Service of prison,	3·	1·	4·	—			60	7	6	60	7	6
Washing clothing and bedding,	—	4·55	4·65	6	0	0	06	16	6	101	18	6
Making bedding and clothing. Repairing bedding and clothing,	—	3·	3·	—			22	13	0	22	13	0
Rope-picking,	15·48	—	10·48	—			57	15	0	57	15	0
Sewing sacks,	25·	—	25·	72	15	0	—			72	15	0
Cooking,	2·	—	2·	—			30	0	0	30	0	0
Stone-breaking,	21·32	—	21·32	50	2	8	—			64	8	8
Knitting,	—	4·45	4·45	2	2	6	16	0	0	15	2	6
Sick,	2·20	·17	2·37	—			—			—		
Unemployed,	5·	5·	—	—			—			—		
Total,	83·58	13·17	96·75	142	5	2	486	8	6	626	13	8

Hard labour is carried out in this prison at the crank mill, crushing Indian corn. Stone-breaking tasked, a total of 886 tons 13 cwt. having been broken during the past year, of which 254 tons 2 cwt. was brought into the prison by the road contractors, and for which they only pay 6d. per ton for breaking, the balance of 632 tons 11 cwt. was stone obtained from the removal of small walls in the exercising yards in the prison, and for which I received 1s. 8d. per ton when broken. Sack sewing tasked; picking rope tasked, 3 tons and a half were picked during the year, 2 tons of which were disposed of to the Anglo-American Rope and Oakum Company, Liverpool, at £16 10s. per ton.

NENAGH PRISON.

Description of Employment.	Males.	Females.	Total.	Net Profit £	s.	d.	Estimated Value £	s.	d.	Total £	s.	d.
Mat-making, picking coir, &c.,	9	—	9	0	17	0	—			6	17	6
Gardening,	1	—	1	8	0	6	—			8	0	6
Shoemakers,	1	—	1	—			22	10	0	22	10	0
Carpenters,	1	—	1	—			30	8	0	30	8	0
Bricklayers and labourers,	9	—	9	—			198	0	0	198	0	0
Pumping water,	1	—	1	—			15	4	0	15	4	0
Service of prison,	1	1	2	—			30	8	0	30	6	0
Washing clothing and bedding,	1	2	3	—			24	4	0	24	4	0
Repairing bedding and clothing,	—	1	1	—			2	6	0	2	5	0
Stone-breaking,	9	—	9	2	0	6	—			2	0	6
Picking oakum,	6	—	6	—			—			—		
Cooking,	1	—	1	—			15	4	0	15	4	0
Picking rope-junk,	6	—	0	—			—			—		
Knitting,	—	2	2	—			0	0	0	0	0	0
Sick,	1	—	1	—			—			—		
Unemployed,	5	1	6	—			—			—		
Total,	52	7	59	16	18	6	347	3	0	364	1	6

RETURN by the GOVERNORS, showing how Prisoners have been employed during the year ending 31st March, 1882, and the Earnings of those engaged in such Employment; also showing the average daily number of Unemployed from Sickness and other reasons.

NAAS PRISON.

Description of Employment.	Daily Average Number of Prisoners employed, unemployed, &c. Males.	Females.	Total.	Net Profit on Work done by Prisoners. £ s. d.	Estimated Value of the Work done for the Prison. £ s. d.	Total. £ s. d.
Mat-making, picking coir, &c.,						
Upholstering,	·25	—	·25	4 14 9	—	4 14 9
Brush-making,						
Tailors,	·5	—	·5	—	3 16 8	3 16 8
Shoemakers,	·25	—	·25	—	4 18 0	4 18 0
Carpenters,	2·	—	2·	—	78 5 0	78 5 0
Bricklayers and labourers,	2·	—	2·	—	72 12 0	72 12 0
Painters and glaziers,						
Tinsmiths,						
Blacksmiths,	·63	—	·63	—	10 10 4½	10 10 4½
Whitewashers,						
Pumping water,	2·	—	2·	—	18 5 0	18 5 0
Washing clothing and bedding,	·75	—	·75	—	20 10 6	20 10 6
Repairing bedding & clothing,	—	1·78	1·78	—	32 9 9	32 9 0
Cleaning prison,	5·	·28	5·28	—	96 7 3	96 7 3
Cooking,	2·	—	2·	—	30 10 0	38 10 0
Rope-picking and stone-breaking,	2·	·25	2·25	22 5 8	—	22 5 8
Sack-making,	6·08	—	6·08	10 7 7½	—	16 7 7½
Sick and unemployed,	9·54	·69	10·23	—	—	—
Total,	33·	3·	36·	43 7 10½	383 4 5½	426 12 4

By Order in Council female prisoners were removed on the 28th June, 1881, and male prisoners on the 15th December, 1881, and not committed after the respective dates.

OMAGH PRISON.

Description of Employment.	Males.	Females.	Total.	Net Profit on Work done by Prisoners. £ s. d.	Estimated Value of the Work done for the Prison. £ s. d.	Total. £ s. d.
Mat-making, picking coir, &c.,	5	—	5	62 7 8	—	62 7 8
Tailors,	1	—	1	—	13 0 10	13 0 10
Shoemakers,	1	—	1	—	15 13 0	15 13 0
Carpenters,	1	—	1	—	7 16 6	7 16 6
Bricklayers and labourers,	0	—	0	—	45 19 0	45 19 0
Painters and glaziers,	1	—	1	—	15 13 0	15 13 0
Tinsmiths,	1	—	1	—	10 8 8	10 8 8
Blacksmiths,	1	—	1	—	10 8 8	10 8 8
Whitewashers,	1	—	1	—	7 10 6	7 10 6
Treadwheel,	(13)	—	(13)	—	—	—
Pumping water,	2	—	2	—	15 13 0	15 13 0
Service of prison,	3	3	6	—	—	—
Washing clothing and bedding,	1	1	2	—	56 10 4	60 10 4
Making bedding and clothing,	—	4	4	—	20 17 4	20 17 4
Repairing bedding & clothing,	—	1	1	—	3 18 1	3 18 1
Stone-breaking,	10	—	10	27 9 7	—	27 9 7
Picking oakum,	10	2	12	—	—	—
Knitting,	—	8	8	—	12 6 10	12 6 10
Wood-splitting and bundling,	1	—	1	—	10 0 0	10 0 0
Sick,	1	—	1	—	—	—
Unemployed,	7	1	8	—	—	—
Total,	53	15	68	89 17 3	246 1 9	335 19 0

The price obtained for the teazed oakum being so near to that paid for the oakum rope that no actual profit has arisen on oakum picking during the past year.

RETURN by the GOVERNORS or CHIEF WARDERS, showing how Prisoners have been employed during the year ending 31st March, 1882, and the Earnings of those engaged in such Employment; also showing the average daily number of Unemployed from Sickness and other reasons.

RICHMOND PRISON.

Description of Employment.	Daily Average Number of Prisoners employed, unemployed, &c.			Net Profit on Work done by Prisoners.*	Estimated Value of the Work done for the Prison.	Total.
	Males.	Females.	Total.			
				£ s. d.	£ s. d.	£ s. d.
Mat-making,	15·53					
Weaving mats,	5·15					
Plaiting yarn,	16·28	—	45·19	273 15 9	—	273 15 9
Weaving matting,	6·51					
Warping and winding,	4·52					
Gardening,	6·41	—	6·41	25 7 0	—	25 7 0
Tailors,	5·71	—	5·71	147 1 4	—	147 1 4
Shoemakers,	5·52	—	5·52	70 7 5	—	70 7 5
Carpenters and slaters,	5·55	—	5·55	—	73 10 0	73 10 0
Bricklayers and labourers,	25·21	—	25·21	—	134 6 6	134 6 6
Painters and glaziers,	4·61	—	4·61	—	73 0 0	73 0 0
Tinsmiths,	1·	—	1·	65 11 3	—	65 11 3
Blacksmiths,	1·	—	1·	—	15 0 0	15 0 0
Whitewashers,	4·21	—	4·21	—	33 10 0	33 10 0
Treadwheel,	20·	—	20·	—	—	—
Cooks,	4·	—	4·	—	54 0 0	54 0 0
Cleaning prison,	15·	—	15·	—	80 0 0	80 0 0
Mattress-making,	12·	—	12·	167 16 4	—	167 16 4
Weaving frieze,	5·13	—	5·13	182 1 5	—	182 1 5
Weaving linsey,	4·	—	4·	25 10 0	—	25 10 5
Lime-burning,	5·26	—	5·26	74 9 0	—	74 9 0
Oakum-picking,	14·21	—	14·21	13 11 0	—	13 11 0
Stone-breaking,	27·12	—	27·12	15 13 4	—	15 13 4
Sick,	24·	—	24·	—	—	—
Unemployed,	20·	—	20·	—	—	—
Total,	271·12	—	271·12	1,057 4 4	482 6 8	1,539 11 0

* Net profit as shown under the several heads of manufacture in "Productive Ledger."

ROSCOMMON PRISON.

Description of Employment.	Males.	Females.	Total.	Net Profit on Work done by Prisoners.	Estimated Value of the Work done for the Prison.	Total.
				£ s. d.	£ s. d.	£ s. d.
Gardening,	0·5	—	0·5	—	3 0 0	3 0 0
Tailors,	0·054	—	0·054	—	1 10 0	1 10 0
Carpenters,	0·08	—	0·08	—	0 18 0	0 18 0
Labourers,	0·37	—	0·37	—	2 11 0	2 11 0
Tinsmiths, Blacksmiths,	0·025	—	0·025	—	0 14 0	0 14 0
Whitewashers,	0·11	—	0·11	—	2 5 0	2 5 0
Pumping water,	0·206	—	0·286	—	5 0 0	5 0 0
Service of prison,	0·985	0·126	1·112	—	7 12 0	7 12 0
Washing clothing and bedding,	—	0·17	0·17	—	2 8 0	2 8 0
Repairing bedding and clothing,	—	0·05	0·05	—	0 15 0	0 15 0
Rope-picking,	0·052	—	0·052	—	—	—
Sick,	0·054	—	0·054	—	—	—
Unemployed,	0·81	—	0·81	—	—	—
Total,	3·456	0·356	3·834	—	26 14 0	26 14 0

RETURN by the GOVERNORS, showing how Prisoners have been employed during the year ending 31st March, 1882, and the Earnings of those engaged in such Employment; also showing the average daily number of Unemployed from Sickness and other reasons.

SLIGO PRISON.

Description of Employment.	Daily Average Number of Prisoners employed, unemployed, &c.			Net Profit on Work done by Prisoners.	Estimated Value of the Work done for the Prison.	Total.
	Males.	Females.	Total.			
				£ s. d.	£ s. d.	£ s. d.
Tailors,	1·28	—	1·28	—	24 8 9	24 8 9
Shoemakers,	1·	—	1·	—	18 12 6	18 12 6
Carpenters,	·21	—	·21	—	8 0 0	8 0 0
Painters and glaziers,	·42	—	·42	—	8 1 3	8 1 3
Whitewashers,	·29	·18	·47	—	8 7 6	8 7 6
Treadwheel,	9·	—	9·	—	—	—
Pumping water,	2·78	—	2·78	—	42 5 0	42 5 0
Service of prison,	5·	1·13	6·13	—	94 0 0	94 0 0
Washing clothing and bedding,	—	1·	1·	—	13 16 0	13 15 0
Making bedding and clothing,	—	1·73	1·73	—	8 15 4	8 15 4
Repairing bedding and clothing,	—	2·	2·	—	9 10 4	9 10 4
Stone-breaking,	1·	—	1·	3 6 8	—	3 6 8
Rope-picking,	20·38	3·47	23·85	—	—	—
Splitting wood,	1·	—	1·	5 2 0	1 5 0	6 7 0
Sick,	1·61	·46	2·07	—	—	—
Unemployed,	6·48	1·40	7·88	—	—	—
Total,	50·40	11·42	61·82	8 8 8	287 0 8	295 9 4

TRALEE PRISON.

Description of Employment.	Males.	Females.	Total.	Net Profit on Work done by Prisoners.	Estimated Value of the Work done for the Prison.	Total.
				£ s. d.	£ s. d.	£ s. d.
Mat-making, picking coir, &c.,	8·2	—	8·2	5 19 5	*16 16 5	22 15 10
Gardening,	—	—	—	—	5 0 5	5 0 5
Tailors,	·4	—	·4	—	10 3 4	10 3 4
Shoemakers,	·3	—	·3	—	6 6 3	6 6 3
Carpenters,	·1	—	·1	—	3 3 7	3 3 7
Bricklayers and labourers,	§2·	—	2·	—	39 5 0	39 5 0
Painters and glaziers,	·3	—	·3	—	3 7 0	3 7 0
Tinsmiths,	·1	—	·1	—	3 5 3	3 5 3
Blacksmiths,	—	—	—	—	1 2 4	1 2 4
Cranks,	4·	—	4·	—	—	—
Service of prison,	·3	·8	1·1	—	15 17 0	15 17 0
Washing clothing and bedding,	—	1·4	1·4	—	38 13 1	38 13 1
Making bedding and clothing,	—	1·7	1·7	—	11 8 9	11 8 9
Stone-breaking,	7·7	—	7·7	7 14 10	†14 0 0	21 14 10
Splitting or chopping wood for fire-lights,	1·	—	1·	0 4 6	‡7 8 0	7 12 6
Sick,	·3	·3	·6	—	—	—
Unemployed,	19·9	2·	21·9	—	—	—
Total,	44·8	6·2	51·	13 18 9	180 11 8	194 10 5

* Net value of mats and plait on hands.
† Net value of fine gravel on hands.
‡ Net value of fire-lights on hands.
§ Raising stones in quarry on the prison premises, and drawing them into the prison to be broken.

Hard labour has been carried out by cranks, picking rope junk, and stone-breaking, tasked for Probation Class Prisoners.

The unemployed were untried prisoners

RETURN by the GOVERNORS or CHIEF WARDERS, showing how Prisoners have been employed during the year ending 31st March, 1882, and the Earnings of those engaged in such Employment; also showing the average daily number of Unemployed from Sickness and other reasons.

TRIM PRISON.

Description of Employment.	Daily Average Number of Prisoners employed, unemployed, &c. Males.	Females.	Total.	Net Profit on Work done by Prisoners. £ s. d.	Estimated Value of the Work done for the Prison. £ s. d.	Total. £ s. d.
Gardening,	1	—	1	10 6 0	1 0 0	11 6 0
Pumping water,	·00137	—	·00137	—	1 10 0	1 10 0
Service of prison,	·00137	—	·00137	—	2 10 0	2 10 0
Washing clothing and bedding,	—	·0470	·0479	—	2 10 0	2 10 0
Stone-breaking,	1	—	1	3 10 0	—	3 10 0
Total,	—	—	—	13 10 0	7 10 0	21 0 0

TULLAMORE PRISON.

Description of Employment.	Males.	Females.	Total.	Net Profit £ s. d.	Estimated Value £ s. d.	Total. £ s. d.
Tailors,	1	—	1	—	15 3 0	15 3 0
Shoemakers,	1	—	1	—	15 6 0	15 3 0
Carpenters,	·5	—	·5	—	18 18 9	18 18 9
Bricklayers and labourers,	3	—	3	—	43 13 6	45 13 6
Painters and glaziers,	1	—	1	—	37 17 6	37 17 6
Tinsmiths, Blacksmiths,	1	—	1	—	30 12 0	30 12 0
Whitewashers,	·5	—	·5	—	11 8 4	11 8 4
Pumping water,	8	—	8	—	80 0 0	80 0 0
Service of prison,	4	1	5	—	50 0 0	50 0 0
Washing clothing and bedding.	—	1·5	1·5	6 5 2	22 10 0	28 15 2
Making bedding and clothing, Repairing bedding and clothing,	—	2·5	2·5	—	25 0 0	25 0 0
Picking oakum,	2	—	2	4 3 8	—	4 3 8
Cooking,	2	—	2	—	40 0 0	40 0 0
Sack-making,	43	—	43	240 13 1	—	240 13 1
Sick,	1	—	1	—	—	—
Unemployed,	5	—	5	—	—	—
Total,	73	5	78	257 1 11	392 6 1	649 8 0

Sack-making has been successfully carried on in this prison for the past year the prisoners have worked well with some exceptions.

WEXFORD PRISON.

Description of Employment.	Males.	Females.	Total.	Net Profit £ s. d.	Estimated Value £ s. d.	Total. £ s. d.
Mat-making, picking coir, &c.,	6	—	6	2 0 8	—	2 0 8
Gardening,	1	—	1	—	15 0 0	15 0 0
Carpenters,	1	—	1	—	2 10 0	2 10 0
Bricklayers and labourers,	8	—	8	—	62 18 0	62 18 0
Whitewashers	2	—	2	—	30 10 0	30 10 0
Pumping water,	2	—	2	—	—	—
Service of prison,	2	1	3	—	48 10 0	48 10 0
Washing clothing and bedding,	2	1	3	—	46 10 0	48 10 0
Picking oakum,	8	—	8	18 7 6	—	18 7 6
Sewing,	—	1	1	—	12 0 0	12 0 0
Knitting,	—	1	1	—	12 0 0	12 0 0
Stone-breaking,	6	—	6	4 9 10	—	4 9 10
Unemployed,	1	—	1	—	—	—
Total,	39	4	43	24 18 0	237 16 0	262 14 0

RETURN by the GOVERNORS or CHIEF WARDERS, showing how Prisoners have been employed during the year ending 31st March, 1882, and the Earnings of those engaged in such Employment; also showing the average daily number of Unemployed from Sickness and other reasons.

WATERFORD PRISON.

Description of Employment.	Daily Average Number of Prisoners employed, unemployed, &c.			Net Profit on Work done by Prisoners.	Estimated Value of the Work done for the Prison.	Total.
	Males.	Females.	Total.			
				£ s. d.	£ s. d.	£ s. d.
Mat-making, picking coir, &c.,	5	—	5	20 12 4	—	20 12 4
Tailors, ... } Shoemakers, ... }	1	—	1	—	18 3 0	18 3 0
Bricklayers and labourers, .	3	—	3	—	40 10 0	40 10 0
Painters and Glaziers, . } Tinsmiths, ... }	1	—	1	—	5 10 0	5 10 0
Whitewashers, ...	1	—	1	—	14 14 0	14 14 0
Pumping water, ...	2	—	2	—	17 7 0	17 7 0
Service of prison, ...	3	1	4	—	60 0 0	60 0 0
Washing clothing and bedding,	2	6	8	31 15 0	68 0 0	99 15 0
Repairing bedding and clothing, ...	—	2	2	—	25 16 0	25 16 0
Knitting, ...	—	5	5	8 4 8	33 0 6	41 5 2
Picking, packing, and sorting oakum, ...	18	2	20	22 10 10	—	22 10 10
Cooking, ...	2	—	2	—	56 10 0	56 10 0
Stoking and stone-breaking,	1	—	1	—	17 12 0	17 12 0
Cutting wood, ...	4	—	4	—	52 2 0	52 2 0
Sick, ...	1	1	2	—	—	—
Unemployed, ...	4	1	5	—	—	—
Total, . . .	48	18	66	78 2 10	394 18 6	473 16 4

WICKLOW PRISON.

Description of Employment.	Males.	Females.	Total.	Net Profit on Work done by Prisoners.	Estimated Value of the Work done for the Prison.	Total.
				£ s. d.	£ s. d.	£ s. d.
Service of prison, ...	1	—	1	—	12 0 0	12 0 0
Washing clothing and bedding, ...	—	1	1	—	15 0 0	15 0 0
Picking oakum, ...	3	—	3	1 5 0	—	1 5 0
Total, . . .	4	1	5	1 5 0	27 0 0	28 5 0

[MOUNTJOY PRISON.

RETURN by the GOVERNOR and SUPERINTENDENT, showing how Prisoners (not Convicts) have been employed during the year ending 31st March, 1882, and the Earnings of those engaged in such Employment; also showing the average daily number of Unemployed from Sickness and other reasons.

MOUNTJOY (MALE) PRISON. [LOCAL PRISONERS.]

Description of Employment.	Daily Average Number of Prisoners employed, unemployed, &c.			Net Profit on Work done by Prisoners.	Estimated Value of the Work done for the Prison.	Total.
	Males.	Females.	Total.			
				£ s. d.	£ s. d.	£ s. d.
Mat-making, picking coir, &c.,	93·20	—	93·29	353 14 6	—	353 14 6
Tailors,	16·82	—	16·82	284 16 9	—	284 16 9
Shoemakers,	19·20	—	19·20	241 8 6	—	241 8 6
Carpenters,	8·51	—	8·51	—	323 7 7	323 7 7
Painters and glaziers,	2·24	—	2·24	—	85 2 5	85 2 5
Tinsmiths,	2·82	—	2·82	—	107 8 2	107 8 2
Whitewashers,	·28	—	·28	—	10 12 10	10 12 10
Service of prison,	9·05	—	9·05	—	240 14 7	240 14 7
Picking oakum,	14·28	—	14·28	16 14 5	—	16 14 5
Making fendoffs,	3·86	—	3·86	28 0 6	—	28 0 6
„ nets, &c.,	1·74	—	1·74	3 2 9	—	3 2 9
Cutting firewood,	12·53	—	12·53	172 14 2	—	172 14 2
Sick,	6·50	—	6·50	—	—	—
Unemployed,	3·33	—	3·33	—	—	—
Total,	194·28	—	194·28	1,102 8 7	767 0 7	1,869 8 2

MOUNTJOY (FEMALE) PRISON. [LOCAL PRISONERS.]

Description of Employment.	Males.	Females.	Total.	Net Profit on Work done by Prisoners.	Estimated Value of the Work done for the Prison.	Total.
				£ s. d.	£ s. d.	£ s. d.
Service of prison,	—	12·41	12·41	—	125 15 1	125 15 1
Washing clothing and bedding,	—	19·85	19·85	—	1,002 19 3	1,002 19 3
Making bedding and clothing,	—	18·48	18·48	—	60 8 6	60 8 6
Sick,	—	3·61	3·61	—	—	—
Unemployed,	—	0·38	0·38	—	—	—
Total,	—	54·73	54·73	—	1,189 2 10	1,189 2 10

B.—CONVICT PRISONS.

1.—MOUNTJOY MALE CONVICT PRISON.

MOUNTJOY MALE CONVICT PRISON.

Governor's Report.

GOVERNOR'S REPORT.

Mountjoy Male Prison,
17th May, 1882.

SIR,—I beg to forward my annual report, and also the statistical returns for the year ended, 31st March, 1882.

There have been many changes in the staff since my last report. The late chief warder has been promoted to the position of deputy-governor of Spike Island Convict Prison. Consequent on same, a principal warder from this staff was promoted to the vacancy, a first class warder to that of principal warder, and a second class warder to that of first class warder. A second class warder was promoted to be chief warder at Tullamore Prison, and his place was filled by a warder transferred from Grangegorman Prison. One second class warder was dismissed the service for misconduct, and his place was filled by a transfer from Spike Island Convict Prison. A vacancy existing for a first class warder was also filled by transfer from Spike Island.

Owing to the re-establishment of a tailors class in this prison a second class warder was promoted to first class, and put in charge of that department. A second class warder was transferred from Richmond Prison and appointed tailor warder.

Four officers have been appointed, and are now doing duty here as temporary ordinary warders, to fill the places of four warders from this staff who are ordered for special duty at local gaols.

I can report favourably of the general conduct of the staff, with the exception of the one occurrence already referred to.

Owing to the large and varied increase in the number of prisoners, the staff is numerically weak, and a great strain exists in carrying out the duties, so much so that relaxation for the officers in the shape of leave is almost now impossible.*

The industry of the prisoners has, during the past twelve months, been further developed in the making of mattresses and palliasses for public departments.

A large branch of employment has also been added to the occupation of the prisoners by the manufacture of firewood, which is cut and made up into bundles for public departments—this, in addition to their former industries, has found ample employment for the prisoners.

I regret to say that corporal punishment was inflicted on two convicts within the past twelve months for gross misconduct.

No attempt at escape was made, with the exception of one prisoner, who was noticed to have tampered with the window in his cell, but he was detected in time and the effort was frustrated.

The prisoners attend school as heretofore; they are reported as being attentive and making average progress in their studies.

Two prisoners died in hospital through natural causes. An inquest was held in each case, as laid down by regulations.

The prison buildings and fittings pertaining thereto have been kept in repair by the General Prisons Board with the assistance of prison labour, with the exception of such cases where special contracts had been entered into with parties outside.

I certify that the rules laid down for the government of the prison

* Arrangements have been made by which some of the officers are now permitted to go on leave, and the Board, having duly considered the numerical strength of the staff of this prison, are of opinion that it is ample for the duties required if they are judiciously disposed.

have been strictly complied with, except such particular cases as have been reported and brought under the notice of the General Prisons Board. MOUNTJOY MALE CONVICT PRISON. Governor's Report.

I have the honour to be, sir, your most obedient servant,

P. W. HACKETT, Governor.

The Chairman, General Prisons Board,
Dublin Castle.

CLASSIFIED STATEMENT of the NUMBER of OFFENCES committed by the Convicts during the year ended 31st March, 1882.

Offences.	No.	Offences.	No.
Assaults on Officers,	4	Indecent Conduct,	2
Assaults on convicts,	6	Idleness,	9
Disobedience,	9	Injuring prison property,	13
Disobedience and insolence,	66	Malingering,	1
Disorderly conduct,	29	Prohibited articles,	13
Fighting,	1	Other offences,	57
Insolence,	6		
Insubordination,	1	Total,	217

CLASSIFICATION of CRIMES for which those Convicts have been sentenced who were received during the year ended 31st March, 1882.

Crimes.	No.	Crimes.	No.
Assault,	1	Larceny,	24
Assault and larceny,	2	Larceny and previous conviction of felony,	18
Assault with intent to rob,	1	Larceny with violence,	2
Assault on wife,	1	Larceny and burglary,	1
Assault on police,	9	Larceny from the person,	16
Assault with bodily harm,	5	Larceny of money from a Railway Company,	1
Assault (grievous),	1	Larceny of money from a post letter,	1
Assault by kicking,	1	Larceny of cattle and previous conviction,	1
Arson,	4	Larceny of wearing apparel,	2
Burglary,	7	Larceny of a watch and chain,	1
Burglary and robbery,	5	Murder,	4
Burglary and previous conviction,	5	Manslaughter,	13
Burglary and prison breach,	1	Maliciously broke glass,	1
Breaking into a chapel with intent,	1	Malicious wounding,	1
Cattle stealing,	3	Military offences,	7
Coining,	2	Obtaining money under false pretences,	1
Demanding money,	1	Perjury,	1
Embezzlement,	1	Posting threatening notice,	2
Entering a building with intent to commit a felony,	1	Placing an obstruction on a railway,	1
Felony,	8	Riot and assault,	2
Felonious assault with intent to rob,	2	Robbery with violence,	1
Felony and previous conviction,	1	Rape,	10
Feloniously breaking and entering a dwelling-house,	1	Rape on a child under 10 years,	1
Felony (breaking prison),	1	Receiving stolen goods,	6
Feloniously wounding with intent to maim,	2	Stealing sheep,	2
Forgery,	1	Stealing a watch and chain,	1
Forgery of Inland Revenue stamps,	1	Shooting at,	1
Garrotting,	2	Uttering base coin,	1
Housebreaking,	11	Unlawful possession,	1
Housebreaking and larceny,	4	Wounding,	4
House attack, assault, and appearing armed by night,	1	Whiteboy offences,	14
Having in possession coining stamps,	1		
Highway robbery,	1	Total,	241

NUMBER of CONVICTS admitted in association during the year ended 31st March, 1882.

Trades.	No.	Trades.	No.
Received:—		Removed, viz.:—	
Labourers,	55	Carpenters,	1
Painters,	1	Labourers,	44
Plumbers,	1	Masons,	1
Plasterers,	1	Smiths,	1
Shoemakers,	1	Shoemakers,	7
Tailors,	24	Tailors,	8
Remaining on 31st March, 1881,	64	Remaining on 31st March, 1882,	85

RETURN showing how CONVICTS have been Employed during the year ending 31st March, 1882, and the Earnings of those engaged in such employment; also showing the average daily number of Unemployed from sickness and other reasons.

Description of Employment.	Daily Average Number of Prisoners employed, unemployed, &c.			Net Profit on Work done by Prisoners.			Estimated Value of the Work done for the Prison.			Total.		
	Males.	Females.	Total.	£	s.	d.	£	s.	d.	£	s.	d.
Mat-making, picking coir, &c.,	47·10	—	47·10	160	0	7	—			160	0	7
Gardening, ...	17·72	—	17·72	—			471	7	0	471	7	0
Tailors, ...	16·78	—	16·78	309	11	7	—			309	11	7
Shoemakers, ...	18·88	—	18·88	229	0	4	—			229	0	4
Carpenters, ...	2·78	—	2·78	—			105	12	10	105	12	10
Bricklayers, ...	1·87	—	1·87	—			71	1	2	71	1	2
Tinsmiths, ...	·41	—	·41	—			15	11	7	15	11	7
Blacksmiths and Plumbers, .	2·83	—	2·83	—			107	10	10	107	10	10
Whitewashers, ...	·83	—	·83	—			22	1	7	22	1	7
Service of prison, . . .	12·23	—	12·26	—			325	0	4	325	0	4
Making bedding, . . .	4·95	—	4·95	41	0	0	81	18	4	122	18	4
Picking oakum, . . .	38·38	—	38·38	16	14	4	—			16	14	4
Fire wood, ...	5·74	—	5·74	53	7	3	—			53	7	3
Sick, ...	7·14	—	7·14	—			—			—		
Unemployed, ...	3·23	—	3·23	—			—			—		
Total, ...	—	—	182·06	809	14	1	1,200	9	8	2,010	3	9

RETURN of WORK for the year ended 31st March, 1882.

SHOEMAKING DEPARTMENT.

Making.

Blucher boots, - -	pairs	478
Navvy ,, - - -	,,	33
Men's shoes, - - -	,,	681
Women's shoes, - - -	,,	331
Warders' slippers, - -	,,	69
Matron's ,, - - -	,,	67
Canvas ,, - - -	,,	528
Frieze ,, - - -	,,	338
Children's shoes, - -	,,	10
Boots, P. C., - - -	,,	18
Restraint muffs, - -	,,	4
Shoe laces, - - - -	gross	6

Repairing.

Men's shoes, - -	pairs	1,128
Women's ,, - - -	,,	391
Blucher boots, - - -	,,	170
Slippers, - - - -	,,	34
Prisoners' boots, - - -	,,	130

TAILORING DEPARTMENT.

Making.

Warders' coats, - - - - -	221
,, trousers, - - - - -	260
,, capes, - - - - -	263
,, top coats, - - - - -	112
,, tweed suits, - - -	46
Frieze jackets, - - - - -	551
,, trousers, - - - - -	1,370
,, vests, - - - - -	530
,, caps, - - - - -	408
,, braces, - - - - -	700

TAILORING DEPARTMENT—*continued.*

P. C. frieze suits, - - - - -	28
Men's canvas suits, - - - -	30
Women's ,, - - - - -	27
Aprons (tradesmen's), - - -	39
Barragon vests, - - - - -	43
Cord trousers, - - - - -	47
Serge suits, - - - - - -	165
Monkey jackets, - - - - -	39
Blouse, - - - - - -	11
Frock coats, - - - - - -	16
Black trousers, - - - - -	36
Tweed ,, - - - - -	8
Top coats, - - - - - -	8
Vests, - - - - - - -	16

Repairing.

Jackets, - - - - - -	450
Trousers, - - - - - -	1,035
Vests, - - - - - -	127
Over-coats, - - - - - -	24

MAT, MATTING, &c., DEPARTMENT.

Brush mats made, - - -	2,978
Chain ,, - - -	1,107
Bordered ,, - - -	2,025
Hearthrugs, - - - - -	86
Matting, sq. yds., - - -	3,434
Coir brushes, - - - -	1,042
,, scrubs, - - - -	2,136
Fend-offs, - - - - -	380
Oakum picked, - - - cwt.	267½

MOUNTJOY MALE CONVICT PRISON.

Governor's Report.

STATEMENT of the NUMBER of CONVICTS committed and disposed of, from 1st April, 1881, to 31st March, 1882.

Received—	No.	Removed—	No.
Convict depôts,	109	Convict depôts,	154
Local prisons,	164	Discharged,	45
Licence revoked cases,	16	Died,	2
Military barracks,	6	Dundrum Lunatic Asylum,	1
In custody on 31st March, 1881,	150	Remaining in custody on 31st March, 1882,	243

TABLE showing the reported PREVIOUS IMPRISONMENT of the Convicts received during the year ended 31st March, 1882.

Not reported to have been in prison before,	54	Seven times,	9
Once,	32	Eight „	6
Twice,	31	Nine „	3
Three times,	27	Ten and under fifteen times,	18
Four „	16	Fifteen times and over,	16
Five „	19	Total,	241
Six „	10		

AGES of CONVICTS on CONVICTION, received during the year ended 31st March, 1882.

Fifteen and under twenty years of age,	25	Fifty and under sixty,	9
Twenty and under twenty-five,	81	Sixty and over,	5
Twenty-five and under thirty	46		
Thirty and under forty,	46	Total,	241
Forty and under fifty,	29		

SENTENCES of the CONVICTS committed to the Prison during the year ended 31st March, 1882.

Five years' penal servitude,	146	Twenty years' penal servitude,	2
Seven „ „	57	Twenty-five „ „	1
Ten „ „	20	Life, „ „	6
Twelve „ „	2		
Fourteen „ „	3	Total,	241
Fifteen, „ „	4		

Single, 171. Married, 70.
Roman Catholics, 208. Protestants, 24. Presbyterians, 7.
Baptist, 1. Unitarian, 1.

SCHOOL.

	Convicts.	Local Prisoners.
At the close of the past year there were on school rolls,	122	64
Admitted during the year 1881–82,	163	92
Transferred from school to other prisons, &c., in 1881–82,	116	113
Remaining on school rolls 31st March, 1882,	169	43

TABLE showing the promotions in the several classes.

	Convicts.	Local Prisoners.
Advanced during the year:—		
From First to Second Book,	66	56
From Second to Third Book,	54	70
From Third to Fourth Book,	58	–
Total,	148	126

TABLE showing the proficiency attained by the Prisoners who passed through Mountjoy Male Prison School during the year ended 31st March, 1882.

Subjects examined in and Proficiency attained.	Numbers.				Per-centage.			
	On Admission.		On Removal.		On Admission.		On Removal.	
	Con-victs.	Local Prisoners.	Con-victs.	Local Prisoners.	Con-victs.	Local Prisoners.	Con-victs.	Local Prisoners.
Reading:								
Not able, ...	52	70	3	7	31·9	76·09	2·58	6·19
Badly, ...	80	22	35	19	49·08	23·91	30·17	16·81
Fairly, ...	31	–	78	87	19·02	–	67·25	77·
Totals, . .	163	92	116	113	100·	100·	100·	100·
Writing:								
Not able, ...	75	70	11	10	46·01	76·09	9·48	8·85
Badly, ...	68	22	45	35	41·72	23·91	38·79	30·97
Fairly, ...	20	–	60	68	12·27	–	51·73	60·18
Totals, . .	163	92	116	113	100·	100·	100·	100·
Arithmetic:								
Perfectly ignorant of, .	80	75	11	10	49·08	81·52	9·48	8·85
Part of Simple Rules,	63	17	25	39	38·65	18·48	21·55	34·51
Part of Compound Rules, ...	13	–	30	59	7·98	–	25·87	52·21
Proportion and above,	7	–	50	5	4·29	–	43·10	4·43
Totals, . .	163	92	116	113	100·	100·	100·	100·

MOUNTJOY MALE CONVICT PRISON.

Medical Officer's Report.

MEDICAL OFFICER'S REPORT.

Mountjoy Male Convict Prison,
18th April, 1882.

SIR,—I have the honour to submit my annual report of the sanitary condition of this Prison for the year ending 31st March, 1882, which is so far satisfactory that there is little to remark.

The general health of the officers and of the prisoners has been good. Of the officers, nine were received into hospital, four from the staff of the Female Prison, two from Lusk Prison, and one, on temporary duty here, from Kilmainham Prison. None of their complaints, however, were of a grave character.

Among the sixty-one prisoners in hospital, only two deaths occurred. Both were worn-out returned convicts who had spent many years in prison.

It was found necessary to transmit one prisoner to the Central Lunatic Asylum.

Only one prisoner was sent here for treatment from Lusk Prison, and no case of contagious or epidemic disease occurred during the year.

I beg to express my acknowledgments to all the officers for the facilities afforded me by them in the discharge of my duties.

I have the honour to be, sir,

Your obedient servant,

J. W. YOUNG, M.D., Medical Officer.

The Chairman, General Prisons Board, Dublin Castle.

MOUNTJOY MALE CONVICT PRISON.

Medical Officer's Report.

TABLE I.—HOSPITAL RETURN for the year.

Number of patients in hospital, 1st April, 1881,	3	64
" " admitted during the year,	61	
" " discharged "	49	64
" " sent to Central Asylum,	1	
" " died,	2	
" " remaining in hospital, 1st April, 1882,	12	

Daily average number in hospital,	6
Number of Externs prescribed for,	1,872
Daily average,	5·1

TABLE II.—DISEASES of those admitted to HOSPITAL.

Debility,	4	Hæmorhoids,	1
Observation,	5	Sore throat,	2
Gastric,	3	Ophthalmia,	2
Nervous,	2	Infirm,	5
Scald,	2	Diarrhœa,	1
Syphilis,	4	Erysipelas,	2
Pulmonic,	2	Bronchitis,	3
Abscess,	2	Stricture,	2
Colds,	4	Do. of heart,	2
Fistula,	2	Sinus,	1
Wound,	1	Anthrax,	1
Scrofula,	5	Rheumatism,	1
Swelled knee,	1	Concussion,	1

TABLE III.—DEATHS during the year.

Register No.	Initials of Name.	Received in Prison.	Admitted to Hospital.	Died.	Cause of Death.
A 25	L. D.	21 Mar., 1879,	9 May, 1881,	13 June, 1881,	Malignant disease of abdomen.
A 224	J. B.	7 April, 1881,	31 Oct., 1881,	14 Feb., 1882,	Tubercular disease of intestines.

TABLE IV.—CONVICTS sent to Central Lunatic Asylum.

Register No.	Initials of Name.	Where Convicted.	Date of Conviction.	Removal to Prison.	Transferred o Asylum
10067	J. B.	Cork,	16 April, 1877.	30 June, 1881,	29 Sept., 1881.

PROTESTANT CHAPLAIN'S REPORT.

Protestant Chaplain's Report.

H.M. Prison, Mountjoy, Dublin,
May, 1882.

SIR,—As is usual, during the past year the services of the Church have been held, religious instruction given, and the convicts and prisoners visited in their cells.

I respectfully ask that the rule which prevents the attendance of local prisoners at divine service upon week-days, may be so altered as to give at least the well conducted amongst those prisoners the privilege of attending such services.

My intercourse with convicts and prisoners adds every year to my conviction that drink is all but the universal cause of crime, and that

H

Mountjoy Male Convict Prison.

Protestant Chaplain's Report.

until further restrictions are put upon the drink traffic, there is but little prospect either of lessening crime or of the reformation of criminals.

I am, sir, your faithful servant,

ROBERT FLEMYNG, M.A.,
Church of Ireland Chaplain.

To the Chairman, General Prisons Board,
Dublin Castle.

Roman Catholic Chaplain's Report.

ROMAN CATHOLIC CHAPLAIN'S REPORT.

Mountjoy Male Prison,
24th May, 1882.

SIR,—I beg to submit my report for the year commencing 1st April, 1881, and ending 31st March, 1882.

It is my duty to report that the prisoners under my care have been, on the whole, well conducted, obedient to those placed over them, and disposed to avail themselves of the means afforded for moral improvement. I can also speak well of the manner in which the prison discipline was carried out. Whereas the prison discipline was administered strictly, and in accordance with the spirit of the regulations, due allowance was at the same time made for human weakness, and, in consequence, I rarely, if ever, heard prisoners complain of harsh and unfair treatment on the part of officers.

I am pleased to have to report that the classification by which the convicts undergoing imprisonment for the first time, are separated from habitual criminals, who, as a general rule, are so eager to initiate others in the secrets of their own evil ways, has been attended with very considerable advantages to the discipline of the prison, and the moral reformation of the former class of prisoners. I regret to have to report to you that the evil habits and conduct of prisoners from the cities of Dublin and Belfast, and also from Reformatories, even when kept in separate confinement in the same prison, are calculated to do much mischief to the entire body of prisoners from other parts of the country. I am of the opinion that a great deal of contamination would be prevented among the prisoners of Mountjoy if some means could be adopted by which entire and complete separation could be effected of Reformatory boys, Dublin and Belfast prisoners, from the other prisoners of the country at large. I feel grateful in reporting that every facility has been afforded me in the exercise of my ministry, and that every one of the officers with whom my duties brought me into relation, has treated me very kindly.

From the commencement of the year to its close, the number of local prisoners and convicts having been so large that almost every available cell in either prison was occupied, my duties there increased in proportion. I have never been able to discharge all my duties towards the convicts, and the local prisoners confined in Mountjoy consequent on the passing of the Act of 1877; and so I have been compelled to beg the constant help of another clergyman. He is not, however, a paid assistant. I very respectfully call your attention to this matter, with the view of obtaining for him a salary.

I have the honour to be, sir,

Your most obedient humble servant,

MICHAEL CODY, R.C. Chaplain.

The Chairman, General Prisons Board, Dublin Castle.

PRESBYTERIAN CHAPLAIN'S REPORT.

MOUNTJOY MALE CONVICT PRISON.

Presbyterian Chaplain's Report.

Mountjoy Male Convict Prison,
May 9, 1882.

SIR,—In compliance with instructions from the General Prisons Board, I have, during the past year, added a second day in the week to the discharge of my duties.

Divine service has been regularly performed every Sabbath during the year, generally by myself, and occasionally by my assistant minister, the Rev. Dr. Tait.

I have in no case observed anything objectionable in the conduct of the prisoners under my care, and my ministrations have been received with attention, and I trust have not been fruitless, indeed, I think some good has resulted from the religious instruction I have been enabled to impart. Cellular visits, advice, and admonitions, have been accepted with respect and gratitude. In the privacy secured by the chaplain's visits to the cells, appeals can be made to individual conscience which cannot be so efficiently done in a congregation.

I have given some attention to the schools, and noted some progress in several instances in reading and writing.

Every assistance is given me in the performance of my duties by the efficient governor and the entire staff of officers.

I am, sir, your faithful servant,

S. G. MORRISON.

The Chairman of the General Prisons Board, Dublin Castle.

MOUNTJOY FEMALE CONVICT PRISON.

MOUNTJOY FEMALE CONVICT PRISON.

SUPERINTENDENT'S REPORT.

Superintendent's Report.

Mountjoy Female Prison,
24th April, 1882.

SIR,—I have the honour to submit my annual report for the year ended 31st March, 1882, with usual statistical returns.

The Officers (except those specially brought under the notice of the Board) discharged their duties efficiently.

During the year the conduct of both convicts and local prisoners has been good, and all were most industrious.

The numbers continue to decrease, so that it has not been found necessary to fill up seven vacancies which occurred on the staff.

The school works well.

The religious instruction of the prisoners has been carefully attended to by the respective chaplains and lady visitors.

I certify that the rules laid down for the government of the prison have been complied with, except in such cases as have been reported to you.

I have the honour to be, Sir,

Your obedient servant,

ANNE SHEERAN, Superintendent.

The Chairman, General Prisons Board, Dublin Castle.

MOUNTJOY FEMALE CONVICT PRISON.

Superintendent's Report.

RETURN of the Number of CONVICTS received and disposed of from 1st April, 1881, to 31st March, 1882.

	Convicts.	Children.
In confinement 1st April, 1881,	139	2
Received during the year,	40	-
Born,	-	-
Total,	179	2
Discharged, sentence completed,	11	-
Discharged on license,	17	-
Transferred to Lunatic asylum,	2	-
Transferred to Refuges, viz.:—Protestant, 5; Roman Catholics, 35,	40	-
Died,	1	-
Sent to Nurse,	-	2
Total disposed of,	71	2
Remaining in custody 31st March, 1882,	108	-

AGES (ON CONVICTION) OF CONVICTS NOW IN CUSTODY.

15 years and under 20 years,	2
20 " 25 "	9
25 " 30 "	14
30 " 35 "	14
35 " 40 "	14
40 " 45 "	20
45 years and upwards,	35
Total,	108

Age of oldest prisoner on conviction, 73 years.

Age of youngest prisoner on conviction, 15 years.

NUMBER OF PRISONERS NOW IN CUSTODY WHO WERE CONVICTED IN THE FOLLOWING YEARS.

In the year 1864,	1
" 1868,	1
" 1871,	1
" 1872,	2
" 1873,	2
" 1874,	1
" 1875,	6
" 1876,	2
" 1877,	18
" 1878,	11
" 1879,	20
" 1880,	15
" 1881,	22
" 1882,	5
Total,	108

SENTENCES of PRISONERS now in CUSTODY.

Penal Servitude for Life,	18
" 20 years,	2
" 10 "	7
" 8 "	1
Penal Servitude for 7 years,	51
" 5 "	34
Total,	108

CRIMES of PRISONERS now in CUSTODY.

Assault and robbery, and previous conviction,	1
Assault,	1
Arson,	3
Base coin,	2
Child stealing,	1
Feloniously receiving stolen goods,	1
Felony from dwelling, and previous conviction,	1
Felony, and previous conviction,	5
Housebreaking,	1
Infanticide,	1
Larceny,	23
Larceny, and previous conviction,	37
Manslaughter,	7
Murder,	12
Malicious assault, causing bodily harm,	1
Perjury,	1
Receiving stolen goods, and previous conviction,	7
Stealing money from person,	3
Total,	108

Number of CONVICTS in CUSTODY on the first day of each month during the year ended 31st March, 1882.

April,	139
May,	134
June,	133
July,	135
August,	133
September,	113
October,	110
November,	109
December,	109
January,	110
February,	112
March,	110

School.

SCHOOL.

Number of days on which prisoners were taught,	298
Average on rolls for the year,	112
Average daily attendance,	46
Newly admitted,	34

Mountjoy Female Convict Prison. — *Superintendent's Report.*

Those received during the year were examined on reception, and classified as under:—

First Book, wholly illiterate, - - - - -	6
Able to read badly, - - - - - -	22
„ fairly, - - - - - - -	6
Total, - - -	34

The annexed table shows the advances in the several classes:—

Advanced during the year:—

From First to Second Book, - - - - -	10
„ Second to Third „ - - - - -	12
„ Third to Fourth „ - - - - -	16
Learned to write, - - - - - - -	29
„ to make figures, - - - - - -	23
Advanced from Simple Addition to Simple Subtraction, - -	15
„ to Compound Rules, - - - - -	12

Return by the Superintendent, showing how Convicts have been Employed during the year ending 31st March, 1882, and the Earnings of those engaged in such Employment; also showing the average daily number of Unemployed from Sickness and other reasons.

Description of Employment.	Daily Average Number of Prisoners employed, unemployed, &c.			Net Profit on Work done by Prisoners.	Estimated Value of the Work done for the Prison.			Total.		
	Males.	Females.	Total.							
				£ s. d.	£	s.	d.	£	s.	d.
Tailors, ...	—	3·85	3·85	—	64	15	9	64	15	9
Service of prison, ...	—	25·91	25·91	—	262	11	1	262	11	1
Washing clothing and bedding, ...	—	40·96	40·96	—	2,004	17	7	2,004	17	7
Making bedding and clothing,	—	37·20	37·20	—	110	14	2	110	14	2
Sick, ...	—	7·42	7·42	—	—			—		
Unemployed, ...	—	3·70	3·70	—	—			—		
Total, . . .	—	110·04	119·04	—	2,442	18	7	2,442	18	7

Estimated Value of Convict Prisoners' Labour for the year ended 31st March, 1882.

How employed.	Average No. of Prisoners employed daily.	Estimated Value of the Work performed.		
		£	s.	d.
Sewing and knitting prison materials, - -	37·20 (Sewing and knitting prison materials; Sewing for customers)	95	7	11
Sewing for customers, - - - - - -		15	6	3
Tailoring, - - - - - - -	3·85	64	15	9
Washing prison clothing, bedding, &c., - -	40·96 (Washing prison clothing, bedding, &c., and all washing for others below)	118	9	9
„ for Mountjoy Male Prison, - - -		178	17	7
„ for Lusk Prison, - - - - -		7	0	0
„ for General Prisons Board, - - -		9	7	6
„ for prison officers, - - - - -		17	10	8
„ for Royal Irish Constabulary Depot, - -		90	8	6
„ for Department of National Education, -		421	7	5
„ for Royal Hospital, - - - -		221	8	2
„ for Royal Hibernian Military School, -		936	4	0
„ for Mountjoy Barracks, - - - -		4	4	0
Cooking, nursing, cleaning for 304 working days, at 6*d*. per day, - - - - - - -	25·91	262	11	1
Total, - - - - -	—	2,442	18	7

Daily average number of convict prisoners in custody during the year,	119·04
Per-centage on prison population working, - - - -	90·56
„ „ in punishment, - - -	3·09
„ „ sick or infirm, - - -	6·35

MOUNTJOY FEMALE CONVICT PRISON.

Medical Officer's Report.

MEDICAL OFFICER'S REPORT.

Mountjoy Female Convict Prison,
18th April, 1882.

SIR,—I have the honour to submit my annual report of the sanitary condition of this prison, for the year ending 31st March, 1882, which has been most satisfactory. Only one death occurred during the year—that of a prisoner (M. A. T.) sent here on 19th December last, in very delicate health. She was admitted to hospital on the day following. It soon became evident she was in an advanced stage of pulmonary phthisis, and her death occurred on 28th March, 1882.

The prison was free from any epidemic or contagious disease, and the daily average of complaining sick was light, as were also the admissions to hospital—which is owing in a great measure to the decrease in the number of committals, as well as to the healthy state of the population.

It was found necessary to transmit two convicts to the Central Asylum—one of whom was stated to have been in an asylum previously, the other exhibited unmistakeable symptoms of mental debility on her reception.

Eleven matrons were treated in hospital, and six were obliged to retire from the service on the ground of health.

I have to reiterate what has been said in previous reports, that were it not for the assistance and co-operation of Mrs. Sheeran, the superintendent, it would be difficult for me to manage the capricious and sometimes irresponsible characters brought before me, but with her help it is made comparatively easy.

I have the honour to be, sir,
Your obedient servant,
J. W. YOUNG, M.D., Medical Officer.

The Chairman, General Prisons Board,
Dublin Castle.

TABLE I.—HOSPITAL RETURN for the year ending 31st March, 1882.

Number of patients in hospital, 1st April, 1881,	6	48
" " admitted during the year,	42	
" " discharged,	37	48
" " sent to lunatic asylum,	2	
" " died in hospital,	1	
" " remaining in hospital 1st April, 1882,	8	
Daily average of sick in hospital,		7·42
Externs prescribed for,		368
Daily average prescribed for,		1

TABLE II.—DISEASES of those admitted to Hospital.

Tonsillitis,	2	Abscess,	1
Cutaneous,	2	Epilepsy,	1
Debility,	6	Tumour,	1
Ulcer,	1	Swelled knee,	1
Febrile attacks,	3	Bilious attacks,	3
Syphilis,	1	Phthisis,	1
Gumboil,	1	Bronchitis,	1
Ranula,	1	Scald,	1
Colds,	4	Diarrhœa,	1
Asthma,	1	Hysteria,	1
Observation,	3	Uterine,	1
Rheumatism,	3	Hæmorrhoids,	1

Mountjoy Female Convict Prison.

TABLE III.—CONVICTS transferred to Central Asylum.

Medical Officer's Report.

Register No.	Initials of Name.	Where convicted.	Date of Conviction.	Removed to Prison.	Transferred to Asylum.
B. 51	E. R.	Parsonstown, .	8 June, 1881,	16 June, 1881,	11 Oct., 1881.
B. 54	E. R.	Dublin, . .	10 June, 1881,	20 June, 1881,	10 Sep., 1881.

PROTESTANT CHAPLAIN'S REPORT.

Protestant Chaplain's Report.

Mountjoy Female Prison,
April 24th, 1882.

SIR,—In submitting my report for the year ending 31st March, 1882, I have much pleasure in stating that the prisoners under my care have been earnestly attentive to the Sunday and week-day services in the Church, and that they have earned throughout the prison the character of being well-conducted women.

Their industry is spoken of, most favourably, by the matrons who have charge of them.

Order and peace prevail, and this is doubtless owing in a great degree to the mild and considerate, but withal, firm rule of the Superintendent; the advantage of whose knowledge and judgment I have availed myself in dealing with the prisoners, and always with satisfaction. The different officers of the prison have been without an exception—kindly and attentive.

Our lady visitors continue to attend for the purpose of giving religious and moral instruction; and to their influence likewise, we are indebted for the satisfactory account of the prisoners, which, as I have before said, I have much satisfaction in giving.

I remain, sir, your obedient servant,

DAVID STUART, Protestant Chaplain.

To the Chairman, General Prisons Board,
Dublin Castle.

ROMAN CATHOLIC CHAPLAINS' REPORT.

Roman Catholic Chaplains' Report.

Mountjoy Female Convict Prison,
April, 1882.

SIR,—We beg to submit our report for the year ending March, 1882

The conduct of the Catholic prisoners, with few exceptions, was good, and their attention to their religious duties marked. Habits of industry acquired during their stay in prison, combined with a more accurate knowledge of the truths of faith and the strengthening grace of the Sacraments, give good grounds for hope that most of them will never return to their evil ways again.

We recommend the wayward amongst them to the kindness and charity of the officers, for it is only in this way that good impressions can be made on them.

We beg to return our best thanks to the Superintendent and the other officers who have kindly assisted us in the discharge of our duties.

We have the honour to be, sir,

Your obedient servants,

MICHAEL WALSH, R.C.C.
TERENCE O'DONNELL, A.R.C.C.

To the Chairman, General Prisons Board.

MOUNTJOY FEMALE CONVICT PRISON.

Presbyterian Chaplain's Report.

PRESBYTERIAN CHAPLAIN'S REPORT.

Mountjoy Female Prison,
April 20, 1882.

SIR,—In perusing my journal for 1881, I notice nothing calling for any particular remarks. With a very few exceptions I have performed all the duties of my chaplaincy, and in my absence, by permission of the Prisons Board, my assistant, the Rev. William Tait, LL.D., officiated for me.

From the beginning of the year, for some time, I visited the Prison once during the week, and performed divine service every Sabbath; but from February 27th, I have visited, in addition to Sabbath attendance, two days during each week.

I have had but few prisoners under my care during the year, and the year closed with but two—one convict and one county prisoner.

As in all former years I have had continued all the attention and assistance that could be rendered to me, from the active and efficient Superintendent, to the most recently appointed assistant,

I am, sir, your faithful servant,

S. G. MORRISON.

The Chairman of the General Prisons Board,
Dublin Castle.

SPIKE ISLAND CONVICT PRISON.

Governor's Report.

3.—SPIKE ISLAND CONVICT PRISON.

GOVERNOR'S REPORT.

Spike Island Government Prison,
May, 1882.

SIR,—I have the honour to submit my annual report for the year ended the 31st March, 1882.

The usual statistical returns for the year have been already forwarded.

Twenty-two warders joined the staff, eighteen of which were on promotion from other prisons; eight were transferred to other prisons; three on promotion; three were dismissed the service from Maryborough Prison, where they were at the time on special duty from this staff; six resigned the service; and four were discharged on medical grounds. The general conduct of the staff has been, on the whole, very satisfactory; the chief warder and principal warders were attentive and zealous in the discharge of their respective duties; and Mr. Murphy, Deputy-Governor, rendered me very efficient assistance in the supervision generally.

Nothing requiring special notice occurred during the year. The daily routine has been strictly observed in all its details, and the prisoners were employed precisely in the same manner as described in former reports—that is, the larger proportion on the Government Dock at Haulbowline Island, the remainder at Spike Island, some on Royal Engineer works, the others in the service of the prison at their respective trades, such as shoemakers, tailors, carpenters, smiths, gardening, and fatigue work generally. The invalids were employed either in the prison garden or at oakum-picking. With some few exceptions, I observed a willing desire on the part of the prisoners generally to work in a steady, regular manner, and their conduct generally was satisfactory.

SPIKE ISLAND CONVICT PRISON.

Governor's Report.

Selections for trades were made from the well-conducted as usual, viz., masons, stone-cutters, carpenters, smiths, &c., and it is a matter of surprise that they become handy and useful in so short a time. Of course they are allowed to select the trade for which they may have a taste or fancy, and in this way they take to it so much more kindly and with better will. I would again respectfully submit that if the convict labour could be carried on under the direct control of the prison department, supervised by an experienced and responsible officer, a very much greater amount of work could be obtained. I have long since arrived at this conclusion, from many years close observation of the present system.

The statistical returns show the number of prisoners received during the year, and how disposed of. Three prisoners were sent to Dundrum Lunatic Asylum on medical certificates.

There were no attempts at escape, and no case of corporal punishment. Some few cases of assaults were committed on warders, but none of a serious or aggravated nature.

Small parties of convicts from here, with their officers, are still employed at Cork and Maryborough prisons in carrying out alterations and repairs.

Daily average number employed, . .	355
Not employed (in cells and hospital), . .	22
Total daily average, . .	377

The prison buildings (with the exception of the roof of one block, and the flooring in a portion of another block) may be considered in fair order. The necessary repairs have been provided for in the estimates of the current year. The respective chaplains have been punctual in their attendance both on Sundays and week-day duties. The school duties were carried on by Mr. Ryan with his usual zeal and attention.

I have not seen or received intimation of any abuse or abuses not reported by me; and I hereby certify that the rules laid down for the government of the prison have been complied with during the past year, except in such cases as have been reported to or brought under the notice of the Board.

I have the honour to be, sir,

Your most obedient servant,

P. HAY, Governor.

The Chairman, General Prisons Board,
Dublin Castle.

[ABSTRACT.

SPIKE ISLAND CONVICT PRISON.

(Governor's Report.)

ABSTRACT ACCOUNT showing the ESTIMATED VALUE of the PRODUCTIVE LABOUR of the Prisoners, and the NUMBER EMPLOYED during the Year ended 31st March, 1882.

How Employed.	Daily Average Number Employed for 304 days.		Estimated Value of Work performed.			Total.		
			£	s.	d.	£	s.	d.
PRISON WORKS.								
Tailors, - - - - -	12		456	0	0			
Shoemakers, - - - - -	9		342	0	0			
Carpenters, - - - - -	2		76	0	0			
Smiths and Nailers, - - -	1		45	12	0			
Do. beginners, -	1		22	16	0			
Painters, - - - -	1		38	0	0			
Masons, - - - - -	2		91	4	0			
Bakers, - - - - -	6		273	12	0			
Tinsmiths and Coopers, - -	1		30	8	0			
Repairing Beds, Socks, &c., - -	6		91	4	0			
Labourers in Prison Garden and on Prison Works generally, - -	36		449	9	10			
Washing in Laundry, - -	6		182	8	0			
Cooks, - - - - -	5		76	0	0			
Fatigue work, Cleaning, and Messing,	17		258	8	0			
Boatmen, - - - - -	6		91	4	0			
		111				2,524	5	10
ROYAL ENGINEER WORKS.								
Labourers, - - - - -	50		760	0	0			
		50				760	0	0
WAR DEPARTMENT (HAULBOWLINE).								
Labourers, - - - - -	9		205	4	0			
		9				205	4	0
ADMIRALTY WORKS.								
Stonecutters and Masons, - -	37		1,499	14	8			
Do. do. beginners, -	9		182	8	0			
Carpenters, - - - - -	5		202	13	4			
Do. beginners, - -	4		91	4	0			
Smiths, - - - - -	2		81	1	4			
Do. beginners, - - -	9		205	4	0			
Labourers, Quarrymen, &c., -	98		1,986	2	8			
Picking oakum (on wet days and penal class), - - -	8		30	8	0			
Do. (Invalids), - -	13		16	9	4			
		185				4,295	5	4
Total, - - -		355				7,784	15	2

Daily average number employed, - - - -	355
" " not employed (in cells and hospital), -	22
Total daily average, - - -	377

[RETURN.

SPIKE ISLAND CONVICT PRISON.

Governor's Report.

RETURN showing the CRIMES of 379 CONVICTS in CUSTODY, 31st March, 1882.

Murder,	11	Stealing from the person,	27
Shooting at with intent to murder,	3	Larceny and previous conviction,	97
Assault with intent to murder,	1	Cattle stealing,	7
Attempting to kill and murder,	1	Horse stealing,	3
Manslaughter,	35	Sheep stealing,	7
Stabbing, cutting, and wounding,	7	Receiving stolen goods,	10
Felonious, grievous, malicious, and other assaults,	14	Obtaining goods and money by false pretences,	6
Assault and robbery,	10	Having base coin in possession,	4
Assault with intent to rob,	7	Sodomy,	4
Unlawfully assembling and breaking into habitation,	2	Buggery,	1
Highway robbery,	2	Carnal knowledge of females under 12 years of age,	3
Burglary and robbery, and previous conviction,	26	Abduction,	1
Robbery and attempt to rob,	9	Arson,	6
Rape and aiding,	17	Placing wood and an iron bar on a railway,	2
Housebreaking and robbery,	37	Military offences,	9
Felony and previous conviction,	6	Misdemeanour,	1
Forgery,	1		
Uttering forged bank-notes	2	Total,	379

RETURN showing the NUMBER of CONVICTS in CUSTODY, committed and disposed of during the Year ended 31st March, 1882.

		HOW DISPOSED OF.	
1st April, 1881—		31st March, 1882—	
In custody,	395	Remaining in custody,	379
Committed from—		Removed during the year to—	
Mountjoy Male Prison,	92	Mountjoy,	22
Cork Male Prison,	17	Mountjoy for Lusk,	28
Maryborough Prison	18	Mountjoy for discharge on completion of sentence,	9
		Mountjoy for release on license,	5
		Maryborough Prison,	12
		Cork Male Prison,	12
		Dundrum Lunatic Asylum,	3
		Released on license,	33
		Released on license on Medical Grounds,	1
		Discharged on completion of sentence,	13
		Discharged on commutation of sentence,	1
		Died,	4
Total,	522	Total,	522

RETURN showing the SENTENCES and the AGES on CONVICTION of 379 CONVICTS in CUSTODY, 31st March, 1882.

SENTENCES.

Five Years' Penal Servitude,	129	Life penal servitude,	22
Seven " "	139	Life transportation,	1
Ten " "	50		
Twelve " "	2		
Fourteen " "	15		
Fifteen " "	9		
Twenty " "	12		
	356		23

Total, 379.

AGES ON CONVICTION.

Under Twenty Years,	38	Fifty and under Sixty,	21
Twenty and under Twenty-five,	85	Sixty and under Seventy,	5
Twenty-five and under Thirty,	66	Seventy and under Eighty,	4
Thirty and under Thirty-five,	58	Eighty and under Ninety,	2
Thirty-five and under Forty,	39		
Forty and under Fifty,	61	Total,	379

Spike Island Convict Prison.

Governor's Report.

Return by the Governor, showing how Prisoners have been Employed during the year ending 31st March, 1882, and the Earnings of those engaged in such Employment; also showing the average daily number of Unemployed from Sickness and other reasons.

Description of Employment.	Daily Average Number of Prisoners employed, unemployed, &c.			Net Profit on Work done by Prisoners.			Estimated Value of the Work done for the Prison.			Total.		
	Males.	Females.	Total.	£	s.	d.	£	s.	d.	£	s.	d.
Gardening,	15	—	15	130	5	10		—		130	5	10
Tailors,	16	—	16		—		570	0	0	570	0	0
Shoemakers,	12	—	12		—		440	16	0	440	16	0
Carpenters,	22	—	22		—		810	13	4	810	13	4
Bricklayers, masons and labourers,	198	—	198		—		3,700	0	4	3,700	0	4
Painters and glaziers,	3	—	3		—		114	0	0	114	0	0
Tinsmiths and coopers,	2	—	2	48	0	0	33	8	0	81	8	0
Blacksmiths and nailors,	15	—	15		—		436	15	4	436	15	4
Whitewashers,	2	—	2		—		36	10	0	36	10	0
Pumping water,	6	—	6		—		91	4	0	91	4	0
Service of prison,	23	—	23		—		361	16	0	361	16	0
Washing clothing and bedding,	7	—	7		—		202	8	0	202	8	0
Repairing bedding & clothing,	6	—	6		—		91	4	0	91	4	0
Stonecutters,	52	—	52		—		1,830	12	0	1,830	12	0
Bakers,	6	—	6		—		273	12	0	273	12	0
Cooks,	8	—	8		—		121	12	0	121	12	0
Boatmen,	6	—	6		—		91	4	0	91	4	0
Plasterers,	3	—	3		—		106	8	0	106	8	0
Picking oakum,	31	—	31		—		46	17	4	46	17	4
Sick,	13	—	13		—			—			—	
Unemployed,	0	—	0		—			—			—	
Total,	445	—	445	178	5	10	8,439	8	4	8,617*	14	2

Return of the several Industrial and Trades' pursuits in which Convicts were employed during the year ended 31st March, 1882, viz.:—

Tailoring.
Shoemaking.
Carpentering.
Bricklaying and masoning.
Plastering.
Stonecutting.
Painting.
Tinsmith work.
Coopering.
Blacksmith work.
Nail making.
Baking.
Cooking.
Washing in laundry.
Repairing beds and socks.
Boatmen.
Labouring.
Picking oakum.
Fatigue work, cleaning and messing.

Medical Officer's Report.

MEDICAL OFFICER'S REPORT.

Spike Island Convict Prison,
28th April, 1882.

Sir,—I have the honour to submit the annual report on the state of health of the officers and prisoners, and on the general sanitary condition of this prison, with the usual medical statistics, for the year ended 31st March last.

During the year there were forty-seven warders admitted into hospital for ordinary ailments, four of whom, being found medically to be permanently unfitted for the further performance of their duties, were discharged the service. There was no death.

* £1,833 of this sum is the estimated value of the labour of the convicts belonging to Spike Island, and temporarily employed at Cork and Maryborough Prisons.

Spike Island Convict Prison.

Medical Officer's Report.

There were ninety-two convicts received here from Mountjoy Male Prison during the year, ten of whom being found in delicate health received special attention and treatment, and were placed at labour most suitable to their conditions.

During the year there were 149 convicts treated in hospital, chiefly for diseases of the respiratory and digestive systems, debility, simple continued fever, rheumatism, tonsillitis, ulcers, abscesses, wounds, and contusions. There were four deaths—one from chronic bronchitis, one from effusion on the brain, one from cancer of the stomach, and one from pneumonia.

During the year there were three prisoners transferred to Dundrum Criminal Lunatic Asylum, one of whom, on reception, was reported to be labouring under melancholy; in either of the other two cases there was no record of any mental disturbance. There was one convict released from prison on medical grounds; he was delicate when received into this prison.

It is pleasing to be able to state that during the year no epidemic appeared. There was no case of infectious or contagious disease, no serious accident occurred, nor was there any attempt at suicide.

The general sanitary condition of the prison has been, as in past years, most satisfactory; the prison dietaries were wholesome, ample, and sufficiently varied; the water was good in quality, and the supply abundant; the ventilation was good; the clothing and bedding supplied to the prisoners being comfortable and warm; the labour was well regulated and exercised no unfavourable influence on their state of health.

The Governor and the other prison officials invariably rendered me effective assistance. The resident apothecary performed his duties in a most satisfactory manner.

I have the honour to be, sir,

Your most obedient servant,

P. O'Keeffe, M.D., Medical Officer.

The Chairman, General Prisons Board,
Dublin Castle.

MEDICAL STATISTICS for the Year ended 31st March, 1882.

Number of sick remaining in hospital on the 1st April, 1881, -	18
" admitted during the year, - - - -	149
Total, - - - - - - -	167
Of these were discharged from hospital, - - - -	138
Died during the year, - - - - - -	4
Remaining in hospital on the 1st April, 1882, - - -	25
Total, - - -	167
Daily average number of sick treated in hospital during the year, -	12·82
Number of externs treated during the year, - - -	11,707
Daily average number of externs treated during the year, - -	32
Number of Warders treated in hospital during the year, - -	47
Number of Warders who died during the year, - - -	–
Number of Warders discharged the service on medical grounds, -	4
Number of Prisoners released from Prison on medical grounds, -	1
Number of Prisoners transferred to Dundrum Criminal Lunatic Asylum, - - - - - - - -	3

Spike Island Convict Prison.

Medical Officer's Report.

Number of Diseases treated in Hospital during the Year.

Pneumonia, bronchitis, and other diseases of the respiratory organs,	43	Retention of urine, - - -	1
Diseases of the digestive system, -	27	Periostitis, - - - -	1
Tonsillitis, - - - - -	7	Fracture of rib, - - -	1
Diseases of the circulatory system,	2	Wounds and contusions, - -	6
Febrile diseases, - - -	11	Abscess, - - - -	6
Cancer of the stomach, - -	1	Epilepsy, - - - -	3
Rheumatism, - - -	6	Erysipelas, - - - -	2
Ulcers, - - - -	7	Herpes, - - - -	1
Hæmorrhoids, - - -	1	Furuncula, - - - -	1
Stricture of the urethra, - -	1	Œdema, - - - -	1
Debility, - - - -	16	Total, - - -	149
Ophthalmia, - - -	1		

MORTALITY TABLE.

Register Number.	Initials of Name.	Date of Admission into Hospital.	Date of Death.	Cause of Death.
14,283	D. D.	17 July, 1877,	21 May, 1881,	Chronic bronchitis.
14,635	J. Q.	14 March, 1881,	1 July, 1881,	Effusion on the brain.
14,846	T. H.	23 April, 1881,	29 Aug., 1881,	Cancer of stomach.
A 236	D. M.	7 Feb., 1882,	8 March, 1881,	Pneumonia.

List of Prisoners released from Prison on Medical Grounds.

Register No.	Initials of Name.	Date of reception at Spike Island.	Where convicted.	Crime.	Disease.
14,873	F. D.	24 Sep., 1879,	Londonderry	Manslaughter,	Bronchitis.

List of Prisoners transferred to Dundrum Criminal Lunatic Asylum.

Register No.	Initials of Name.	Date of reception at Spike Island.	Where convicted.	Crime.	Date of removal to Asylum.
A 242	J. C.	9 Sep., 1881,	Dublin, .	Burglary, . .	28 Nov., 1881.
14,935	E. W.	10 Jan., 1882,	Dublin, .	Housebreaking, .	17 Feb., 1882.
14,898	J. F.	22 July, 1880,	Galway, .	Manslaughter, .	15 March, 1882.

Protestant Chaplain's Report.

PROTESTANT CHAPLAIN'S REPORT.

Queenstown, April 29, 1882.

SIR,—I am thankful to report favourably of the Episcopalian convicts committed to my charge during the year closing March 31, 1882.

The services of the Church have been attended with much reverence and devotion. The Sacrament of the Lord's Supper administered to several of the convicts desiring it. The weekly instructions regularly conducted, and the cells and hospital duly visited during the past year, I believe with spiritual benefit to many of the prisoners.

In some cases I have been cheered by an evident improvement in conduct as reported to me by others, as well as observed by myself, and one who recently died gave satisfactory proof of sincere repentance and humble faith in the merits and salvation of Christ.

The circulation of religious books each Sunday is welcomed by many who seem to enjoy and profit by their perusal. The library is very limited, and some new well-selected works would be a great boon and benefit to the prisoners.*

SPIKE ISLAND CONVICT PRISON.

Protestant Chaplain's Report.

With the Governor's sanction, I have formed a very efficient choir, and allow only well conducted prisoners to join it. The church service is thus rendered more interesting, whilst the memories of all are being stored with instructive truths which I find in my hospital visits and occasional intercourse, influential and consoling.

The Sunday School held outside the Prison for the children of Protestant warders increases in attendance and interest.

If the prison admitted of a better classification more could be done, but under the circumstances I believe the best is done.

I have the honour to be, sir,

Your faithful servant,

M. A. COOKE COLLIS, D.D., Protestant Chaplain.

To the Chairman, General Prisons Board.

ROMAN CATHOLIC CHAPLAIN'S REPORT.

Roman Catholic Chaplain's Report.

Spike Island, 10th May, 1882.

SIR,—I beg leave to forward to you my report for the year ending 31st March, 1882, as the Roman Catholic Chaplain of Spike Island Convict Prison.

I regret that it is not in my power to give a more favourable report of the religious and moral condition of the Roman Catholic prisoners during the last year than during several previous years, although it was a year of jubilee when the greatest efforts were made to produce a better sense and a better practice among them. I even got a religious mission to be conducted in the prison by six neighbouring clergymen to accomplish that desirable object, but the corrupting influence of the close association of the prisoners here, soon destroyed all the good that was done by the jubilee and by the mission, as well as by the discipline of the prison. And this uncontrollable evil must continue until the prison is reconstructed into proper separate cells as at Mountjoy prison, and now in all the county gaols in Ireland. It is then much to be regretted that Spike Island Prison, where all the convicts pass most of their penal servitude, and where their chief reformation should be effected, is still left without that essential improvement.

I have the honour to be, sir,

Your very obedient servant,

T. F. LYONS, R.C. Chaplain.

The Chairman of the Prisons Board, Dublin Castle.

ASSISTANT ROMAN CATHOLIC CHAPLAIN'S REPORT.

Assistant Roman Catholic Chaplain's Report.

Spike Island, April, 1882.

SIR,—I have the honour to submit my report for the year ending 31st March, 1882.

In doing so, I am glad to be able to state that the religious and moral condition of the Roman Catholic prisoners has been, on the whole, satisfactory.

The great majority of them have been attentive to their religious duties, having approached the Sacrament once or twice at least during the year, whilst a large number have been frequent communicants. I

* The Governor has been communicated with about this matter.

SPIKE ISLAND CONVICT PRISON.

Assistant Roman Catholic Chaplain's Report.

have pleasure also in bearing testimony to their edifying demeanour in the chapel during mass and religious instruction.

I regret, however, to be obliged to repeat what I have already adverted to in former reports, viz., the sad results arising from the indiscriminate association of the good and bad on the public works, as well as from the defective construction of the prison. These are matters that have been already condemned by competent authorities, and until they be rectified I fear it is hopeless to expect a thorough reformation of the criminal classes. The truth of the maxim "Evil communications corrupt good morals" have no where, I venture to say, been more strikingly exemplified than in the case of the unfortunate convicts located in this prison.

During the year, I have, as usual, celebrated mass twice a week for the warders and prisoners, and visited daily the sick in hospital, as well as the defaulters in the punishment cells.

I beg, in conclusion, to bear testimony to the uniform kindness and efficient support I have invariably received at the hands of the Governor and the entire prison staff.

I have the honour to be, sir,

Your most obedient servant,

J. O'CONNOR, A.R.C.C.

The Chairman, General Prisons Board, Dublin Castle.

Presbyterian Chaplain's Report.

PRESBYTERIAN CHAPLAIN'S REPORT.

Spike Island, 22nd April, 1882.

SIR,—I beg to present to you my report for the year ending the 31st March, 1882.

Nothing has arisen in the bygone year calling for any special notice beyond what I have had the honour of laying before you in former reports.

I have regularly performed all the duties of my office, including the visitation of the sick in the Hospital, and of the misdemeanants in the punishment cells.

I have the honour to be, sir,

Your very obedient servant,

WM. J. KERTLAND, LL.D., Presbyterian Chaplain.

To the Chairman of the General Prisons Board, Dublin Castle

LUSK CONVICT PRISON.

Superintendent's Report.

4.—LUSK CONVICT PRISON.

SUPERINTENDENT'S REPORT.

Lusk Convict Prison, 23rd April, 1882.

SIR,—I beg leave to submit the usual annual report on this prison and farm for the year ending 31st March, 1882.

On the 1st April, 1881, in custody at Lusk 37 convicts; received during the year, 60, making a total of 97. They have been disposed of as follows:—61 released on licence; removed to Mountjoy Male Prison, misconduct, 5; removed to Spike Island, own request, 1; removed to Mountjoy Male Prison, 1, own request; leaving at Lusk on the 31st

March, 1882, convicts, 29; the daily average being 32·3 for the year. The conduct and industry has been very good, with one or two exceptions, and owing to the constant attention given by the warders, who work with the men and encourage them on, many have been made good farm labourers who have had no knowledge of such work, the larger portion being from the cities and other large towns of Ireland. We have had no absconding, or attempts at such, during the year. The convicts attend school each evening after working hours, and Mr. Daly reports willingness to learn and improve themselves. We have had two changes on the prison staff during the year. The Protestant chaplain resigned, and the Rev. A. D. Purefoy was appointed chaplain. The R. C. Chaplain, the Rev. N. O. Farrell, died during the year, and Rev. M. J. Gibney was appointed chaplain. Both Protestant and R. C. chaplains were very kind to the convicts, and took a deep interest in their future well-doing, which caused much regret at their loss.

LUSK CONVICT PRISON.

Superintendent's Report.

The usual farm works have been carried out, and the crops, cattle, sheep, and horses and pigs have done well, without any loss by accident or disease. Fifty-two cattle have been stall fed, 5 milch cows attended to, their calves reared, nearly 200 sheep and lambs, and young horses broken in and worked. The quarry only in part worked, as we have not a sufficient number of hands for the purpose. Buildings kept in repair with usual tradesmen—smith, carpenter, mason, tailor, and shoemaker. I have much pleasure in reporting that I have been well assisted by every officer of the prison, which the present state of the farm and works show.

The usual statistics are annexed.

I have the honour to be, sir,

Your most obedient servant,

R. GUNNING, Superintendent.

The Chairman, General Prisons Board.

RETURN showing the Number of Convicts in custody during the year ended 31st March, 1882, and how they have been disposed of.

In custody 1st April, 1881,	37
Received from Mountjoy Male Convict Prison,	6
" from Spike Island "	28
" from Cork Male "	11
" from Maryborough "	15
Total,	97
Released on licence,	61
Removed to Mountjoy Male Prison—misconduct,	5
" " " own request,	1
" Spike Island *via* Mountjoy "	1
Remaining in custody, 31st March, 1882,	29
Total,	97
Daily average number in custody,	32·3

LUSK CONVICT PRISON.

Superintendent's Report.

CRIMES of 60 Prisoners received during the year ended 31st March, 1882.

Army offences,	1
Arson,	1
Assault and robbery,	3
,, with intent to rob,	1
,, felonious, and robbery from the person,	3
,, and stabbing,	1
Burglary,	4
Breaking and entering shop, and previous conviction,	1
,, into dwelling-house with intent to steal,	1
Felony of money with violence,	1
Forgery,	1
Housebreaking, and robbery,	4
Having in possession stolen money,	1
Larceny,	9
,, and previous conviction,	9
,, from person,	3
,, of cow, and previous conviction,	1
Manslaughter,	2
Rape,	3
Robbery,	2
,, and previous conviction,	1
,, with violence, and previous conviction,	2
Receiving stolen goods,	2
Setting fire to house to defraud,	1
Sheep stealing and previous conviction,	1
Stealing from person ,,	1
Total,	60

SENTENCES of 60 Convicts received during the year ended 31st March, 1882.

5 years' penal servitude,	37
7 ,, ,,	21
10 ,, ,,	1
14 ,, ,,	1
Total,	60

AGES on reception of 60 Convicts received during the year ended 31st March, 1882.

20 years and under 30,	29
30 ,, ,, 40,	16
40 ,, ,, 50,	11
50 ,, ,, 60,	3
60 years and upwards,	1
Total,	60

RETURN showing the reported Previous Convictions of 60 Convicts received in this Prison during the year ended 31st March, 1882.

Not reported to have been previously convicted,	10	Seven times,	2
Once,	11	Eight ,,	1
Twice,	9	Ten ,,	1
Three times,	8	Eleven ,,	3
Four ,,	4	Thirty-two ,,	1
Five ,,	6	Total,	60
Six ,,	4		

Of the above, 20 were convicted in Dublin.
,, 3 ,, Cork.
,, 7 ,, Belfast.
,, 25 ,, in other towns in Ireland.

ACCOUNT showing the value of Productive Labour of Prisoners at Lusk for the year ended 31st March, 1882.

Lusk Convict Prison.

Superintendent's Report.

Trades.	Amount. £	s.	d.	Observations.
Masons, - - -	71	12	6	
Carpenters, - - -	49	5	6	
Smiths, - - -	47	5	0	Daily average number, - - 32·3
Painters, - - -	8	3	6	Less sick, - - - ·46
Shoemakers, - -	31	1	7	
Tailors, - - -	36	6	0	31·84
	243	14	1	
25·45 prisoners employed quarrying and at general farm work, for 52 weeks, at 11s. per week, -	720	14	5	Average earning of each effective prisoner, £30 5s. 10d.
Total, - -	964	8	6	

MEDICAL OFFICER'S REPORT.

Medical Officer's Report.

Lusk Prison, 21st April, 1882.

SIR,—I have the honour of making the usual annual medical report of the state of this prison during the past year.

The health of the officers and prisoners has been excellent; their dietary has been carefully looked after; and the huts, bedding, &c., have been kept in the best order by Mr. Superintendent Gunning, and the other officers. Any medical requisites necessary for them have been promptly provided.

I have the honour to be, sir, your obedient servant,

F. J. B. QUINLAN, M.D., Dub., M.R.I.A.,
Fellow of the College of Physicians and Medical Superintendent.

To the Chairman of the General Prisons Board.

PROTESTANT CHAPLAIN'S REPORT.

Protestant Chaplain's Report.

The Vicarage, Lusk,
April 25, 1882.

GENTLEMEN,—Owing to the recent date of my appointment to the chaplaincy of Lusk Prison, I have not much matter for comment.

The demeanour of the convicts, both in church and at my Scripture classes, has been attentive and respectful.

I have not found them in most cases familiar with their Bibles, but they take an interest in the subject we consider weekly, and generally answer intelligently.

I always meet with every attention on the part of the officials connected with the prison.

I remain, gentlemen, obediently yours,

A. D. PUREFOY, Clk.

To the General Prisons Board.

LUSK CONVICT PRISON.

Roman Catholic Chaplain's Report.

ROMAN CATHOLIC CHAPLAIN'S REPORT.

The Presbytery, Lusk,
April 22nd, 1882.

GENTLEMEN,—It is with very great pleasure I write this, my first report, as R. C. Chaplain of the Reformatory Prison of Lusk. For, fully acquainted as I had been with the beneficent designs of the system carried out here, and knowing from past experience, as acting R. C. Chaplain in Smithfield Prison, how thoroughly effective that system had been in realizing the object it had in view—the honest, sincere reform of the criminal—I did feel it a pleasure indeed to find myself once more engaged in the same good and satisfactory work.

On my appointment, I found, as I had expected, that cordial goodwill and harmony between the officials and prisoners, that is, as it were, the keynote to the honest reform of the prisoner's heart. Where that honest confidence between prisoners and officials has been established and is maintained, together with the strict observance of the prison rules, the chaplain's duty is made a labour of love—for he finds ready and willing hearts to deal with, and at the same time every facility to move them, and open them to the influence of Divine Grace, on which alone in after life they must rely for perseverance in their good intentions and resolutions.

Hence it affords me no small or unexpected pleasure to report to your Board the very great gratification and satisfaction I have felt in my ministry at the prison. The prisoners are docile, orderly, and anxious to avail themselves of the aids of religion. The officials are courteous, attentive, and most willing to afford us every facility consistent with the prison rules. The superintendent (thoroughly imbued with the spirit of the system) is firm, yet gentle, determined, yet duly considerate, and hence esteemed and respected by all.

I am, gentlemen, faithfully yours,

M. J. GIBNEY.

RETURN by the SUPERINTENDENT, showing how Prisoners have been employed during the year ending 31st March, 1882, and the Earnings of those engaged in such Employment; also showing the average daily number of Unemployed from Sickness and other reasons.

Description of Employment.	Daily Average Number of Prisoners employed, unemployed, &c.			Net Profit on Work done by Prisoners.	Estimated Value of the Work done for the Prison.			Total.		
	Males.	Females.	Total.		£	s.	d.	£	s.	d.
Tailors,	1·16	—	1·16	—	36	6	0	36	6	0
Shoemakers,	·72	—	·72	—	31	1	7	31	1	7
Carpenters,	1·26	—	1·26	—	49	5	6	49	5	6
Bricklayers or masons, and labourers,	1·63	—	1·63	—	71	12	0	71	12	6
Painters and glaziers,	·21	—	·21	—	8	3	6	8	3	6
Blacksmiths,	1·21	—	1·21	—	47	5	0	47	5	0
Service of prison,	2·	—	2·	—	87	4	0	87	4	0
General farm labour, quarrying, &c.,	23·45	—	23·45	—	663	10	5	663	10	5
Sick,	·46	—	·46	—	—			—		
Total,	32·3	—	32·3	—	964	6	6	964	6	6

LUSK CONVICT PRISON.

Superintendent's Report.

RETURN of the several Industrial and Trades' pursuits in which Prisoners were employed during the year ending 31st March, 1882, viz.:—

Tailoring.—Repairing prisoners' clothing, &c. *Shoemaking.*—Repairing prisoners' navvy boots, &c. *Carpentry.*—Remaking prison carts, making cart wheels, erecting hay barn, repairing out-offices, farm implements, &c. *Masonry.*—Building new stables, repairing buildings, &c. *Painting.*—Painting farm implements, buildings, &c. *Smith-work.*—Repairing ploughs, harrows, and other farm machines and tools, shoeing horses, &c. *Labourers.*—General farm works, stall feeding, and attending cattle, sheep, and pigs, quarrying stones, making drains, levelling old fences, repairing roads, &c.

TABLE I.—RETURN showing the PROPORTION of SICK and DEATHS to the Number of Convicts, in the Irish Convict Prisons for the years 1854, 1855, 1856, 1857, 1858, and 1859.

—	1854.					1855.				
	Spike Island and Philipstown.	Cork and Grange-gorman.	Newgate and Smithfield.	Mountjoy.	Totals, 1854.	Spike Island and Philipstown.	Cork and Grange-gorman.	Newgate and Smithfield.	Mountjoy.	Totals, 1855.
No. of Convicts, .	2,290	339	556	443	3,628	1,777	488	430	452	3,147
Average daily No. of Sick, . .	276	25	46	21	368	203	36	65	17	321
No. of Deaths, .	241	6	33	9	289	101	8	31	9	149
Per-centage of Deaths on prison population, .	10·5	1·8	5·9	2·	8·	5·7	1·0	7·2	2·	4·7

—	1856.					1857.				
	Spike Island and Philipstown.	Cork and Grange-gorman.	Newgate and Smithfield.	Mountjoy.	Totals, 1856.	Spike Island and Philipstown.	Cork, Grange-gorman, and Newgate.	Smithfield and Lusk.	Mountjoy.	Totals, 1857.
No. of Convicts, .	1,619	613	199	421	2,852	1,329	686	70	357	2,442
Average daily No. of Sick, . .	101	42	35	16	194	67	37	6	16	126
No. of Deaths, .	35	11	5	3	54	34	6	2	3	45
Per-centage of Deaths on prison population, .	2·1	1·8	2·5	·7	1·9	2·6	·	2·9	·8	1·8

—	1858.					1859.				
	Spike Island and Philipstown.	Female Prisons.	Smithfield and Lusk.	Mountjoy Male.	Totals, 1858.	Spike Island and Philipstown.	Mountjoy Female.	Smithfield and Lusk.	Mountjoy Male.	Totals, 1859.
No. of Convicts, .	1,008	593	97	320	2,018	887	464	99	393	1,698
Average daily No. of Sick, . .	41	41	4	12	98	32	14	8	18	62
No. of Deaths, .	16	12	2	8	38	11	3	.	1	15
Per-centage of Deaths on prison population,	1·6	2·	8·6	0·9	1·6	1·3	0·6	·	0·3	0·9

RETURN showing the PROPORTION of SICK and DEATHS to the Number of Convicts in the Irish Convict Prisons for the years 1860, 1861, 1862, 1863, 1864, and 1865.

—	1860.					1861.				
	Spike Island and Philipstown.	Mountjoy Female.	Smithfield and Lusk.	Mountjoy Male.	Totals, 1860.	Spike Island and Philipstown.	Mountjoy Female.	Smithfield and Lusk.	Mountjoy Male.	Totals, 1861.
No. of Convicts, .	783	423	105	251	1,562	676	394	94	205	1,369
Average daily No. of Sick, . .	22	17	4	11	54	15	20	4	11	50
No. of Deaths, .	3	11	—	1	15	1	6	1	3	11
Per-centage of Deaths on Prison population, .	·3	2·6	—	·4	·96	·1	1·5	1·1	1·5	·80

—	1862.					1863.				
	Spike Island and Philipstown*	Mountjoy Female.	Smithfield and Lusk.	Mountjoy Male.	Totals, 1862.	Spike Island.	Mountjoy Female.	Smithfield and Lusk.	Mountjoy Male.	Totals 1863.
No. of Convicts, .	708	416	79	316	1,519	783	460	75	370	1,688
Average daily No. of Sick, .	14	27	4	17	62	9	26	4	17	56
No. of Deaths, .	8	10	—	5	23	10	4	—	5	19
Per-centage of Deaths on Prison population, .	1·1	2·4	—	1·5	1·5	1·2	·8	—	1·3	1·1

—	1864.					1865.				
	Spike Island	Mountjoy Female.	Smithfield and Lusk.	Mountjoy Male.	Totals, 1864.	Spike Island.	Mountjoy Female.	Smithfield and Lusk.	Mountjoy Male.	Totals, 1865.
No. of Convicts, .	918	499	99	290	1,806	901	486	105	221	1,713
Average daily No. of Sick, . .	8	30	8	16	62	8	28	5	19	60
No. of Deaths, .	7	13	2	10	32	10	10	2	2	24
Per-centage of Deaths of Prison population, .	·7	2·	2·0	3·4	1·7	1·1	·2	1·9	·9	1·

* Philipstown Prison was closed on the 31st March, 1863.

RETURN showing the PROPORTION of SICK and DEATHS to the Number of Convicts in the Irish Convict Prisons for the years 1866, 1867, 1868, 1869, and 1870.

1866.

—	Spike Island.	Mountjoy Female.	Smithfield and Lusk.	Mountjoy Male.	Total, 1866.
No. of Convicts,	799	462	96	191	1,548
Average daily No. of Sick,	12	23	3	10	48
No. of Deaths,	12	5	–	6	23
Per-centage of Deaths on prison population,	1·5	1·	–	3·1	1·4

1867.

—	Spike Island.	Mountjoy Female.	Smithfield and Lusk.	Mountjoy Male.	Total, 1867.
No. of Convicts,	722	426	80	159	1,387
Average daily No. of Sick,	12	24	3	8	47
No. of Deaths,	9	3	–	1	13
Per-centage of Deaths on prison population,	1·2	·7	–	·6	·9

1868.

—	Spike Island.	Mountjoy Female.	Smithfield and Lusk.	Mountjoy Male.	Total, 1868.
No. of Convicts,	696	409	74	154	1,333
Average daily No. of Sick,	12	24	3	3	42
No. of Deaths,	8	5	–	1	14
Per-centage of Deaths on prison population,	1·1	1·2	–	·6	·1

1869.

—	Spike Island.	Mountjoy Female.	Smithfield* and Lusk.	Mountjoy Male.	Total, 1869.
No. of Convicts,	682	389	81	144	1,296
Average daily No. of Sick,	12	22	3	3	40
No. of Deaths,	3	7	–	1	11
Per-centage of Deaths on prison population,	·4	1·7	–	·6	·8

1870.

—	Spike Island.	Mountjoy Female.	Lusk.	Mountjoy Male.	Total, 1870.
No. of Convicts,	675	340	61	157	1,233
Average daily No. of Sick,	15	19	·6	·4	38·6
No. of Deaths,	2	6	1	–	9
Per-centage of Deaths on prison population,	·2	1·7	1·5	–	·7

* Smithfield Prison was closed and the Prisoners transferred to Lusk on 18th June, 1869.

Return showing the **Proportion** of **Sick** and **Deaths** to the Number of Convicts in the Irish Convict Prisons for the years 1871, 1872, 1873, 1874, and 1875.

1871

—	Spike Island.	Mountjoy Female.	Lusk.	Mountjoy Male.	Total, 1871.
No. of Convicts,	694	333	61	135	1,223
Average daily No. of Sick,	11	22	·2	8	30·2
No. of Deaths,	4	5	–	1	10
Per-centage of Deaths on prison population,	·5	1·4	–	·7	·8

1872.

—	Spike Island.	Mountjoy Female.	Lusk.	Mountjoy Male.	Total, 1872.
No. of Convicts,	664	320	57	131	1,172
Average daily No. of Sick,	13	13	·4	8	31·4
No. of Deaths,	8	5	–	–	13
Per-centage of Deaths on prison population,	1·2	1·5	–	–	1·1

1873.

—	Spike Island.	Mountjoy Female.	Lusk.	Mountjoy Male.	Total, 1873.
No. of Convicts,	640	299	45	145	1,129
Average daily No. of Sick,	11	13	·2	6	30·2
No. of Deaths,	8	5	–	1	14
Per-centage of Deaths on prison population,	1·2	1·6	–	·6	1·2

1874.

—	Spike Island.	Mountjoy Female.	Lusk.	Mountjoy Male.	Total, 1874.
No. of Convicts,	664	282	33	154	1,133
Average daily No. of Sick,	13	12	·4	5	31·4
No. of Deaths,	7	3	–	1	11
Per-centage of Deaths on prison population,	1·0	1·0	–	·6	·9

1875.

—	Spike Island.	Mountjoy Female.	Lusk.	Mountjoy Male.	Total, 1875.
No. of Convicts,	670	282	44	153	1,149
Average daily No. of Sick,	14	13	·5	7	34·5
No. of Deaths,	7	5	–	1	13
Per-centage of Deaths on prison population,	1	1·7	–	·6	1·1

RETURN showing the PROPORTION of SICK and DEATHS to the Number of Convicts in the Irish Convict Prisons for the years 1876, 1877, 1878, from 1st April, 1879, to 31st March, 1880, and from 1st April, 1880, to 31st March, 1882.

1876.

—	Spike Island.	Mountjoy Female.	Lusk.	Mountjoy Male.	Total, 1876.
No. of Convicts, ...	681	279	42	150	1,152
Average daily No. of Sick, .	11	13	·3	7	31·3
No. of Deaths, ...	6	3	-	1	10·0
Per-centage of Deaths on prison population, ...	·8	1·0	-	·6	0·9

1877.

—	Spike Island.	Mountjoy Female.	Lusk.	Mountjoy Male.	Total, 1877.
No. of Convicts, ...	669	249	48	167	1,133
Average daily No. of Sick, .	15	15	·4	8	38·4
No. of Deaths, ...	10	4	-	2	16
Per-centage of Deaths on prison population, ...	1·5	1·6	-	1·2	1·4

1878.

—	Spike Island.	Mountjoy Female.	Lusk.	Mountjoy Male.	Total, 1878.
No. of Convicts, ...	583	229	52	191	1,055
Average daily No. of Sick, .	14·5	6	·3	10·8	31·3
No. of Deaths, ...	6	2	.	3	11
Per-centage of Deaths on prison population, ...	1	·88	.	1·5	1

From 1st April, 1879, to 31st March, 1880.

—	Spike Island.	Mountjoy Female.	Lusk.	Mountjoy Male.	Total.
No. of Convicts, ...	430	182	40	412	1,064
Average daily No. of Sick, .	17·76	7·77	0·6	8·45	34·58
No. of Deaths, ...	7	2	-	-	9
Per-centage of Deaths on prison population, ...	1·63	1·1	-	-	2·73

From 1st April, 1880, to 31st March, 1881.

—	Spike Island.	Mountjoy Female.	Lusk.	Mountjoy Male.	Total.
No. of Convicts, ...	496	192	100	416	1,204
Average daily No. of Sick, .	15 416	5·60	·42	6·39	27·826
No. of Deaths, ...	1	4	-	-	5
Per-centage of Deaths on prison population, ...	·244	2·8	-	-	3·044

From 1st April, 1881, to 31st March, 1882.

—	Spike Island.	Mountjoy Female.	Lusk.	Mountjoy Male.	Total.
No. of Convicts, ...	378	119	32	391	920
Average daily No. of Sick, .	13	7·42	·46	5·74	26·62
No. of Deaths, ...	4	1	-	2	7
Per-centage of Deaths on prison population, ...	1	·84	-	1·09	2·93

TABLE II.—NUMBER of PRISONERS in each of the CONVICT PRISONS on the First

PRISONS.	1st April, 1880.			1st May, 1880.			1st June, 1880.			1st July, 1880.			1st August, 1880.			1st September, 1880.		
	M.	F.	Tot.	M.	F.	Tot.	M.	F.	Tot.	M.	F.	Tot.	M.	F.	Tot.	M.	F.	Tot.
Cork (Male), . .	83	–	83	30	–	30	26	–	26	26	–	26	31	–	31	35	–	35
Maryborough, .	45	–	45	44	–	44	44	–	44	46	–	46	46	–	46	44	–	44
Mountjoy (Male), . .	205	–	205	186	–	186	192	–	192	188	–	188	176	–	176	171	–	171
Mountjoy (Female),	–	163	163	–	161	161	–	158	158	–	158	155	–	156	156	–	151	151
Spike Island, .	415	–	415	419	–	419	415	–	415	418	–	416	427	–	427	424	–	424
Lusk, . . .	26	–	26	24	–	24	35	–	35	29	–	29	27	–	27	32	–	32
Total, . .	734	163	887	713	161	874	704	158	862	704	155	859	718	156	866	706	151	857

PRISONS.	1st April, 1881.			1st May, 1881.			1st June, 1881.			1st July, 1881.			1st August, 1881.			1st September, 1881.		
	M.	F.	Tot.	M.	F.	Tot.	M.	F.	Tot.	M.	F.	Tot.	M.	F.	Tot.	M.	F.	Tot.
Cork (Male), . .	36	–	36	32	–	32	36	–	36	34	–	34	36	–	36	31	–	31
Maryborough, .	56	–	56	53	–	53	49	–	49	51	–	51	49	–	49	46	–	46
Mountjoy (Male), .	151	–	151	140	–	140	140	–	140	164	–	164	175	–	175	178	–	178
Mountjoy (Female),	–	139	139	–	134	134	–	133	133	–	135	135	–	134	134	–	113	113
Spike Island, .	396	–	396	401	–	401	398	–	398	377	–	377	366	–	366	364	–	364
Lusk, . . .	30	–	30	38	–	38	40	–	40	31	–	31	23	–	23	28	–	28
Total, . .	670	139	809	668	134	802	655	163	766	649	135	784	649	134	783	647	113	760

TABLE III.—RETURN of PRISON OFFENCES and PUNISHMENTS in

PRISON.	Total Number of Prisoners during the Year.	Corporal Punishment.	Irons or Handcuffs.	Prison Punishments.		Total number of Prisoners Punished.
				Punishment Cells.	Dietary Punishment.	
Mountjoy Male Convict Prison, ...	391	2	3	170	178	161
Mountjoy Female Convict Prison, ...	179	–	3	107	64	47
Spike Island Convict Prison,* . . .	634	–	45	41	561	234
Lusk Convict Prison, .	97	–	–	–	–	5
Totals 1881–82, . .	1,301	2	51	318	795	387
Totals 1880–81, . .	1,428	2	36	168	668	465

* See Memo. on page 149.

Day in each Month of the Years ended 31st March, 1881 and 1882.

1st October, 1880. M.	F.	Tot.	1st November, 1880. M.	F.	Tot.	1st December, 1880. M.	F.	Tot.	1st January, 1881. M.	F.	Tot.	1st February, 1881. M.	F.	Tot.	1st March, 1881. M.	F.	Tot.	Prisons.
28	-	28	41	-	41	40	-	40	38	-	38	33	-	33	33	-	38	Cork (Male).
70	-	70	86	-	86	60	-	60	58	-	50	56	-	58	53	-	53	Maryborough.
156	-	156	137	-	137	149	-	149	155	-	155	149	-	149	150	-	150	Mountjoy (Male).
-	150	150	-	149	149	-	148	146	-	146	148	-	147	147	-	144	144	Mountjoy (Female).
396	-	396	393	-	393	405	-	405	407	-	407	407	-	407	485	-	485	Spike Island.
31	-	31	30	-	30	28	-	28	29	-	29	37	-	37	34	-	34	Lusk.
681	150	831	687	149	836	682	148	828	688	128	836	682	147	829	675	144	818	Total.

1st October, 1881. M.	F.	Tot.	1st November, 1881. M.	F.	Tot.	1st December, 1881. M.	F.	Tot.	1st January, 1882. M.	F.	Tot.	1st February, 1882. M.	F.	Tot.	1st March, 1882. M.	F.	Tot.	Prisons.
32	-	32	32	-	32	24	-	24	23	-	23	31	-	31	18	-	18	Cork (Male).
37	-	37	60	-	60	20	-	28	24	-	24	24	-	24	18	-	18	Maryborough.
171	-	171	178	-	170	185	-	185	228	-	228	213	-	213	231	-	231	Mountjoy (Male).
-	110	110	-	109	109	-	108	109	-	110	110	-	111	111	-	109	109	Mountjoy (Female).
364	-	364	378	-	376	380	-	380	378	-	378	383	-	383	384	-	384	Spike Island.
29	-	29	33	-	33	32	-	32	41	-	41	39	-	39	36	-	36	Lusk.
623	110	748	647	109	759	647	109	758	604	110	804	690	111	881	688	109	787	Total.

Convict Prisons from 1st April, 1881, to 31st March, 1882.

Prison Offences. Violence.	Escapes and attempts to Escape.	Idleness.	Other breaches of Regulations.	Total Offences.	Deprivation of Marks.	Prison.
6	1	9	207	223	34	Mountjoy Male Convict Prison.
102	-	-	108	210	68	Mountjoy Female Convict Prison.
74	1	34	668	777	328	Spike Island Convict Prison.*
-	-	-	5	5	5	Lusk Convict Prison.
182	2	43	988	1,215	427	Totals, 1880–81.
143	4	87	954	1,188	370	Totals, 1879–80.

† Removed to Mountjoy.

Spike Island Convict Prison,
27th April, 1882.

MEMO.

With reference to the return of punishments on Form No. 1, I beg to explain that the total number of punishments shown is 180 less than the number of offences, the difference being made up of 75 cases that were dealt with by stoppage of marks or suspension of classification only, 51 by admonitions, 2 by the forfeiture of a portion of their gratuity, and 2 by the civil power.

Of the 234 individual prisoners shown as punished, many were punished several times during the year.

All dietary punishments at Spike Island, except stoppage of suppers, of which there were 31 cases during the year, have been carried out in the punishment cells; the 41 cases entered under heading "Punishment Cells," comprise 33 who were placed in dark refractory cells at Spike Island Prison, and 8 who were committed to dark cells at Cork male Prison.

There were only 75 cases of deprivation of marks where no other punishment was ordered, and the remainder of the 320 cases of deprivation of marks shown were in addition to the dietary punishment.

Thirty-four of the 777 offences were committed at Cork and Maryborough Prisons.

PETER HAY, Governor.

The Chairman, General Prisons Board,
Dublin Castle.

C.—REGISTRATION OF CRIMINALS.

I.—RETURN of the Number of Criminals sentenced to Police Supervision during each of the following years:—

Year.	Males.	Females.	Total.	Year.	Males.	Females.	Total.
*1870,	–	–	–	1877,	29	8	37
1871,	4	2	6	1878,	41	8	49
1872,	66	32	98	1879,	43	9	52
1873,	46	26	72	1880,	32	7	39
1874,	50	15	65	1881,	19	5	24
1875,	34	19	53				
1876,	30	7	37	Total,	394	138	532

* No record kept.

	Males.	Females.	Total.
Number sentenced during year ended 31st March, 1882,	21	10	31

II.—RETURN of Criminals discharged from Prison in each of the following years, and subject to Police Supervision:—

Year.	Males.	Females.	Total.	Year.	Males.	Females.	Total.
1870,	4	6	10	1877,	48	25	73
1871,	54	36	90	1878,	25	12	37
1872,	63	33	96	1879,	43	10	53
1873,	40	20	60	1880,	39	14	53
1874,	34	14	48	1881,	34	11	43
1875,	34	13	47				
1876,	61	29	90	Total,	447	223	670

	Males.	Females.	Total.
Number discharged during year ended 31st March, 1882,	34	9	43

III.—Return of Licence Holders discharged from Prison during each of the following years:—

Year.	Males.	Females.	Total.	Year.	Males.	Females.	Total.
1870,	141	64	205	1877,	117	60	177
1871,	151	72	223	1878,	149	62	211
1872,	137	58	195	1879,	185	48	233
1873,	134	56	190	1880,	111	44	155
1874,	106	68	174	1881,	122	60	182
1875,	133	64	197				
1876,	104	50	154	Total,	1,590	706	2,296

	Males.	Females.	Total.
Number discharged during year ended 31st March, 1882,	114	40	154

IV.—Return of Convicts discharged from Prison on completion or commutation of their sentences during each of the following years:—

Year.	Males.	Females.	Total.	Year.	Males.	Females.	Total.
1870,	28	20	48	1877,	48	18	66
1871,	18	24	42	1878,	54	15	69
1872,	35	25	60	1879,	53	19	72
1873	37	23	60	1880,	46	8	54
1874,	42	13	55	1881,	26	8	34
1875,	27	14	41				
1876,	29	12	41	Total,	443	199	642

	Males.	Females.	Total.
Number discharged during year ended 31st March, 1882,	48	9	57

V.—Return of Licence Holders discharged during each of the following years, subject to Police Supervision on expiration of Licence:—

Year.	Males.	Females.	Total.	Year.	Males.	Females.	Total.
1870,	–	–	–	1877,	24	12	36
1871,	–	–	–	1878,	14	9	23
1872,	–	–	–	1879,	13	6	19
1873,	–	–	–	1880,	14	5	19
1874,	2	1	3	1881,	9	3	13
1875,	6	3	9				
1876,	33	18	51	Total,	115	57	172

	Males.	Females.	Total.
Number discharged during year ended 31st March, 1882,	12	1	13

VI.—Return of Convicts discharged on expiration of sentence during each of the following years, and subject to Police Supervision:—

Year.	Males.	Females.	Total.	Year.	Males.	Females.	Total.
1870,	–	–	–	1877,	7	4	11
1871,	–	–	–	1878,	2	–	2
1872,	–	–	–	1879,	5	1	6
1873,	–	–	–	1880,	5	-	5
1874,	–	–	–	1881,	6	2	9
1875,	–	–	–				
1876,	2	–	2	Total,	27	7	34

	Males.	Females.	Total.
Number discharged during year ended 31st March, 1882,	6	4	10

VII.—Return showing the number of queries as to Prisoners in Custody awaiting Trial, received from Prisons and Police during each of the following years, and showing the per-centage known :—

Year.	Queries received from		Per-centage known.	
	Prisons.	Police.	Prisons.	Police.
1870*a*, - -	–	–	-	–
1871*b*, - -	47	27	31·9	15·
1872, - -	99	40	36·36	35·
1873, - -	151	24	37·08	46·
1874, - -	133	42	40·6	38·09
1875, - -	164	32	33·54	15·62
1876, - -	130	25	26·15	8·
1877, - -	92	24	19·56	29·
1878, - -	78	28	26·	25·
1879, - -	57	35	21·	8·6
1880. - -	153	75	54·9	1·07
From 1/4/80 to 31st March, '81,	146	52	60·8	·6
From 1/4/81 to 31st March, '82,	140	13	79·3	7·7

a. No record kept. *b.* Commencing August, 1871.

VIII.—Return showing the number of habitual criminals registered in :—

Year.	No.	Year.	No.
1870, . . .	907	1877, . . .	609
1871, . . .	1,058	1878, . . .	272
1872, . . .	840	1879, . . .	305
1873, . . .	1,118	1880, . . .	294
1874, . . .	1,062	From 1st April, 1880, to 31st March, 1881, .	223
1875, . . .	986	Year ended 31/3/82, .	224
1876, . . .	964		

D. EXPENDITURE—CONVICT AND LOCAL PRISONS

(INCLUSIVE OF BRIDEWELLS).

RETURN

SHOWING

THE EXPENDITURE UNDER EACH HEAD OF SERVICE,

IN THE YEAR ENDED 31ST MARCH, 1882.

D.—EXPENDITURE—CONVICT AND LOCAL

RETURN showing the Expenditure under each Head

HEADS OF SERVICE.	TOTAL EXPENSES.	Mountjoy, Male.	Mountjoy, Female.	Lusk.
Daily Average, inclusive of Minor Prisons, and exclusive of Bridewells.	—	377	173	32
	£ s. d.	£ s. d.	£ s. d.	£ s. d.
COST OF STAFF.				
Pay and allowances of officers, including uniforms, &c.	80,084 0 2	4,803 11 1	8,607 1 4	804 10 0
MAINTENANCE OF PRISONERS.				
Victualling for prisoners, ...	28,201 8 8	2,910 7 2	1,002 13 7	413 2 2
Medicines, surgical instruments, &c., .	057 2 0	83 11 2	68 16 6	4 17 9
Soap, scouring and cleaning articles, .	1,404 1 4	160 18 10	125 9 11	0 12 2
Clothing for prisoners, ...	6,060 1 5	1,234 10 8	272 18 6	195 17 7
Fuel, light, and water, ...	15,368 16 10	1,413 6 11	1,816 12 2	107 1 2
Total expenses of Maintenance, .	46,781 10 2	5,800 14 4	3,388 10 8	760 10 10
OTHER EXPENSES.				
Bedding for prisoners, ...	1,448 10 9	5 9 9	*516 6 11	—
Gratuities to prisoners, ...	2,051 14 4	206 9 9	480 2 10	456 12 8
Buildings, including furniture, repairs, alterations, &c.	11,308 1 11	287 17 2	432 15 0	149 12 0
Kitchen utensils, crockery, &c., . .	208 17 0	31 10 0	6 17 3	0 10 0
Rent, ...	021 5 1	—	6 10 2	1 15 0
Incidental expenses, ...	2,352 14 10	142 7 2	105 13 10	27 15 10
Total of Other Expenses, . . .	18,186 12 11	760 14 4	981 19 7 *515 8 11 460 12 8	638 12 6
Gross Total Expenses, . . .	125,008 3 4	11,878 10 9	7,522 4 8	2,304 3 1

HEADS OF SERVICE.	Clonmel.	Cork, Male.	Cork, Female.	Downpatrick.
Daily Average, inclusive of Minor Prisons, and exclusive of Bridewells.	97	231	80	67
	£ s. d.	£ s. d.	£ s. d.	£ s. d.
COST OF STAFF.				
Pay and allowances of officers, including uniforms, &c.	1,583 12 11	2,574 4 6	1,008 8 10	1,162 11 8
MAINTENANCE OF PRISONERS.				
Victualling for prisoners, ...	435 0 10	1,035 4 9	203 12 0	386 17 4
Medicines, surgical instruments, &c., .	18 17 2	14 15 2	13 14 4	0 4 4
Soap, scouring and cleaning articles, .	88 5 4	57 16 8	18 10 7	12 19 6
Clothing for prisoners, ...	36 17 3	246 10 7	40 10 0	53 12 4
Fuel, light, and water, ...	412 16 9	606 7 11	344 6 11	299 10 2
Total expenses of Maintenance, .	949 6 4	1,960 14 8	710 15 10	763 3 8
OTHER EXPENSES.				
Bedding for prisoners, ...	141 6 1	8 3 4	12 7 11	17 5 10
Gratuities to prisoners, ...	10 1 2	47 6 6	7 0 1	28 7 5
Buildings, including furniture, repairs, alterations, &c.	341 5 7	489 18 3	190 7 1	109 0 1
Kitchen utensils, crockery, &c., . .	23 14 4	2 15 5	0 6 4	1 6 6
Rent, ...	69 11 0	—	57 16 0	27 13 10
Incidental expenses, ...	63 1 0	74 14 8	34 15 0	24 9 3
Total of Other Expenses, . . .	650 10 2	618 18 2	302 14 5	268 1 10
Gross Total Expenses, . . .	3,183 15 5	5,153 12 4	2,032 17 1	2,195 17 2

* NOTE.—Mountjoy Female Prison supplied bedding from its store during the year to other prisons to the [illegible] 4s. 8d. There is thus a credit in favour of Mountjoy Female Prison of £515 6s. 11d.

PRISONS (inclusive of Bridewells).

of Service, in the year ended 31st March, 1882.

Spike Island.	Armagh.	Belfast.	Castlebar.	Heads of Service.
378	124	491	44	Daily Average, inclusive of Minor Prisons, and exclusive of Bridewells.
£ s. d.	£ s. d.	£ s. d.	£ s. d.	
				Cost of Staff.
9,546 1 0	1,578 7 4	2,983 15 7	754 10 3	Pay and allowances of officers, including uniforms, &c.
				Maintenance of Prisoners.
3,709 0 1	483 9 1	1,048 8 3	216 10 6	Victualling for prisoners.
76 11 4	42 3 10	95 9 11	22 5 0	Medicines, surgical instruments, &c.
87 0 5	18 15 8	92 10 5	6 5 11	Soap, scouring and cleaning articles.
938 17 8	174 3 1	506 5 0	28 16 9	Clothing for prisoners.
879 11 4	407 13 4	859 5 5	162 3 8	Fuel, light, and water.
5,774 8 10	1,126 5 7	3,434 0 0	435 10 10	Total expenses of Maintenance.
				Other Expenses.
134 6 0	189 14 4	85 9 0	4 3 7	Bedding for prisoners.
257 15 5	15 7 11	52 14 5	10 12 5	Gratuities to prisoners.
330 12 6	1,016 18 2	1,370 4 1	207 3 9	Buildings, including furniture, repairs, alterations, &c.
2 17 0	14 0 0	10 3 5	8 0 5	Kitchen utensils, crockery, &c.
—	—	0 14 5	—	Rent.
145 1 3	137 15 11	71 18 7	25 10 5	Incidental expenses.
871 12 4	1,372 16 4	1,539 14 11	250 16 7	Total of Other Expenses.
15,192 0 2	4,077 9 3	7,947 10 5	1,457 17 8	Gross Total Expenses.

Drogheda.	Dundalk.	Galway.	Grange-gorman.	Heads of Service.
30	99	155	272	Daily Average, inclusive of Minor Prisons, and exclusive of Bridewells.
£ s. d.	£ s. d.	£ s. d.	£ s. d.	**Cost of Staff.**
522 9 11	1,439 4 11	1,501 18 7	2,796 3 9	Pay and allowances of officers, including uniforms, &c.
				Maintenance of Prisoners.
90 10 4	477 14 8	488 5 7	1,151 18 6	Victualling for prisoners.
—	13 15 4	95 1 1	8 3 10	Medicines, surgical instruments, &c.
7 4 10	18 11 8	62 1 5	183 1 0	Soap, scouring and cleaning articles.
42 18 8	84 2 8	174 12 4	318 8 6	Clothing for prisoners.
95 1 8	320 5 8	501 17 0	1,108 12 7	Fuel, light, and water.
235 10 4	921 11 5	1,346 17 6	2,755 4 7	Total expenses of Maintenance.
				Other Expenses.
4 11 11	82 4 9	116 18 11	53 14 3	Bedding for prisoners.
2 19 11	23 18 10	2 11 5	40 15 11	Gratuities to prisoners.
108 6 9	441 13 10	380 19 1	253 15 9	Buildings, including furniture, repairs, alterations, &c.
2 6 2	12 8 11	9 15 5	15 10 1	Kitchen utensils, crockery, &c.
—	87 17 2	—	—	Rent.
6 9 3	71 9 2	145 9 8	96 11 5	Incidental expenses.
119 18 0	649 11 8	637 0 4	481 8 6	Total of Other Expenses.
877 18 3	3,010 8 8	3,485 16 5	5,034 16 9	Gross Total Expenses.

amount of £659 11*s*. 7*d*. The cost of bedding supplied to Mountjoy Female Prison during the year was which is shown as a deduction in relief of expenditure under that prison.

CONVICT AND LOCAL PRISONS

RETURN showing the Expenditure under each Head

HEADS OF SERVICE.	Kilkenny.	Kilmainham.	Limerick, Male.	Limerick, Female.
Daily Average, inclusive of Minor Prisons, and exclusive of Bridewells.	87	178	162	46
COST OF STAFF.	£ s. d.	£ s. d.	£ s. d.	£ s. d.
Pay and allowances of officers, including uniforms, &c.	1,298 3 5	2,454 6 8	2,034 3 11	758 4 1
MAINTENANCE OF PRISONERS.				
Victualling for prisoners, ...	257 7 2	455 13 4	488 7 11	214 4 7
Medicines, surgical instruments, &c., .	21 8 10	19 1 11	35 11 10	4 0 0
Soap, scouring and cleaning articles, .	11 10 0	66 10 0	25 15 7	16 10 10
Clothing for prisoners, ...	89 16 8	62 15 5	114 15 11	82 17 0
Fuel, light, and water, ...	200 11 10	708 3 4	465 8 2	210 2 3
Total expenses of Maintenance, .	580 14 6	1,312 18 0	1,129 17 5	487 10 9
OTHER EXPENSES.				
Bedding for prisoners, ...	182 2 10	150 17 4	120 8 0	—
Gratuities to prisoners, ...	18 7 3	24 11 5	18 14 11	5 12 0
Buildings, including furniture, repairs, alterations, &c.	517 19 4	1,330 7 0	338 17 9	211 6 4
Kitchen utensils, crockery, &c., . .	11 4 6	23 17 0	14 1 2	4 14 3
Rent, ...	—	—	—	—
Incidental expenses, ...	54 13 6	385 13 5	57 12 10	10 3 6
Total of Other Expenses, . . .	784 7 8	1,937 3 11	565 10 4	240 19 0
Gross Total Expenses, ...	2,763 5 7	5,704 6 7	3,749 10 8	1,495 5 9

HEADS OF SERVICE.	Omagh.	Richmond.	Sligo.	Tralee.
Daily Average, inclusive of Minor Prisons, and exclusive of Bridewells.	83	276	03	81
COST OF STAFF.	£ s. d.	£ s. d.	£ s. d.	£ s. d.
Pay and allowances of officers, including uniforms, &c.	1,403 6 7	3,041 10 5	1,049 0 5	1,137 3 7
MAINTENANCE OF PRISONERS.				
Victualling for prisoners, ...	441 13 2	1,346 19 7	349 17 0	220 8 3
Medicines, surgical instruments, &c., .	3 13 3	83 1 9	21 6 11	6 5 3
Soap, scouring and cleaning articles, .	23 16 8	140 12 4	14 8 6	11 11 3
Clothing for prisoners, ...	33 7 5	431 3 7	07 0 8	34 1 5
Fuel, light, and water, ...	329 7 6	1,078 1 3	123 11 6	236 0 7
Total expenses of Maintenance, .	005 9 3	5,333 10 11	010 12 7	303 7 4
OTHER EXPENSES.				
Bedding for prisoners, ...	106 13 3	10 5 9	36 15 4	14 9 3
Gratuities to prisoners, ...	20 4 10	75 16 3	12 18 0	2 13 3
Buildings, including furniture, repairs, alterations, &c.	097 19 2	330 3 6	187 5 10	113 1 3
Kitchen utensils, crockery, &c., . .	8 19 3	11 11 2	0 10 11	3 1 1
Rent, ...	—	117 4 4	51 13 10	42 0 0
Incidental expenses, ...	124 3 9	87 4 5	44 16 7	84 17 11
Total of Other Expenses, . . .	760 6 3	032 4 11	344 0 3	215 7 0
Gross Total Expenses, ...	3,137 11 9	7,080 0 3	2,008 13 8	1,684 16 11

(inclusive of Bridewells)—*continued.*

of Service, in the year ended 31st March, 1882—*continued.*

Londonderry.	Maryborough.	Mullingar.	Naas.	Nenagh.	Heads of Service.
99	87	102	122	58	Daily Average, inclusive of Minor Prisons, and exclusive of Bridewells.
£ s. d.	£ s. d.	£ s. d.	£ s. d.	£ s. d.	Cost of Staff.
1,584 9 4	1,028 3 5	1,324 15 2	1,578 4 8	881 3 10	Pay and allowances of officers including uniforms, &c.
					Maintenance of Prisoners.
869 17 11	898 18 10	541 15 7	388 1 1	202 0 5	Victualling for prisoners.
0 1 0	13 9 5	3 9 5	6 11 8	10 7 5	Medicines, surgical instruments, &c.
48 3 7	6 18 1	36 1 4	11 12 3	18 11 7	Soap, scouring and cleaning articles.
200 7 7	57 11 4	149 0 5	41 8 9	101 8 6	Clothing for prisoners.
498 17 5	468 12 6	340 4 11	632 10 0	289 3 2	Fuel, light, and water.
1,941 9 6	1,337 5 2	1,071 11 8	1,079 2 8	691 11 1	Total expenses of Maintenance.
					Other Expenses.
17 13 8	182 18 1	82 5 10	60 0 2	3 3 9	Bedding for prisoners.
34 14 8	7 0 5	18 18 4	10 18 5	16 14 7	Gratuities to prisoners.
348 11 8	580 19 5	241 6 1	402 15 10	86 8 3	Buildings, including furniture, repairs, alterations, &c.
4 15 4	5 7 8	3 18 0	28 16 4	5 10 8	Kitchen utensils, crockery, &c.
—	—	—	—	0 17 10	Rent.
21 14 8	84 15 3	52 15 5	87 16 0	57 8 8	Incidental expenses.
322 5 0	770 2 0	400 5 8	611 7 0	167 0 1	Total of Other Expenses.
3,187 19 10	3,080 10 7	2,696 10 6	3,218 14 5	1,739 15 0	Gross Total Expenses.

Tullamore.	Waterford.	Wexford.	Total Expenses.		Heads of Service.
81	36	48	—		Daily Average, inclusive of Minor Prisons, and exclusive of Bridewells.
£ s. d.	£ s. d.	£ s. d.	£ s. d.		Cost of Staff.
1,387 16 2	1,338 0 8	955 10 5	80,084 0 2		Pay and allowances of officers including uniforms, &c.
					Maintenance of Prisoners.
442 9 8	580 6 8	246 7 0	28,291 8 8		Victualling for prisoners.
0 10 0	9 18 8	5 12 1	657 2 0		Medicines, surgical instruments, &c.
28 18 4	17 8 7	12 19 4	1,404 1 4		Soap, scouring and cleaning articles.
87 10 3	79 0 1	50 7 2	6,080 1 5		Clothing for prisoners.
298 5 8	362 12 5	204 15 7	15,368 16 10		Fuel, light, and water.
857 3 8	729 0 9	520 4 2	42,751 10 2		Total expenses of Maintenance.
					Other Expenses.
10 14 8	12 0 5	72 17 9	1,448 19 8		Bedding for prisoners.
24 11 3	21 4 2	12 10 3	2,061 14 4		Gratuities to prisoners.
119 16 8	121 10 8	60 8 11	11,868 1 11		Buildings, including furniture, repairs, alterations, &c.
5 9 11	0 19 3	8 11 11	293 17 0		Kitchen utensils, crockery, &c.
—	—	207 11 8	623 5 1		Rent.
83 18 8	17 3 6	17 19 3	2,852 14 10		Incidental expenses.
304 12 9	173 18 6	379 14 7	19,188 12 11		Total of Other Expenses.
2,339 17 7	2,240 0 1	1,785 8 2	195,002 3 4		Gross Total Expenses.

(E. BRIDEWELLS.)

RETURN showing the names and situation of the BRIDEWELLS referred to, par. 14, page 7, discontinued since the date of last report, viz.:—

Bridewell.	County.
Skibbereen, . . .	Cork.

DUBLIN: Printed by ALEX. THOM & Co., 87, 88, & 89, Abbey-street,
The Queen's Printing Office.
For Her Majesty's Stationery Office.

www.ingramcontent.com/pod-product-compliance
Lightning Source LLC
Chambersburg PA
CBHW022127160426
43197CB00009B/1181
* 9 7 8 3 7 4 1 1 0 4 4 9 7 *